Y. H. Wong, PhD
Thomas K. P. Leung, PhD

Guanxi
Relationship Marketing in a Chinese Context

Pre-publication
REVIEW

"This book shows a thorough grasp of Western and Chinese approaches to network relationships. It also compares and contrasts those two approaches, incorporating cultural reasons for why they are different. Its treatment of guanxi is exceptional. Their many forms are outlined, and the reasons for their existence in China over many years are sympathetically examined. The authors then develop a most comprehensive model of guanxi and test it with quantitative and qualitative research. All researchers of networks and relationship marketing in Asia should read this book because of its modern, complete, and knowledgeable treatment of guanxi. The final guanxi model is for business executives, so business readers will find value in the book, too. They should especially like the discussion of the step-by-step development of a guanxi relationship, and the detailed case studies of modern, China-owned businesses that were built through guanxi."

Chad Perry, PhD
*Professor of Marketing and Management,
Southern Cross University,
Australia*

Guanxi
Relationship Marketing
in a Chinese Context

INTERNATIONAL BUSINESS PRESS®
Erdener Kaynak, PhD
Executive Editor

Guanxi
Relationship Marketing in a Chinese Context

Y. H. Wong, PhD
Thomas K. P. Leung, PhD

International Business Press®
An Imprint of The Haworth Press, Inc.
New York • London • Oxford

Published by

International Business Press®, an imprint of The Haworth Press, Inc., 10 Alice Street, Binghamton, NY 13904-1580.

Company and personal names mentioned in case studies have been changed to protect confidentiality.

Cover design by Jennifer M. Gaska.

Library of Congress Cataloging-in-Publication Data

Wong, Y. H., 1953-
 Guanxi : relationship marketing in a Chinese context / Y.H. Wong, Thomas Leung.
  p. cm.
 Includes bibliographical references and index.
 ISBN 0-7890-1289-8 (alk. paper) — ISBN 0-7890-1290-1 (pbk. : alk. paper)
 1. Relationship marketing—China. I. Leung, Thomas K. II. Title.

HF5415.55 .W66 2001
658.8'12—dc21

00-066455

To my wife, Daisy, and my sons Andrew and Michael, with love.

Y. H. Wong

To my wonderful family—my wife May and my son Nelson.

T. K. P. Leung

ABOUT THE AUTHORS

Y. H. Wong, PhD, MBA, BSocSc (Hons), is Associate Professor of Marketing at The Hong Kong Polytechnic University. Prior to joining the university, he worked as regional export manager and general manager for several multinationals in the Asia-Pacific region, including Continental (USA) Corp, Swire Pacific Group in Hong Kong, and Amcor Group (Australia) for more than 12 years. In 1989 his export department received the Export Award from the Australian government. His article, "Insider Selling to China: *Guanxi,* Trust, and Adaptation," was given a Citation of Excellence (Highest Quality Rating) by Anbar Electronic Intelligence in 1998. His research has been published in journals, including *European Journal of Marketing, International Business Review, Journal of Business Ethics, Journal of International Consumer Marketing, Industrial Marketing Management, International Marketing Review, Journal of Services Marketing,* and *Marketing Planning and Intelligence.* For more information, contact Dr. Wong at <www.yhwong.com>.

T. K. P. Leung, PhD, MCom, BA, is Assistant Professor of Marketing at The Hong Kong Polytechnic University. He has more than twenty years of experience in business and academic services. He worked as a marketing and sales manager in various companies, including Nestle Ltd., Rheem Australia Ltd., and Plating Engineering Ltd. He has published articles in refereed journals, including *European Journal of Marketing, Journal of Business Ethics, Journal of Small Business Management,* and *Asia Business Law Review.* For more information, contact Dr. Leung at <www.tkpleung.com>.

CONTENTS

Foreword

This book is a major contribution for those who are interested in relationships, and in comparing relationships in China to those in Western cultures. Many businesspeople and scholars in the West recognize the existence and importance of guanxi in the Chinese culture, but I am not sure many people really understand its genesis—why it has, for such a long time, been a much more important and reliable medium of exchange than money, or how and why it substitutes for contract law in China.

I doubt if two writers anywhere are in a better position to develop a theoretical model to explain how guanxi is the basis of complex industrial relationship behavior in the Chinese culture, or how the emphasis is different from the foundation for industrial relationships in the West. Such a model certainly stimulates one to ponder the advantages of reduced transaction costs and quick, reliable decision making, which are features of a guanxi relationship.

Both authors have been researching guanxi for many years. They have combined their knowledge by designing a survey to measure guanxi constructs and how they affect business, and particularly marketing efficiency. They have indeed made a valuable gift to businesspeople and academics alike.

In a world that is moving toward regionalization, some may even argue globalization, it is important that researchers such as Y. H. and Thomas outline how relationships form and develop in a particular culture, as their work will help to reduce misunderstandings and oil the wheels of international trade. Their theory and approach will serve businesspeople and academics well in coping with understanding complex relationships in business and marketing. It is a very valuable contribution to the business literature and understanding of relationships in the Chinese context.

The book is also a timely piece of work, as the world is keen to understand Sino-Western relationships and feel confident to contribute to globalization trends by developing closer relationships with Chinese businesspeople.

E. Alan Buttery, PhD
Professor of Marketing
University of Western Sydney, NSW, Australia
Fellow of the Chartered Institute of Marketing U.K.

Preface

Exciting. Confusing. Challenging. These words have been used to describe the cultural aspect of marketing in China. No doubt, the country has the greatest market potential in the Asia-Pacific region based on the size of its population alone. Because of the "four modernization" programs and China's accession to the WTO, foreign businesspeople are eager to enter China to negotiate investment projects. However, they always find the Chinese cultural environment very difficult to understand because it is different from that in the West. This is specifically true when the Chinese use guanxi (personal relationships) to cement informal alliances with other members of a network, such as kinfolk and friends, to create strategically important personal ties with bureaucrats in large Chinese state-owned enterprises. The informality of this guanxi network always makes it very difficult for outsiders to penetrate, and hence difficult to do business with insiders. Thus, it is of paramount importance for foreign businesspeople to understand how this guanxi network evolves and how an outsider can become an insider in order to effectively negotiate investment projects within the complex Chinese business context.

Over the last two decades, numerous scholars have given their views on different aspects of guanxi. Their views are insightful, but often a holistic picture of the establishment and maintenance of guanxi in the Chinese market cannot be found. Therefore, we set forth to finish this task by producing this book. The legal, social, and economic environments are perceived as vital to the evolution of guanxi. From a holistic perspective, we have developed an integrated guanxi model. We propose a way that guanxi can be positioned and "routed" to navigate the complex network of relationships in China. We also include case studies to test the validity of this model in real business situations.

The book is organized as follows. Chapter 1 explains the conceptual framework and scope of the book. Chapter 2 presents the Western views of relationship from different perspectives, and Chapter 3 puts forward the Chinese views of guanxi. The comparison of the Western and Chinese perspective allows us to develop a comprehensive guanxi framework to address the complex issues of guanxi. Chapter 4 covers the methodology of this study. Chapter 5 gives the theoretical and practical aspects of guanxi and also addresses the positioning, routing, and strategic aspects of guanxi. Chapter 6 contains the detailed guanxi model and case studies to test the model. Also, the implications for business negotiation are included in this chapter.

Writing this book was an intellectual journey that required the combination of an in-depth search of Western and Chinese literature and modern research techniques. The successful completion of these tasks depended on the support of many individuals and firms. We are particularly grateful to Professor Alan Buttery, University of Western Sydney; Professor Chad Perry, University of Southern Queensland; and Professor Peter Graham, Southern Cross University for their useful comments. We are deeply indebted to Professor Erdener Kaynak, Pennsylvania State University, Harrisburg; and Andrew Chan, Monica Law, Regina Lau, and Catherine Ho. All deserve sincere thanks for their valuable encouragement and assistance. For a research grant, we are grateful to Hong Kong Polytechnic University. We also thank all participants from those firms in Hong Kong, China, the United States, Germany, and Indonesia who provided us with their stories of establishing guanxi in China. Their positive feedback on the validity of our guanxi model warrants our heartfelt appreciation.

Finally, we are deeply indebted to our families, whose patience and encouragement have been important for the completion of this book. We are blessed with close relationships with each member of our families. We could not have completed this book without the caring and passion of our family members along our path to understanding the most important element in our lives, human relationships.

Y. H. Wong
T. K. P. Leung

Acknowledgments

Y. H. Wong gratefully acknowledges the following publications for allowing the use of material originally published by them:

Journal of Business and Industrial Marketing; Journal of Business Ethics; Journal of Segmentation in Marketing; Thexis; Marketing Planning and Intelligence; International Marketing Review; Singapore Management Review; Journal of Professional Services Marketing; International Journal of Management; Journal of International Marketing and Marketing Research; IIMB Management Review; Journal of International Consumer Marketing; European Journal of Marketing

Chapter 1

Introduction

Marketing is a system in which people or groups are interrelated, engaged in reaching a shared goal, with a relationship with one another. Considerable research has been done on relationship marketing. Relationship marketing is the development, growth, and maintenance of long-term relationships with customers and other partners for mutual benefit. However, little empirical research has attempted to model the relationship constructs and the dynamic interaction of relationship marketing in a Chinese context. Researchers have emphasized studying the importance of relationships or guanxi in Chinese society, but they have never attempted to conceptualize a systematic analysis of the concept of guanxi (Palmer and Bejou 1994). This study aims to provide a systematic analysis of guanxi and to describe the complex relationships in a guanxi quality development framework so as to help readers appreciate its importance in import/export trade within a Chinese business context. In doing so, this study operationalizes a set of guanxi constructs (literally relationships) and attempts to model these constructs within this guanxi quality development framework. It further investigates the relationship between guanxi quality development and indicators of guanxi performance such as sales development. These objectives help us present a comprehensive model that provides guidelines for foreign businessmen to handle important guanxi issues in a Chinese context.

There are eight major sections in this introductory chapter:

1. Research background
2. Research objectives
3. Conceptual framework and research boundary
4. Justifications for this research
5. Methodology

6. Definitions of special terms
7. Limitations of the research
8. Study Outline

RESEARCH BACKGROUND

In the 1950s, consumer marketing was of primary interest to marketing scholars. In the 1960s, research in industrial marketing prevailed. In the 1970s, considerable academic effort was devoted to nonprofit and societal marketing. In the 1980s, service marketing became a popular topic. In the 1990s, the number of studies on relationship marketing increased considerably. These studies have impacts on two levels. At a macro level, relationship marketing has affected a wide range of marketing activities, such as customer services, international marketing, and cross-cultural management. At a micro level, the nature of interrelationships with customers, particularly overseas customers, is changing from a short-term transaction type to a long-term partner type (Christopher, Payne, and Ballantyne 1991). Two major trends can be identified:

1. Marketing researchers have shifted their attention from transactional marketing to relationship marketing (Christopher, Payne, and Ballantyne 1991).
2. Their research emphasis has been diverted from vertical integration hierarchies to networking marketing.

The practices of both relationship marketing and networking are significantly affected by cultural context because different cultures have different interactive patterns (Harris and Moran 1991). This cultural impact on relationships is especially important in China. The importance of the Chinese cultural element guanxi in Sino-foreign business environments is repeatedly mentioned by numerous scholars (Pye 1982, 1986; Brunner et al. 1989; Tsang 1998; Hofstede and Bond 1988). This study aims to construct a systematic framework for guanxi development and its relationship to business performance in the complex Chinese environment.

Significance of the China Market

The People's Republic of China (PRC) has been developing into a major economic entity, with a population that constitutes one-fifth of the world's consumers (Population Reference Bureau 2000). However, there has been limited academic research on business behavior in this market and its requirements, probably because until recently China has been largely perceived as a source of low-cost labor and land. This perception changed remarkably in the early 1990s. The former Chinese Communist Party (CCP) leader Deng Xiaoping made a highly publicized tour of rapidly growing areas in South China, giving his explicit support to the moderation of the socialist system and the creation of new market mechanisms. The Fourteenth Communist Party Congress confirmed China's commitment to new market-mechanism reform, inspiring confidence in the country's potential for rapid economic growth. According to Reuters (2000), China's GDP (Gross Domestic Product) exceeded US$1 trillion in 2000, about 8 percent growth compared with the previous year. That strong growth was the result of a number of reforms launched by Premier Zhu Rongji in the past few years. The number of "affluent" consumers was projected to rise from 60 million to 200 million by the year 2000 (Davies et al. 1995).

The economic recession in Europe in the early 1990s encouraged most Western companies to search for new market opportunities in the Southern Hemisphere. China, naturally, has become the focus of their attention because of its enormous size and growth potential. However, penetration of the Chinese market by foreign firms is always described as frustrating and difficult because of their lack of understanding of guanxi (Pye 1982, 1986; Brunner et al. 1989; Leung and Yeung 1995; Leung, Wong, and Tam 1995; Wong 1997, 1999). Paul Cheng (1995), chairman of Inchcape Pacific group, one of the major trading groups in Asia, summarized his company's experience in handling the guanxi issue in China:

- The cultivation of relationships (guanxi) at a personal, provincial, or municipal level and the search for connections with the right local authorities is important.
- The search for the right Chinese partner with the right network, preferably going through Hong Kong import/export companies

with good contacts and track records in China, is a definite help in developing Chinese business.

Guanxi

Guanxi seems to be the lifeblood of the Chinese business community, extending into politics and society. But it can also be broadly translated as "personal relationship" or "connections." It necessitates personal interactions and always involves a reciprocal obligation (Brunner and Koh 1988). It is developed with ingenuity and creativity, supplemented by the flexibility of cultivating a relationship through a person's network of connections.

MacInnes (1993) observed that the major contrast between Western and Chinese management practice is the emphasis on written contracts and procedures in the former, and personal relationships and trust in the latter. He provides perhaps the best elaboration of guanxi:

> To Chinese managers, guanxi is laden with powerful implications. To "la guanxi" (literally to "pull" guanxi) means to get on the good side of someone, to store political capital with them, and carries no negative overtones. To "gua guanxi" (literally to "work on" guanxi) means roughly the same but with a more general, less intense feeling and usually carries negative overtones. "Meiyou guanxi" ("without" guanxi) has become an idiom meaning, "it doesn't matter." "Guanxi gao jiang" (guanxi made ruined) means the relationship has gone bad, usually because of a lack of flexibility of those involved. "Lisun guanxi" ("straighten out" guanxi) means to put a guanxi back into proper or normal order, often after a period of difficulty or awkwardness. "You guanxi" ("to have" guanxi) [which is utterly unlike the American idiom "to have a relationship"], means to have access to needed influence. "Youde shi guanxi" ("what one does have" or "the one thing one does have" is guanxi), is sometimes negative, meaning that one has all the guanxi one needs, but something else essential is lacking. "Guanxi wang" ("guanxi net") means the whole network of guanxi through which the influence is brokered. "Guanxi hu" ("guanxi family") means a person, organization, even government department, occupying a focal point in one's guanxi network. (p. 346)

Brief Review of Guanxi Studies

The concept of guanxi has been researched by Jacobs (1980), Brunner and Taoka (1977), Lee and Lo (1988), Tse et al. (1988), Hwang (1987), Brunner and Koh (1988), and Brunner et al. (1989).

By studying a sample of American and Chinese negotiations, Brunner and Koh (1988) noted the impact of guanxi in China after implementation of an open-door policy in 1979. The underlying element of guanxi is the traditional Confucian concept of the group taking precedence over the individual, and it subtly defines the Chinese moral code. The Confucian social hierarchical theory (i.e., the five relationships—emperor-subject, father-son, husband-wife, brother-brother and friend-friend—*wu-lun* in Chinese) perpetuates its influence in modern China (Yau 1994; Buttery and Leung 1998). The word *lun* is actually a concise description of the guanxi among these five relationships (Tsui and Farh 1997). *"Lun"* means the proper positioning of mankind within the social and political hierarchy. An individual will fall into a natural guanxi web in the socialization process after he or she is born. If every individual takes the proper position, social harmony can be achieved in the vast country of China. This social hierarchical theory has prompted almost all Chinese rulers to adopt Confucianism as a strategic tool to achieve social stability.

The development of a guanxi web depends upon whether some attributes of a guanxi base (e.g., clan membership, friendships, schoolmates, teachers and students) exist among individuals (Brunner et al. 1989; Tsang 1998). The extent of guanxi cultivation among individuals depends upon their positioning within a framework based on some social unit classifications. The social units may be family, work units, and social network. The more attributes individuals have, the more capable they are of establishing guanxi within the social units they belong to provided that they have the time, money, and energy to navigate through this web. Gifts are normally used to cultivate guanxi (Brunner et al. 1989). Gift giving and hospitality are the means to establish and maintain guanxi, but these activities are not equivalent to corruption. Outright bribery may be enough to get a business transaction done on a one-time basis, but it cannot produce interpersonal bonds that constitute an emotional relationship (*ganqing* in Chinese) (Simons, Berkowitz, and Moyer 1970; Tsang

1998). One of the major purposes is to generate ganqing and become an insider in a group; then all deals become easy (Wong 1997).

Brunner et al. (1989) indicated that a major factor motivating the efforts to form guanxi was the prevalent shortages of everyday necessities, housing, and goods, so that the Chinese developed guanxi ties to obtain them. The primitive communication system and bureaucratic maze also prompted the Chinese to depend on guanxi as their "currency" to complete ordinary transactions. This social phenomenon functioned autonomously, parallel to the state distribution and market-oriented systems, involving personal obligations, "face" behavior, reciprocity, and social honor.

Summary of Perspectives

In summary, Western academic literature provides various perspectives on this relationship phenomenon. The first is the analysis of cross-cultural management. The concept of guanxi appears to derive from specifically Chinese cultural characteristics, described variously as "patronal" (MacInnes 1993) or "patrimonial" (Redding 1990). In this patrimonial literature, emphasis is placed upon the significance of a preference for vertical and hierarchical personal relationships in this "networked society."

Another angle is developed by the literature on business ethics. The key concern is to identify major differences in the form of social behavior to be considered, whether it is "ethical" or "unethical."

One other perspective is provided by economic analysis. The cultivation and exploitation of guanxi has been regarded as either an "economic rent-seeking" behavior, or the development of trust between potential business players with the objective of reducing transaction costs and improving the efficiency of a market economy by sharing resources, such as technology. Economic rent-seeking behavior is an act of earning income that an owner of an asset receives over and above the amount required to use that asset (Parkin 1994).

Guanxi is also analyzed in marketing literature as linking within a network. The network approach has four major perspectives—networks as relationships, structures, position, and process.

Finally, guanxi has been perceived as the end product of psychosocial constructs of defense mechanisms, paternalism, personalism, and pragmatism in the ever-changing Chinese environment (Redding 1990).

RESEARCH OBJECTIVES

This research attempts to trace the cultural roots of guanxi, to consider its role in marketing, and to determine its efficiency in the process of networking. In particular, it employs the view of networks as relationships, and it aims to provide exploratory empirical ideas and some evidence on the following dimensions:

- The perceived importance of developing guanxi to executives involved in doing business in China, and their differences in perception regarding this task and its importance
- The perceived importance of guanxi at different stages in the process of negotiation, the time taken to establish key contacts, and the number of channels that require mutual exploration and interaction before such contacts are established
- The nature of the actions taken to build guanxi
- The concept, role, and significance of guanxi in relationship marketing

Scope of the Study

Our exploratory research focuses on the following:

- Describing and identifying five environmental contexts: system, personalism, autocratic management, change of environment, and egocentric.
- Describing the atmosphere of interaction between buyer and seller in terms of behavioral strategies including power dependence, cooperation/competition, closeness/distance, and trust/opportunities.
- Investigating the interaction processes commonly employed by Chinese firms to deal with counterparts. An insider-outsider dichotomy is common in a Chinese environment. It can take extra time and effort to enter into a rewarding relationship with a Chinese person.
- Examining the nature and characteristics of short-term and long-term exchanges of products, services, information, financial interests, and social elements.
- Exploring the impact of cultural values on relationships, particularly Confucianism and nepotism (including favoritism toward insiders).

- Developing a new research tool in the form of a questionnaire, to measure the constructs of guanxi and the interaction of those constructs and relationship performance.
- Proposing a comprehensive guanxi model to incorporate the analysis of context, system dynamic (from perception to positioning), adaptation, and performance evaluation.
- Proposing a theoretical framework by suggesting a new vocabulary for analyzing guanxi strategies in terms of routing and implementation of guanxi by proposing concepts A through G.
- Summarizing implications for management by suggesting the benefits and the dynamic elements of guanxi.

The study is based on previous work and studies, such as those covering environmental aspects (Alder, Brahm, and Graham 1992; Armstrong et al. 1991), dynamic aspects (Alston 1989; Hwang 1987), interaction processes (Lee 1989), and Chinese values and exchange elements (Siu 1992; Tai 1988; Rosemont 1991). This study reflects research in different countries, particularly those of the International Marketing and Purchasing Group (IMP) (e.g., Hakansson 1982).

CONCEPTUAL FRAMEWORK
AND RESEARCH BOUNDARY

The study attempts to draw together the various directions of theory and research on the major elements of the seller-buyer relationship, by developing a comprehensive model that conceptually ties all these elements together. The conceptual framework is presented diagrammatically in Figure 1.1.

The Hong Kong import/export industry is selected as the area of analysis in this research, because import/export is the largest industry in Hong Kong in terms of the number of employees and employers.

Competitiveness of Hong Kong

According to the World Economic Forum report (1995), Hong Kong was the world's fifth largest trading economy after the European Union, the United States, Japan, and Canada in 1994. The world competitiveness report ranked Hong Kong third, one level above Japan. The world's most competitive nations were listed as follows (World Economic Forum, 1995):

1. United States
2. Singapore
3. Hong Kong
4. Japan
5. Switzerland
6. Germany
7. Netherlands
8. New Zealand
9. Denmark
10. Norway

FIGURE 1.1. Conceptual Framework of Guanxi Model

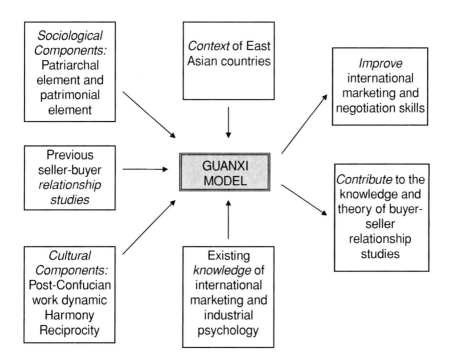

Note: Various social and cultural components, seller-buyer relationship studies, the Asian context, plus marketing and psychological knowledge are the major inputs to the guanxi model. The model aims to provide better understanding of international marketing and to contribute to relationship studies.

A strong service sector, outstanding entrepreneurial spirit, and government efficiency propelled Hong Kong to third place. Hong Kong achieved the world's fastest real growth in services during a ten-year period ending in 1992. Average annual growth in the service sector is 18 percent compared to 11 percent in China. K. Y. Tang, a Hong Kong government economist, indicated that the growth in services came from the strong performance of exports to China. Hong Kong became the world's largest exporter of garments, imitation jewelry, travel goods and bags, umbrellas, toys, and clocks. Hong Kong's major export markets were China, the United States, and the European Union. Approximate 76 percent of Hong Kong's reexports were destined for the PRC, and 50 percent of reexports came from China in 1994 (World Economic Forum 1995).

According to the Hong Kong government's annual report in 1995, the territory was the world's eighth largest trading economy (based on the total value of its merchandise trade) in 1994. The service sector includes 75.9 percent of total employment. Approximately 532,913 people work in the import/export industry, 23 percent of total employment. The outstanding performance of Hong Kong services and the competitiveness of the import/export industry motivated us to carry out this research. The Import/Export Training Center at Hong Kong's Vocational Training Council was selected as the major site of research using questionnaires.

Vocational Training Council

The Vocational Training Council is a Hong Kong government-funded organization offering training via their twenty-four centers for practicing executives, supervisors, and staff in both the industrial and service sectors. The Import/Export Training Center serves more than 3,000 people annually. Most of the courses are one- to three-day free intensive courses, specially designed for employees in the import/export sector.

The import/export industry contributes significantly to the economic prosperity of Hong Kong. In 1994, the total value of domestic exports amounted to HK$222 billion, reexports HK$448.6 billion, and imports HK$1,282 billion. According to the government's 1994 annual report, the workforce in the import/export trades has experienced an average annual growth rate of 17.5 percent since 1992 (Hong Kong Government 1995). Over 93 percent of the establishments in the trade have fewer than ten employees. This implies that very few companies are able to provide in-house training. In addition, few existing educational or training institutions offer courses specially tailored for the trades. Import/export practice, selling skills, and marketing techniques were the most preferred training courses, which required updated research input for better understanding and effective marketing application.

This research aims to provide the theoretical and practical tools to help the import/export industry to be more competitive in developing the PRC market. It contributes to the better understanding of global competition within this important industry, which requires more effective analytical and research tools and models for improving export marketing efficiency.

JUSTIFICATIONS FOR THIS RESEARCH

The relative lack of major empirical studies on guanxi prompted us to implement this research. There is a gap in the existing literature, the details of which are elaborated in Appendix A. Another concern facing researchers is that the research tools are insufficient. No questionnaire has been specially designed to measure guanxi constructs and their interactions with relationship quality and sales performance indicators.

The value of this research lies in:

- The importance of developing a theoretical model to explain complex industrial interactive behavior. In a world of rapid changes in technology combined with shorter product life cycles, a relationship can be appreciated as a competitive advantage.
- The significance of providing practical tools for business executives to understand and analyze the concept of guanxi.
- Following the proposal of Sheth (1985), it is important to focus on competitive behavior in order to pinpoint relative perceptions and behavior within a given culture. This study in a specific setting hopefully contributes greatly to the knowledge of global marketing.

METHODOLOGY

The major research tool of this study is a questionnaire survey supplemented by a case study and in-depth interviews. The purpose of the survey is to identify guanxi constructs and to discover the relationship between these constructs and relationship performance.

Focus groups were formed to generate concepts and ideas. Then two pilot tests were done to test and refine the questionnaires and to provide feedback for improving their quality. Finally, the major survey was carried out.

The analyses of the data consist of the following:

- Analysis of the respondent's profile
- Analysis of the working mechanism of guanxi
- Identification of guanxi constructs
- The relationship between guanxi constructs and relationship quality

Various tests were done to ensure overall reliability. Both correlation and multiple regression tests were performed to find the extent of associations between guanxi constructs and relationship quality and the relationship performance indicators, which include sales performance, relationship termination costs, and formalization. A case study was also carried out to test the model in a real-life situation.

DEFINITIONS OF SPECIAL TERMS

Guanxi

Guanxi can be roughly translated as "personal relationship" or "connections." Guanxi includes relationships and social connections with classmates, people from the same hometown, relatives, superiors and subordinates in the workplace, and so forth (Yang 1988).

Lisun guanxi means "straightening out" guanxi; that is, the reestablishment of guanxi in proper or normal order, often after a period of difficulty or awkwardness (MacInnes 1993).

Guanxi gao jiang means that guanxi is ruined; a relationship has gone bad, usually because of a lack of flexibility in business deals (MacInnes 1993).

Guanxi wang means "guanxi net." It is the whole network of guanxi through which influence is brokered (MacInnes 1993).

Guanxi hu means a person, organization, or even government department, occupying the center of one's guanxi network.

Favor and Renqing

Favor is the special treatment of an individual, the allocation of resources to another party as a "gift" in the process of a market transaction, to tighten up the bonds between parties. Among Chinese, it may be said that the connection between the bestowal and return of favors is stronger than in some other cultures. Renqing is the feedback or payback process of returning a favor.

Face (Mianzi)

Face is essentially the recognition by others of one's social standing and position, and thus may be regarded as situationally defined rather than a facet of one's personality (Ho 1976). *Mianzi* is the Chinese term for face. Mianzi reflects the individual's social position or prestige gained by the successful performance of one or more specific social roles as recognized by others (Hu 1944).

Heart and Mind Management

Heart management refers to the winning of people's hearts, whether those people are employees, workers, suppliers, or business partners (Wee 1994). Mind management implies a rational approach based on laws, regulation, and predefined policies with little appeal to people's emotions.

Insider and Outsider Relations

Insider relations imply the understanding of both parties involved that they share a common network, group, or party of some kind. The result is often the uninhibited exchange of information. Outsider relations imply the interaction of parties outside of any mutually defined group or network. In this case, the exchange of information may well be inhibited.

Fencer and Fiancé

The fencer stage is a period when each party is testing the other's intentions or reactions. Each party regards the other as an outsider. The fiancé stage occurs when each party bargains to establish a relationship depending on how it evaluates its dependence on the other party.

Lubrication and Subornation

Lubrication is payment for requesting a person to do a job rapidly or efficiently. Subornation refers to requests to officials or resource allocators to give special favors, not perform their jobs effectively, or even break the law.

Yin and Yang

Yin and yang are two Taoist concepts. Yin implies a soft approach whereas yang implies a hard approach. The two concepts have a symbiotic relationship and fuse to form a harmonious whole. Each compensates for the other's weakness and supplements its own strength.

Nepotism and de Facto

Nepotism is defined as providing favors to one's relatives. In Chinese society, it is a common phenomenon. A de facto relationship refers to two people living together without a formal marriage certificate. In social perspective, a de facto relationship of a Chinese couple is not allowed. If they really have this kind of relationship, it cannot be discussed in public. It should be kept secret. But in the business world, this type of connection is informally accepted. People are linked by various kinds of undisclosed bonding. The interpretations of this relationship are totally different in some Western countries. For example, in Australia, a de facto relationship of a couple is acceptable, and the relationship is protected by law to some extent. Nevertheless, businesspeople prefer to establish relationships similar to marriage by signing contracts or documents.

Although the Chinese have the same tasks or face similar situations, they may have different behavior or decisions and reactions, because they have their own value judgments and social norms as well as different management approaches. Explanations of these special terms help to provide a basic understanding of Chinese behavior and attitudes. In later chapters, more detailed descriptions and explanations are given.

LIMITATIONS OF THE RESEARCH

This study is the first attempt to propose a comprehensive model for the concept of guanxi, incorporating the constructs of trust, adaptation, favor, and dependence. Thus, it is inevitably subject to certain limitations. Tremendous efforts were made to conduct this study in a rigorous manner. The limitations are as follows:

1. *The location chosen*—The research data were mainly collected from Hong Kong exporters/importers. The scales of the research questionnaire were tested and found to be valid and reliable for the Chinese exporters and importers of Hong Kong. However, it is not appropriate to treat China as one big market. It should be regarded as one country and several markets. Dialects, lifestyles, climates, fashions, beliefs, and diets are quite different among provinces, and these differences imply a drastic change in cultural and personal values. It is necessary to test the measurement scale to avoid the inaccuracy of overgeneralization.
2. *The operationalization of guanxi constructs*—As there is no previous empirical evidence, nor statistics, on the identification of the measurement dimensions, the domains of Chinese values and attitudes may be underspecified or overspecified (not clearly defined).
3. *Study sample*—The data collected come mainly from the Import/Export Training Center, Vocational Training Council, in the form of interviews and questionnaires. The nature of this sample limits potential generalization regarding other industries in Hong Kong.

STUDY OUTLINE

1. Chapter 2, "Literature Review—Western Views," starts with a review of the theoretical foundations of relationship studies in Western literature. The discussion of the conceptualization of relationships and relationship marketing is followed by an in-

vestigation and exploration of factors affecting relationship development.

2. Chapter 3, "Literature Review—Chinese Views," starts with a review of the theoretical foundations of relationship studies in Chinese literature. The discussion of the conceptualization of relationships and relationship marketing is followed by an investigation and exploration of factors affecting relationship development. Western and Chinese views are also compared and contrasted.

3. Chapter 4 presents the context of guanxi, including the components, attributes, and preliminary constructs and framework of the model.

4. Chapter 5, "Theoretical and Practical Aspects," summarizes the findings of research and concludes by elaborating on the implications for both theoretical and practical aspects.

5. Chapter 6 describes a comprehensive guanxi model.

The chapter organization is summarized in Figure 1.2.

SUMMARY AND CONCLUSION

Owing to the ever-changing marketing environment, relationship marketing and networking are becoming popular, in addition to conventional analysis of the four "P"s (product, price, promotion, and place) in understanding buyer behavior. With the growing economic power of China combined with its cultural characteristics in management and marketing, the concept of guanxi plays an important role in the study of relationship marketing. Guanxi refers to special relationship-building between trading partners as well as anyone involved in market transactions. To study guanxi, several perspectives are considered: cross-cultural management, business ethics, economic analysis, network analysis, and psychosocial analysis.

There are four major research areas:

1. The importance of developing guanxi
2. The significance of guanxi in different relationships plus time spent and the number of channels required to establish guanxi
3. The nature of the actions taken to establish guanxi
4. The concept, role, and impact of guanxi in relationship marketing. This research examines the importance of guanxi in China

and how businesspeople build up effective guanxi with their trading partners.

The research justifications are, first, to develop a theoretical model to explain complex behavior; second, to provide practical tools to understand and analyze the concept of guanxi; and third, to contribute to the knowledge of global marketing.

FIGURE 1.2. Chapter Organization and Research Structure

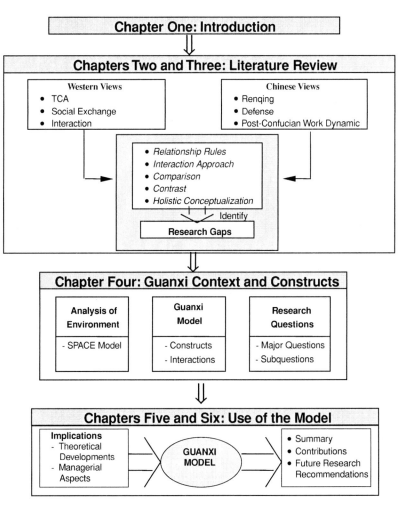

Chapter 2

Literature Review: Western Views

INTRODUCTION

This chapter is concerned with identifying the characteristics of Western approaches to the features of relationships. The Western model is needed to provide a comparison with Chinese approaches in Chapter 3. The major objective of this chapter is to describe and review the major Western theories of buyer-seller relationships: transaction cost analysis, social exchange, and interaction approaches. This chapter includes a critical review of literature on Western-style relationships.

Theoretical Foundation

Western literature includes extensive studies on relationships. In summary, three major categories of relationships are:

1. Economic
2. Sociopsychological
3. Marketing

There are Western and Chinese views on each of these types of relationships.

In Western literature:

1. Transaction cost analysis (TCA)
2. Social exchange
3. Interaction theory

In Chinese literature (discussed in Chapter 3):

1. Defense and network
2. Renqing and face
3. Post-Confucian work dynamic

Table 2.1 provides the classification of both views under different interpretation topics.

WESTERN VIEWS

The Western views are discussed by describing transaction cost analysis, social exchange, and interaction theories with critical comments. In Western literature, economic analysis is one of the major and pioneering contributions to the explanation of economic behavior between persons and organizations. Transaction cost analysis is a popular explanation proposed by economists.

Transaction Cost Analysis

Transaction cost analysis has been used to explain the behavior of a wide range of organizational activities, including bureaucracy (Williamson 1979), vertical integration of production (Williamson 1971; Klein, Craqford, and Alchian 1978), clanlike relations among firms (Ouchi 1980), and organizational culture. It is important to elaborate further on the underlying concepts.

Transaction costs are associated with an economic exchange, such as research and information costs, monitoring costs, and enforcing contractual performance. These costs are independent of the compet-

TABLE 2.1. Types of Interpretation of Relationships: Classification According to Western and Chinese Approaches

Type of Interpretation	Western Approach	Chinese Approach
Economic	Transaction Cost Analysis	Defense and Network
Sociopsychological	Social Exchange	Renqing and Face
Marketing or Business	Interaction Theory	Post-Confucian Work Dynamic

itive market price of goods or services, but they are subject to the influence of different types of exchanges.

The transaction cost approach has addressed the issue of economic exchange mainly in the context of commercial organization. The basic problem for such organizations is to adapt effectively to uncertainty.

Ouchi (1980) claims that the clan mechanism will create better relationships. The clan mechanism involves a long process of interactions leading to common values and beliefs. An interdependent relationship is formed through clan association. Both buyer and seller work together to share information and solve problems. The cooperation between the two parties becomes stronger. An optimal relationship will reduce the transaction costs of searching for information, relationship monitoring, and contract enforcement.

Principles of TCA

One of the principles of TCA is that decision makers have limited information (bounded rationality) and may pursue their self-interest with incomplete or misleading information disclosure (opportunism). Markets may fail to allocate services and goods efficiently due to natural and government-induced operation conditions such as market and regulatory barriers (Kogut 1988; Root 1987; Teece 1986). Transactions may require each party to invest in durable assets, human capital, or technology, since one firm will face a higher cost if it approaches an international market by itself, e.g., in establishing a wholly owned subsidiary in that market. By bringing its transactions under a common cooperative structure with another firm in that market, each of the two partnering firms can improve its efficiency because the costs of transaction in terms of production, technology innovation, etc., are minimized.

As Ouchi (1980) argues, transaction costs are presented in a cooperative relationship in which the parties have difficulty identifying or valuing their respective contributions. Transaction costs are minimized as trading partners attempt simultaneously to coordinate operations to protect their own interests and to adapt to situational uncertainty, thus creating the perception of equity among themselves.

The TCA approach has mainly been used to explain the complex aspects of economic behavior. TCA provides the concept of opportunism but is unable to support the argument of close cooperation because minimum transaction costs may mean greater opportunism and a decrease in the number of transactions. In the real world, most transactions are not "economic," and a minimum number of transactions does not mean maximum efficiency. The aim of this research is to provide an explanation for why there is a tendency toward opportunistic behavior.

Social Exchange

Social exchange theory provides a framework for analyzing different buyer-seller relationships (Dwyer, Schurr, and Oh 1987). Interaction is defined as a process in which two parties are engaged in exchanging valuable resources. They will continue interacting with each other only if they perceive the exchange as valuable.

According to Peter Blau (1964), the concept underlying the building of relations between groups and individuals is the differentiation of the power of the peer group. Social exchange theory serves as an effective tool to analyze how the structure of rewards and costs in relationships affects the patterns of interactions (Linda 1991). There are two major components of social exchange theory: trust and power dependence.

Trust

During the process of exchange, the actors in a relationship gradually build trustworthiness by showing commitment through the processes of adapting to each other.

Sullivan and Peterson (1982) assert that "where the parties have trust in one another then there will be ways by which the two parties can work out difficulties such as power conflict, low profitability, and so forth" (p. 30).

Dwyer, Schurr, and Oh (1987) also argue that "trust is an important concept in understanding expectations for cooperation and planning in a relational contract" (p. 18). Schurr and Ozanne (1985) reveal that the buyer's expectations regarding trust significantly influence the attitudes, communication, and bargaining behavior of its suppliers.

A party that is willing to coordinate with another trusted party may be willing to engage in high-risk coordinative behavior (Pruitt 1981), including:

1. A major concession on getting reciprocation
2. A tendency toward compromise
3. A unilateral tension reduction function
4. Proclaiming motives and priorities to stimulate the other's confidence

Therefore, trust building is an important element in the social exchange process. The parties may demonstrate their trustworthiness by committing themselves to the exchange relationship, and an important way of showing commitment is by adapting to each other. Trust is an important variable in the effectiveness of relationships, which depend on interpersonal acceptance and openness of expression for any joint problem solving.

Table 2.2 suggests that Westerners have high individualism indexes and low long-term orientation. Individualism refers to the ties among individuals, and the high rate indicates that people have loose relationships, whereas low long-term orientation means focusing on the past and present, rather than the future (Hofstede 1999). It shows that Western cultures prefer individual performance. It may be that Westerners do not easily trust others, so they prefer to perform tasks themselves. In most business encounters they give less emphasis to personal relationships and focus on the task. In negotiating with other cultures, Westerners do not give priority to personal relationships. Many Westerners like to do business over the phone, and are not really interested in meeting their clients face to face. However, in many other cultures, a face-to-face meeting is important in order to build

TABLE 2.2. Value Index of Hofstede's Five Dimensions in Western Cultures

Dimension	Power Distance	Individualism	Masculinity	Uncertainty Avoidance	Long-Term Orientation
Australia	36	90	61	51	31
Great Britain	35	89	66	35	25
United States	40	91	62	46	29
Average	37	90	63	44	28

the personal rapport essential to establishing a business relationship (Elashmawi and Harris 1993).

Power Dependence

Power. Weber (1947) provided the definition "Power is the probability that one actor within a social relationship will be in a position to carry out his own will despite resistance" (p. 152). Tawney (1931) stated that "Power may be defined as the capacity of an individual or groups . . . in the manner which he desires, and to prevent his own product being modified in the manner in which he does not" (p. 229). Thus, power is the ability of individuals or groups to impose their will on others despite resistance.

The relative power of the two actors in an exchange relationship is affected by their relative dependence. Power comes from controlling resources required by the other or controlling the alternative sources of the resources.

Dependence. No organization is able to generate internally all the resources and functions it requires. Managers must find the best ways to compete for resources, as resource acquisition is usually problematic and involves uncertainty. Each actor is involved in the dynamic process of acquiring resources that are subject to variations in the control and discretion of each party.

Beyond the normal interdependencies of interorganizational divisions of labor and specialization of functions, some interdependencies are sought (or avoided) on account of the power and control inherent in the development of dependence. Any organizations that manage to acquire monopoly control over important resources are highly able to defend their market position.

To summarize, an organization seeks to avoid being controlled by other parties by securing resource stability and certainty. Firms in a business relationship are expected to adapt to each other according to the degree of their mutual dependence.

The concepts of trust and dependence are very important to the buyer-seller relationship. However, most theories require empirical tests for verification. Also, the verification is ideally carried out in different cultures. Insufficient empirical tests of these concepts prompted us to carry out this study to develop guanxi constructs and to create a model that incorporates the relationship between the constructs and sales effectiveness.

Limitations of Economic and Social Exchange Theories

The limitations of both economic and social exchange theories appear to be, first, that the theories are able to explain major dimensions behind the theories, e.g., the assumption of rational behavior. Second, a relationship is an important topic with special cultural variables, e.g., its symbolic meaning (Dabholkar and Johnston 1994). Apart from TCA and sociopsychological theories, numerous European scholars have proposed interaction theories to account for the dynamic aspects of relationships. The new analytic tool is the interaction approach refined by European scholars in 1980s.

Interaction Approach

Within an interaction approach, there are four key components. First, different individual exchange episodes among two parties, such as for product, service, or information, form the interaction process. The routinization of these exchange episodes leads to further expectations over a period of time. Second, the distinct characteristics of the interaction parties are very important. Third, the interaction environment plays a significant role. It consists of market structure, dynamism, internationalization, and social system. Fourth, the atmosphere can be apprehended as the relationship among two parties, including the context of power dependence, the condition of conflict or cooperation, the overall closeness or distance of the relationship, and the mutual expectations (Leung, Wong, and Tam 1995). Based on the interaction approach, Kutschler (1985) includes all theoretical frames of reference centering on the processes of mutual influence and communication linked to exchange of industrial goods. Organizational interaction approaches regard transactions as joint decision processes between organizations. Emmerson (1962), Heskett, Stern, and Beier (1977), Levine and White (1961), and Litwak and Hylton (1962) advocate the heuristic view that interaction is both the cause and the result of power and dependency relations. The transaction's progress and structure will reflect the constellation of influences stemming from the relevant product technology, the characteristics of the involved organizations, and the dynamics of the environment.

Other key studies on interaction include Hakansson (1982), Cunningham (1980), and Wilson and Mummalaneni (1986). Wilson and Mummalaneni (1986) suggest that the interactive model be tested in non-European settings, and argue that the European International Marketing and Purchasing (IMP) Group's interaction model is the right approach to deal with the various issues of the buyer-seller relationship.

IMP Approach

The IMP model focuses on the factors leading to close relationships and the exchange episodes over time embedded in the framework of a relationship in which the actors adapt to one another, in order to produce mutually beneficial outcomes.

Adaptation

Adaptation is defined as the extent to which the buyer and seller make substantial investments in the business relationship. Adaptations imply a commitment by the buyer or seller to the development of the relationship. One of the preconditions for the maintenance of an interfirm relationship is mutual orientation—whether the firms are prepared and willing to interact with each other and expect each other to do so (Mattsson 1988).

Adaptations may occur in many aspects of business, such as inventory management, the collection and dissemination of information, and product or process technology. Adaptations will probably enhance interfirm bonds.

The adaptation process may be initiated by either party or both parties. Wilson and Moller (1988) indicate that both parties may even adapt their attitudes, values, and goals to enhance their relationship.

According to Hallen, Johanson, and Seyed-Mohamed (1991), adaptation implies considerable investment by one or both parties. It may be of great importance for highly technical products. Investment in adaptation is often difficult to transfer to other business relationships because both parties need time to adapt to each other. However, adaptations may help to improve long-term competitiveness.

The most popular studies on the topic of interfirm adaptation consider the customization of products by suppliers. The extent of adaptation ranges from small-scale variations to the creation of an entirely new product for a single customer (von Hippel 1978). The supplier may adapt production processes by purchasing new equipment, or by using new logistic systems such as just-in-time delivery and new quality control systems (Frazier, Spekman, and O'Neal 1988).

In the development of a close working relationship, each party may obtain benefits in the form of cost reduction or increases in revenue. These benefits include the activities of tailoring their resources for dealing with a specific buyer or seller by making a durable transaction-specific investment.

The major recent theories of interfirm adaptation include the cooperation approach (Metcalf, Frear, and Krishnan 1992), transaction cost approach (Krapfel, Salmond, and Spekman 1991), and social exchange and power-dependence approach (Hallen, Johanson, and Seyed-Mohamed 1991).

Interaction Model

Metcalf, Frear, and Krishnan (1992) tested the interaction model in the U.S. environment. They concluded that the exchange of information and interpersonal contacts produced a cooperative atmosphere between buyer and seller, possibly leading to mutual adaptation. With the establishment of a cooperative environment between buyer and seller and if products were perceived as being important to the purchasing firm, the tendency was for both firms to be more willing to seek close ties. Customers are more likely to join with vendors in mutual adaptations, particularly with regard to joint product development and the coordination of production schedules. This research is particularly based on the interaction model developed by Hakansson (1982), which has four basic elements:

The interaction environment. The interaction between a buying and a selling firm is considered in a wider context including market structure, dynamism, internationalization, and position in the manufacturing channel and social system.

A Western firm's internationalization process is opportunistic in nature. Its concept of opportunism is based either on cost (TCA), opportunity/market/financial analyses (OMF approach), or matching/ level of control analyses. Second, they explore a universal and systematic approach to determining the market entry process. Finally, they recognize that interaction is an effective way to allocate resources of two partnering firms. This research pays special attention to the context of dynamism, but the "dynamic" element in the IMP interaction model is defined vaguely.

The interaction parties. A firm will evaluate its own and its potential partner's organizational context and attempt to create a strategic plan for the interaction that fits the requirements of both partners. This process of interaction and the relationship between the organizations depends not only on the elements of the interaction but also on the characteristics of the parties involved, including both organizations and individuals.

The interaction process. The process consists of individual episodes of exchange between two parties. They include product and service, information, financial, and social exchanges.

For example, the two parties will adopt a problem-solving attitude (PSA) that encourages them to collect further information if they have established mutual interest. PSA allows them to assess the interacting atmosphere. For example, a team may determine that the issue of technology transfer is too important for them. Therefore, they may not be willing to compromise on this issue and attempt to control it. They may compromise on other issues such as production volume in order to maintain the personal relationship between both parties. On other issues such as employment, they may attempt to collaborate to integrate both parties' requirements. A win/win situation can be achieved through mutual understanding of the other's needs and in a cooperative negotiation environment. However, if the two parties cannot establish interpersonal attraction, they may use the distributive attitude, which limits the information exchange between the parties and results in a win/lose situation.

The atmosphere. Atmosphere can be summarized in terms of power dependence, the state of conflict or cooperation, and the overall closeness or distance of the relationship and the expectations.

Table 2.2 shows the value indexes of major Western cultures. The low power distance indexes imply that Western cultures consider humans as basically equal. The high individualism indexes show that Western cultures prefer individual performance. The low long-term orientation indexes indicate that Western cultures aim at short-term performance.

SUMMARY AND CONCLUSION

This chapter aims to explain the general characteristics and major ideas of Western relationship studies, theories, and approaches. After reviews of various research and literature, this chapter elaborates the Western view of relationship marketing. The Western approach to the buyer-seller relationship is illustrated by reviewing TCA, social exchange, and interaction theories.

In Western literature, the interpretation of economic analysis is based on transaction cost analysis, which is used to explain the complex economic aspects of behavior. Social exchange theory has been adopted to deal with sociopsychological dimensions. Trust and power dependence are the two major components of the theory used to explain the buyer-seller relationship. Owing to the limitations of economic and social exchange theories, interaction theory was proposed to explain the dynamic aspects of relationships. In interaction theory, adaptation plays a vital role.

Chapter 3

Literature Review: Chinese Views

INTRODUCTION

This chapter identifies the characteristics of Chinese approaches to relationships and compares them with Western approaches. It is important to the research because it reveals the major research gap (see Appendix A). The research develops an understanding of the guanxi model, which is specific to the Chinese situation.

The major objective of this chapter is to describe the major Chinese theories of guanxi and the related concepts of renqing (favor) and defense theory, one of the exploratory theories used to explain the psychology of Chinese people. In addition, the positive aspects of guanxi, that is, the post-Confucian work dynamic theory, the analysis of relationship rules, and the integration approach of all Chinese theories, are major topics. Finally, comparison and contrast of Western and Chinese views are attempted.

Empirical Study on the Interaction Approach in an Asian Environment

Most empirical research involving the interaction approach has been carried out in the Western world. An empirical study was undertaken by the authors in an Asian context (Leung, Wong, and Tam 1995). This study implies that guanxi is an underlying dimension of business in China. This finding coincides with the research results of Lee and Lo (1988), Tse et al. (1988), Hwang (1987), and Brunner et al. (1989).

Our study revealed the importance of guanxi and the lack of a robust framework for understanding it. To establish a theoretical framework, it is necessary to know exactly what the constructs of guanxi are and how they can be measured.

Adaptation and guanxi in interactions are the major themes of this research. Chapter 6 provides a review of a new theoretical framework and makes suggestions for marketing and business executives in the formulation and implementation of relationship-enhancing programs.

The literature cited previously reflects the importance of guanxi in relationship building, but what are the micro aspects or variables that explain the mechanisms or concepts of relationships? Why are relationships and guanxi unique in terms of symbolic meaning in the Chinese context?

Concepts of Interfirm Adaptation in Business Relationships

Apart from social exchange theory, interaction theory, and TCA theory, a new concept of interfirm adaptation can be developed based on a new Chinese approach (see Figure 3.1).

The social exchange, TCA, and interaction approaches have been regarded as useful tools for analyzing relationship marketing in Western culture. In Chinese culture, social networks emphasize harmony within a given society and demand the appropriate arrangement of interpersonal relationships (Abbott 1970). The study of indigenous concepts, such as renqing or favor, mianzi or face (King and Myers 1977), has played an important role in understanding Chinese social behavior.

CHINESE VIEWS

What Is Guanxi?

In Chinese culture, it is perceived that one's existence is largely influenced by one's relationships with others, and that one cannot change the environment but must harmonize with it. This guanxi concept is embedded in Chinese business decision making even though businesspeople have been exposed to western cultures (Tse et al. 1988).

Guanxi means the relationships built on preexisting relationships. The right guanxi can bring cheap and reliable material supplies, tax concessions, marketing of goods domestically or for export, and assistance when problems arise (Pye 1986; Tai 1988; Osland 1989).

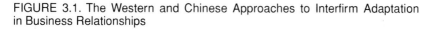

FIGURE 3.1. The Western and Chinese Approaches to Interfirm Adaptation in Business Relationships

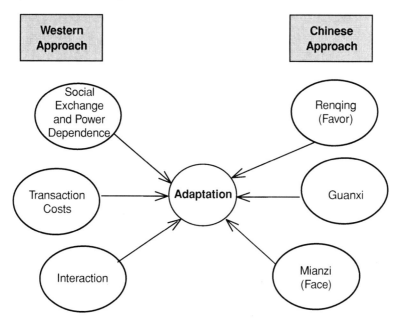

Generally, in Chinese culture, guanxi is a hierarchically structured network of relations. The actor in the relationship network is confined by mutual obligations. Over time, these obligations occur through a conscious manipulation of face, renqing (favor), and related symbols.

Chinese culture emphasizes the value of maintaining personal harmony and social order in hierarchically structured personal relationships. Chinese people usually regard renqing, guanxi, and mianzi (face) as weapons in a power game, to be used to influence people or to obtain social resources controlled by them. Guanxi and renqing are often used to obtain scarce goods and benefits, but only if relationships are developed with some norms of reciprocity. When one uses guanxi to obtain a favor, one is expected to repay the favor at a later stage.

How Can Guanxi Be Developed?

A major factor motivating the efforts to develop guanxi is the prevalent shortage of everyday necessities, including housing and scarce goods. The Chinese developed guanxi to obtain them (Brunner et al. 1989; Wong 1997).

Thus, Yang (1986) suggests that guanxi may be built through the exchange of gifts, favors, and banquets. But money is rarely offered because it is not personal enough, and such an offer may be perceived as bribery. Moreover, the gift should appropriately fit the personal needs of the recipient and be presented at the right occasion, such as a birthday party. Otherwise, the recipient will lose face and the presenter does not have face (Brunner and Koh 1988). This sort of exchange, and knowing how to carry it off, has been referred to as the art of guanxi. The art of guanxi refers to skillful ways to mobilize moral and cultural imperatives, for example, using obligation and reciprocity to fulfill diffused social ends and calculated instrumental ends (Yang 1986).

Expressive, Instrumental, and Mixed Relationships

Traditionally, Chinese people have tended to adopt multiple behavioral standards for interacting with different people around them. Hwang (1987) developed a theoretical model of face and favor in Chinese society. According to this model, Chinese people in different interpersonal relationships use various rules to obtain favor. Interpersonal relationships can be divided into three types: expressive, instrumental, and mixed.

The expressive type is generally a relatively permanent and stable social relationship. This kind of relationship occurs mostly among members of a primary group such as family, close friends, and other congenial groups. The instrumental type refers to personal relationships outside or inside the family that serve only as the means to attain other objectives, and are unstable and temporary. The mixed type is a relationship involving both expressive and instrumental components. In a mixed relationship, an individual seeks to use renqing and mianzi to influence other people. It has a particularistic and personal essence. The actors in the relationship may evaluate their interaction according to their own social standards. Each resource allocator has to consider the rule of renqing whenever he or she is asked to distribute a resource in a beneficial way to any other individual sharing the same personal network.

Moreover, Hwang (1987) also suggested that "establishing guanxi" or "seeking relations" in Chinese society basically involves the establishment of relationships. To establish guanxi, an introduction by a third party is merely the first step in constructing a mixed relationship. To present a gift or to host a feast for a resource allocator are the two tactics most frequently employed by the petitioner for enhancing a relationship with the resource allocator. In addition, two important factors affect relationship development: renqing and face.

Renqing

"Renqing" has three meanings (Hwang 1987):

1. Emotional responses—consisting of happiness, anger, sadness, fear, love, hate, and desire, all of them acquired at birth (p. 70). In psychological terms, renqing is similar to empathy. If someone is indifferent to another person's emotional responses, he or she is described as "not knowing renqing."
2. A gift in social exchange—This gift may be in the form of transfer of resources. Sometimes, gifts are tied up with some abstract components of affection. This affection is difficult to measure. This is why it is difficult to pay back renqing.
3. Social norms—Renqing involves two basic kinds of social behavior: (a) occasional exchanges of gifts and visits within one's social network, and (b) offering help and showing sympathy to other members of the network.

Both parties may negotiate and agree in advance regarding the exact date of reciprocation. In expressive relationships, social exchanges tend to follow the norm of reciprocity. The Chinese saying "I owe him a renqing" signifies that renqing is a certain kind of resource that can be used as a medium of social exchange. But the extent and type of resource used in exchange may be unlimited and the date of reciprocation is unknown. Finally, in the mixed relationship, the rule of "a favor for a favor, an attack for an attack" normally applies. In this case, the recipient owes renqing to the benefactor and should be ready to pay back the debt of gratitude once circumstances permit.

The norm of renqing includes two basic kinds of social behavior:

1. One should keep in contact with the acquaintances in one's social network.
2. When a member of one's social network gets into trouble or faces a difficult situation, another member should sympathize or offer help and "do a renqing" for that member.

In short, the anticipation of repayment is the main motivation for Chinese people to offer renqing to one another (Hwang 1987).

How can rening be valued? Three variables determine the complexities of renqing within mixed relationships:

1. The cost to the resource allocator
2. The anticipation of the petitioner's reciprocation
3. Social personal evaluations within the interpersonal network

Face or Mianzi

"Face" is difficult to define precisely. Face may mean one's respect, status, and moral reputation in Chinese society. It may be a self-image in terms of approved social attributes (Hu 1944; Hwang 1987).

Face is essentially the recognition by others of one's social standing and position, and thus may be regarded as situationally defined rather than a facet of personality (Ho 1976). This definition may imply that face is not solely the responsibility of individuals, but is influenced also by the actions of those with whom they are closely associated, and how they are perceived and dealt with by others. The emphasis is upon the reciprocity of obligations, dependence, and the protection of the esteem of those involved. One should not only protect one's face, but also extend face to others. Both are of equal importance (Brunner and Wang 1988). Face or mianzi work reflects the individual's social position or prestige gained by performing one or more specific successful social roles that are well recognized by others (Hu 1944).

Asian societies are socially stratified and class conscious (Brunner and Wang 1988). The Chinese exercise this social stratification through their bureaucratic system. The practices of "giving face," "losing face," and "face enhancement" can occur at a country or business level as well as a personal level. How does face become social capital?

Face symbols and social capital. The mechanism of face is summarized by Moore (1988). Moore's analysis suggests that face in urban Hong Kong "refers specifically to having a network of useful connections" (p. 52). Having face means that one can make use of a series of linkages to achieve something. Defining face in this way indicates that it is social capital rather than symbolic capital, according to Moore's clarified definitions (Smart 1993). *Symbolic capital* consists of the "prestige and renown attached to a family and a name" (Bourdieu 1977, p. 179). Bourdieu suggests that symbolic capital is a form of credit: "Once one realizes that symbolic capital is always credit, in the widest sense of the word, i.e. a sort of advance which the group alone can grant those who give it the best material and symbolic guarantees, it can be seen that the exhibition of symbolic capital (which is always very expensive in economic terms) is one of the mechanisms which (no doubt universally) make capital go to capital" (Bourdieu 1977, p. 181). "Social capital is the sum of the actual and potential resources that can be mobilized through membership in social networks of actors and organizations" (Anheier, Geshards, and Romo 1995, p. 862).

The concepts of guanxi, renqing, and face are, to some extent, similar to the concepts of Western social theory, but we need to ask: Why is guanxi so important to the Chinese? One must trace the historical background and development of guanxi, individualism, safety, and networks. A good explanation may be provided by theories of defense and insecurity.

Defense Theory

The importance of relationship networks is rooted in Chinese history, which has been characterized by strong government control reinforcing Confucian codes of ethics. These codes include filial piety and pragmatic defense mechanisms in business network building (Figure 3.2).

The following section explains how the behavior of Chinese emperors and officials created mistrust, which eventually led to built-in defense mechanisms in Chinese personality development.

Defense. The defense mechanism in Chinese business organizations is a result of deep-seated mistrust of Chinese legal and political

FIGURE 3.2. Determinants of Defense Mechanisms in Business Networks: The Importance of Defense Mechanisms in the PRC

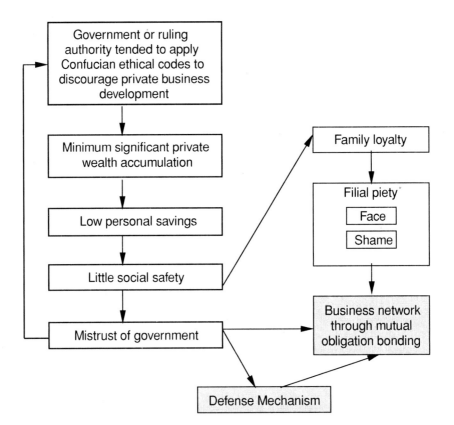

systems. Mistrust is a type of insecurity that derives from a historical combination of (a) the insecurity of wealth in a society without a fully reliable system of property rights, and (b) the general lack of trust outside one's personal network.

Weber (1951) noted that, in the Confucian concept, a gentleman who strove simply for a dignified personality distrusted others, since he believed others distrusted him in general. Sinlin (1976) pointed out that *hsiao,* or filial piety, and *chung,* or loyalty, inevitably caused conflict with the authority figure.

Mistrust and networks. For survival purposes, Chinese people tend to interact with others by building "informal" ties, which become strong bonds leading to the growth of a network. This growth reflects public socialization and customs of hospitality (Redding 1990). Thus, Chinese organization's interactions and exchange processes with other firms in that network develop links of resources and activities. These resources and activities among firms complement one another. Organizations can use the existence of complementarity or competitiveness in their relationships in different ways, as they interact with one another.

Such activities can create not only triangular relationships, but even networks involving four or more participating business organizations (Hakansson and Snehota 1989). One has to be sufficiently trusted to be included in these private systems. Interfirm relations are strategic and ought to be managed with the utmost care and attention.

Networking is mainly used to protect the individual's or group's resources among the members of the network. Chinese people have developed defense mechanisms that are apparent among overseas Chinese businesspeople who have proved to be resilient in the competitive environment of foreign countries (Redding 1990).

Open conflict and overtly self-interested behavior are often regarded by the Chinese as improper. Aggressive desires and emotion are sublimated. Chinese society often has limited guidelines for the management of conflicts of interest.

Avoidance of confrontation. Another common behavior is the tendency to avoid or minimize confrontation in building links. The creation of wealth in one family unit may be achieved by purchasing and sales, exchanges of information, financial interactions, and seeking advice among the family members. To enable such networks to operate efficiently and effectively, Chinese society has paid attention to trust, which is very particularly circumscribed. The number of partners in a bond is highly limited, based on personal obligations and the development and enhancement of reputation and face. Fukuyama (1995) regards Chinese Confucian societies as low-trust societies. He defined the moral bonds of social trust as the unspoken, unwritten bond between citizens. Compared with a high-trust society such as the United States, China is described as less competitive because the low trust value seems to discourage the growth of large-scale business organizations.

Trust and risk management. Networks are built through mutual trust, which is a highly sensitive and powerful norm. The Chinese may have difficulty connecting with an unknown or unestablished network. Normally, trustworthiness is tested by using mutually known intermediary connections or through members of a reputable clan.

In Western business, no personal relationships are involved. Transactions are discrete and purely profit driven (Lee and Lo 1988). However, if foreign negotiators attempt to build relationships with them at a personal level by using a guanxi intermediary, the business scenario will be completely different. At the initial personal contact, the companies may be "new friends." At this stage, the Chinese will test the degree of bonding with foreign firms through various contacts such as formal meetings (company visits) and informal meetings (dining together). After the relationship is consolidated and differences such as business styles and practices are resolved, the "old friends" stage begins and both parties will be bonded by trust.

This "credit" or trustworthiness exercise requires much effort but produces savings in the form of risk avoidance. Most Chinese do not like to enter litigation. There are three principal types of cooperation:

1. Family cooperation—The family is regarded as an important unit, with intense loyalty among members.
2. Network cooperation—As a result of pragmatic needs, bonding and cooperation are cemented effectively by obligation, trust, and friendship.
3. Such relationships are called gentle-type relationships, summed up by a Chinese proverb: "The relationship between gentlemen is as plain as water." Chinese people prefer to have these "gentle-type" relationships. Relationships that are too close lead to misunderstandings, and people do not wish to involve themselves too much in other people's lives.

Chinese history is another factor in Chinese defense strategies. Because of the policy of national isolation and because of Confucian disdain for business for hundreds of years, most governments in Chinese history played a minimal role in the growth of private commercial business. Businesspeople received minimal protection from the government, with limited formal legal systems.

This discussion reflects the interrelationships among defense, mistrust, and risk management in business network building. But another key question is: What is the relationship between Chinese values and guanxi? One perspective is the post-Confucian work dynamic interpretation.

Post-Confucian Work Dynamic

In traditional Confucian ethics, commerce was not highly regarded, because agricultural work was regarded as productive and virtuous, and the individual's social status was often determined by level of education rather than wealth. Material possessions, such as property acquired through business, did not automatically command respect.

These core values of Confucian ethics were strongly upheld by government officials in the interpretation of business law. Emperors constantly reinforced Confucian ethics as a means of maintaining the stability of social systems and civil justice. They tried to prevent the rise of a rich and powerful bourgeoisie, which might undermine the status quo.

The accumulation of wealth was preferably undertaken by the ruling authority. The predominance of the wealth accumulation of the ruling authority was well protected by the fact that most laws were not neutral. Because there was little or no formal system of property rights, Chinese merchants were subject to the vagaries of fiscal policies. There was no formal system of trading shares. Major assets were in the form of cash or tangible assets, which are easily subject to confiscation and taxation.

Merchants were threatened with unfair taxes, unreasonable licensing fees, or unnecessary restrictions on travel or trade. And they had no recourse to take formal legal action against officials in the absence of formal written commercial law.

Chinese merchants have developed substantial negotiating skills and have created defensive contacts or allegiances within an ever-changing superstructure in both benevolent and hostile environments. The survival of many overseas Chinese organizations in highly hostile countries as well as benevolent nations proves this point. Even in China today, guanxi is a very effective way to cope both socially and politically with ever-changing systems. New business features and activities have been developed, such as:

1. Institutions for pooling capital (since only partnerships, lineage common properties, and maritime trade joint ventures began obtaining protection under the open economic system in 1979).
2. Legal, financial, and commercial institutions (e.g., banks, security exchanges, insurance, brokerages, and legal specialists, which are intermediaries to shift capital from household to industry).
3. A reliable currency (but the yuan is still not traded internationally).

Summary

Because of poor legal systems to protect merchants, Chinese businesspeople have always defended their own networks by bonding with members inside a network, and developing bonds of trust with individual persons, suppliers, and government bodies who are considered worthy of mutual obligation. Most businesspeople, who have tried to avoid the bureaucracy, are successful in cities or countries that have supported entrepreneurship, such as Hong Kong and Taiwan.

In a nutshell, the legacy of Chinese social history reflects a lack of security. Chinese people mistrust others with whom they are not familiar, or who are not in a known guanxi network, such as a clan association. In an environment characterized by social insecurity, merchants have had limited confidence in formal institutions or government bodies. They have had to protect themselves. They tend to be motivated by money and the need to gain education, and they defer immediate gratification by saving. In the absence of formal property rights, money is their major wealth, which enhances their living standards and also helps them to develop networks with powerful officials, who can sometimes protect their lives and wealth.

Hodgetts (1993) supported the importance of saving, i.e., the value attributed to thrift. Hofstede called Michael Bond's (1991) new "Confucian dynamism" value a "long-term orientation." This long-term orientation may explain why more capital (in terms of high national saving) is available for investment in economic growth. Moreover, some merchants encourage themselves and their families to get a good education, as most educated people are highly respected in the Confucian world.

RELATIONSHIP RULES

Having explained the nature and implications of insecurity in Chinese society, the next question is: How do Chinese businesspeople develop networks through relationships or bonding? The mechanism of relationship development and consolidation includes vertical bonding or integration through filial piety, face work, shame inculcation, and pragmatism.

The mastery of relationships is required for an individual to fit into and conform well to the basic social order of Chinese society. These relationship rules are well-understood for vertical social linkages. For instance, the notion of *hsiao* (filial duty) is the foundation of Chinese society.

Filial Piety

Weber (1951) stated that China is a "patrimonial" state, in the sense that the ultimate power rests with the state. In order to retain the stability of social systems, authoritarian behavior is always required. Filial piety and patrimonial power are strictly maintained. To ignore the demand for filial piety is considered wrong or something like a sin in the Judeo-Christian context.

In most family settings, possessions normally belong to the group, and while individuals may have a certain stewardship of possessions, they are obliged to return them to common use, if required by other members. Psychological separateness is probably inhibited by this arrangement. Some tensions are created within a family because of the individual's lack of personal control of economic resources. Loyalty to such norms is the price of protection.

The sense of vertical order is also reinforced in the school context, where teachers represent the learning which was traditionally the basis of authority in China.

As shown in Table 3.1, the power distance indexes of Chinese society are consistently higher than those of Western countries, by individual country and by the average of the two groups of countries. This indicates that people in Chinese countries accept the fact that power is vertically ordered and unevenly distributed.

In high power distance cultures, e.g., Taiwan, Singapore, and the PRC, people tend to express a strong sense of vertical order. The people in these cultures believe that society is structured as a ladder. This implies that they are below some people and above others. No one

TABLE 3.1 Value Index of Hofstede's Five Dimensions in Western and Chinese Cultures

Dimension	Power Distance	Individ- ualism	Masculinity	Uncertainty Avoidance	Long-Term Orientation*
Hong Kong	68	25	57	29	96
Taiwan	58	20	45	69	87
Singapore	74	17	48	8	48
Average	67	21	50	35	77
Australia	36	90	61	51	31
Great Britain	35	89	66	35	25
United States	40	91	62	46	29
Average	37	90	63	44	28

Sources: Buttery, A. and Leung, T.K.P. (1998) "The difference between Chinese and Western negotiations," *European Journal of Marketing,* 32(3-4), 374-389; quoted from Hofstede, G. (1991) *Cultures and Organizations, Software of the Mind,* Berkshire, England: McGraw-Hill.

*Based on a Chinese value survey rather than Hofstede (1980) and showing a long-term orientation index for China of 118.

can abuse their responsibilities because this will undermine their own authority, destroying the allegiances of those below them in the series of superior-subordinate relationships. There is rarely an open challenge to formal authority. Occasionally, subtle resistance demonstrates non-Confucian behavior. The heart of the family is filial piety, which is extended to social structures and the state.

Collectivism and Face

With the dominance of family allegiances, horizontal ties tend to be secondary and probably subservient. Even so, such ties are still stronger among Chinese than among Westerners. As shown in Table 3.1, the individualism indexes of the Chinese countries are strikingly lower than those of the Western group of countries, which indicate that human bonds are much tighter in the Chinese countries than in the West. Generally, cultures with high levels of collectivism are also those with a high power distance, e.g., Taiwan. For the Chinese, a social sharing concept guides most behavioral norms. The Chinese have been influenced by the following fundamental beliefs:

1. Confucianism—family, clan, and head of state take precedence over the individual.
2. Taoism—accepting the existing situation and studying the natural order of things and work are better than rejecting and querying them; i.e., simply "be."
3. Buddhism—one's ego is an illusion, and we must try to transcend it to reach the unborn pure being.

In the context of Chinese organizations, the downplaying of self and the emphasis of relationships are quite common, as indicated by empirical studies (Redding 1994).

Shame

Wilson (1970) argued that the system of child rearing in Taiwan, which is generalized to apply to Chinese everywhere, greatly emphasizes the significance of shaming and inculcating a sensitivity to face. Moreover, face and values have an intimate relationship, thus supporting a predominantly vertical group structure (Wilson 1970). The person "invests" in the group, and the investment, which he then cannot afford to lose, becomes his "face." The result of loss of face to the Chinese is, as Hsu (1971) points out, a genuine dread felt in the nervous system more strongly than physical fear.

Work Ethic

There is a common impression that Chinese people are hardworking. Kahn (1979) explained this trait as "seriousness about tasks" in post-Confucian cultures and considered it one of the major factors in East Asia's economic success. Chinese people always tend to force themselves to reach high levels of performance and responsibility. In Chinese society, each family has traditionally had to depend on its own resources rather than on assistance from the government.

Another feature of the Chinese is perseverance. Redding (1994) says that the process of learning Chinese is full of discouragement as thousands of characters need to be memorized; combined with a highly disciplined upbringing, it leads people to be disciplined and accept repetition and boredom while completing a piece of work. This work ethic affects perception of family duties, and plays a part in the acceptance of discipline, fear of insecurity, tolerance of repetition, and the development of a highly tuned pragmatism.

Money, Frugality, and Pragmatism

The Chinese are commonly described as money-minded. Money-mindedness and frugality are types of pragmatism. This pragmatism is explained by the following:

1. Chinese morality is contingent on a situation rather than being based on absolutes.
2. Social control originates principally from one's immediate circle.
3. Dedication to family survival is a dominating motive for behavior (Redding 1994).

These features enable the Chinese to display highly flexible behavior and adaptability.

Favor

A favor is defined as an act of kindness that one does to help somebody, especially when asked (Crowther 1995). Why do the Chinese place so much emphasis on the exchange of favors? One of the key elements here is "renqing."

Dilemma of Compromise versus Favor

The dilemma facing the resource allocator is how to satisfy three norms for justice frequently used in a collective culture, when the allocator has limited resources to distribute to the group. The three norms are:

1. The equity norm—The allocation of resources in proportion to individual contribution.
2. The equality norm—Regardless of individual contribution, resources are distributed equally.
3. The need norm—To satisfy individual legitimate needs, resources are allocated to individual members regardless of their relative contribution.

The problems facing resources allocators are summarized as:

1. How to allocate resources effectively and how to pay back renqing according to the equity norm if other members expect repayment based on the equality or need norms.
2. The difficulty in anticipating the timing and the extent of reciprocation. The Chinese prefer tacit rather than explicit agreements in this case, which requires a subjective evaluation of repayment.
3. The evaluation of guanxi ties—favor is a function of how the individual evaluates important positions within a given guanxi network.

In short, the resource allocator needs to evaluate gain and loss when receiving a favor or requesting a favor, as this implies a future repayment.

The Chinese saying "renqing is as thin as one piece of paper" means that a person is not able to secure good favor during an adverse period because of lower guanxi with others. Foreigners may be surprised to find that the Chinese need such a long time to make business decisions. This is because Chinese prefer to use delay as a form of subtle refusal or because they need more time to evaluate the sophisticated favor and repayment processes.

Integrative Approach of Chinese Research

Most previous studies are fragmented and difficult to integrate. Figure 3.3 demonstrates a holistic way of tying together all variables by proposing a "5 S" approach.

Figure 3.4 shows the holistic perspective of guanxi building within a security network. Each party or player enjoys:

1. Greater flexibility in dealing with an ever-changing environment. For example, the product life cycle of a personal computer is only eight months. Acer (a Taiwanese PC manufacturer) has been successful because of its flexibility in using an integrated network with a trusted and hardworking team through many subcontractors or "insider" members.
2. Through both expressive and instrumental (and mixed) relationships, most members in the network with the overlapping domain of individual and organization interests become a super "mutuality" network to be able to adapt efficiently and effectively.

FIGURE 3.3. A "5 S" Approach to the Guanxi Network Dynamic: A Summary of Sociopsychological Approaches to Understanding the Post-Confucian Work Dynamic

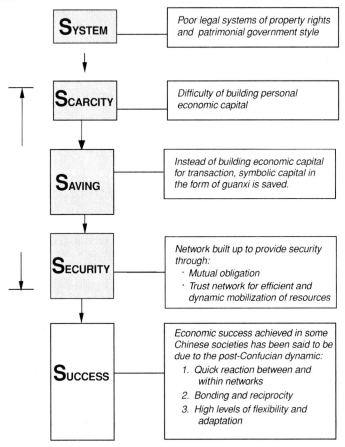

This network is the key reason why newly developed nations, such as Hong Kong and Taiwan, have been successful although they have little or no natural resources. Hong Kong was rated as the world's most competitive city by IMD (International Institute for Management Development) in 1996.

In short, Figures 3.3 and 3.4 are summaries of the psychosocial analysis of the reasons why guanxi networks are so important to Chinese society, as they have been harnessed to provide the energy for the successful growth of some Asian nations.

FIGURE 3.4. Holistic Interpretation of Guanxi Building in a Chinese Environment: Macro and Micro Variables Affecting the Mixed Ties of Reciprocity in Relationship Building

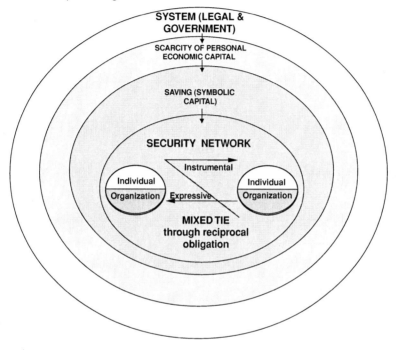

COMPARISON OF WESTERN AND CHINESE VIEWS

As there are many similarities and differences between Western and Chinese theories or views, two frameworks are used in this section to compare and contrast them to identify research gaps.

Gundlach and Murphy's (1993) framework of a continuum of exchange is adapted to make comparisons and Wee's (1994) framework is used for contrast because both give comprehensive scope for understanding complex behavior. Gundlach's continuum of exchange is shown in Table 3.2.

To some extent, values and dimensions such as commitment, trust, and relationship formalization in written contracts are similar in both Western and Chinese views, but they have different degrees of emphasis on a continuum of various types of exchanges, as illustrated in Table 3.3.

TABLE 3.2. Continuum of Exchange

Exchange Element	Forms of Exchange*		
	Transactional	**Contractual**	**Relational**
Temporal Dimensions			
Time horizon	Short	Intermediate to extended	Extended
Nature of transactions	Short duration; transaction has distinct beginning and end	Longer duration; transactions linked together	Longest duration; transactions merged together
Situational/ Strategic Characteristics			
Investment	Small	Moderate	Large
Switching costs	Low	Medium	High
Purpose of exchange	Narrow; economic; substance of exchange	Moderate; economic and social elements; creation of longer-term initiatives	Broad; economic and social elements; creation of longer-term initiatives
Strategic emphasis	Low	Moderate	High
Outcome complexity	Simple offer-acceptance	Increasing complexity	Complex web of operational and social interdependence
Division of benefits and burdens	Distinct, sharp division	Trade-offs and compromise	Blurring as goals converge

Note: This continuum of exchange reflects different degrees of focus on the various types of exchanges. This research focuses on the relational dimensions, which are characterized by a complex web of operational and social interdependence with divisions of benefits and burdens blurring as buyer-seller goals converge.

*Adapted from Dwyer, Schurr, and Oh (1987) and Jackson (1985).

TABLE 3.3. Comparison of Western and Chinese Views

Level of Interaction

Type of Exchange

		Transactional	Contractual Interaction	Relationship Outsider Association	Guanxi Insider Bonding
Western:		TCA	Social	Interaction	
Chinese:		Defense	Renqing	Post-Confucian Dynamic	Guanxi
Exchange Types	**Description**				
Contractual exchange					
Executory bilateral contract	Simple exchange involving a future obligation.	●			
Sequential contingent contract	A series of contracts linked serially and conditional on one another.	●			
Open-ended contract	A contract with certain terms (e.g., price and terms of trade) deliberately open to be agreed later.	●	●	●	
Interparty systems	Interparty exchange relationship involving traditional dimensions (e.g., purchasing).		●	●	☆
Transparty systems	Interparty coalition consists of a system of interpartner roles and responsibilities organized interfunctionally (e.g., R&D, marketing and production) by a network of coordination, liaison, and decision-making linkages (Achrol, Scheer, and Stern, 1992).		●	●	☆

Degree of Adaptation — Theory: Low → High

True Contractual Exchange → Interparty Systems → Transparty Systems → Strategic Alliance → Guanxi Dynamic

TABLE 3.3 *(continued)*

		Type of Exchange			
		Transactional	Contractual Interaction	Relationship Outsider Association	Guanxi Insider Bonding

Level of Interaction

Degree of Adaptation:

- True Contractual Exchange →
- Interparty Systems →
- Transparty Systems →
- Strategic Alliance →
- *Guanxi Dynamic* →

	Transactional	Contractual Interaction	Relationship Outsider Association	Guanxi Insider Bonding
Theory	Low ←→ High			
Western:	TCA	Social	Post-Confucian Dynamic	
Chinese:	Defense	Renqing	*Guanxi Dynamic* Interaction	Guanxi

Exchange Types	Description	Transactional	Contractual Interaction	Relationship Outsider Association	Guanxi Insider Bonding
Strategic alliance	Interparty creation of a network, organized by function, with or without equity positions.			●	☆
Guanxi dynamic	Guanxi dynamic network, integrated by mixed tie of defense–empathy dilemma				Q

Source: Adapted and modified from Goetz and Scott (1981).

Symbol: ● = Focus of Each Approach   ☆ = Minor Research Questions   Q = Major Research Question

Notes: Two major areas of research (in the degree of mutual adaptation) represented by:

☆ = Conventional Types

Exchange types: Interparty systems involving traditional and transactional functions

Coalition types: Transparty systems involving interpersonal and interfunctional coalitions

Partner types: Strategic network alliance with or without equity positions

Q = Guanxi dynamic bonding: Involving outsider-insider and new-old friendship mixed relationship dimensions, which is the major research question

The continuum in Table 3.2 mainly compares the temporal dimensions, situational/strategic characteristics, and outcome of three types of exchanges (i.e., transactional, contractual, and relational). At the transactional end of the continuum, exchange aims at short duration, small investment, narrow focus of purpose, and distinct and sharp division of benefits and burdens. At the other extreme, relational exchange, the exchange aims at extended association, large investment, multiple purposes, and a complex web of operational and social interdependence. The contractual exchange lies between the two extremes.

Table 3.3 shows exchange or association elements along a continuum. The major element is the time horizon or duration of the relationship. At one end is the transactional exchange, which is a single and short-term type with a distinct beginning and end and without any obligations between the parties prior to the exchange (e.g., a spot market type exchange). At the other end of this continuum is guanxi bonding. Between transactional exchange and guanxi bonding, there are two types of relationships; contractual interaction and relational association. Contractual interaction involves an intermediate to extended time horizon while relational association involves an extended period. The relational association is an ongoing process with specific purpose and cooperation.

Table 3.3 shows that Western TCA and Chinese defense theories are, to some extent, similar to transactional exchange because both of them are focused on a short-term time horizon, with low switching costs and strategic involvement. Western social exchange theories and Chinese renqing theories are related to contractual interactions involving traditional links and coordinations, such as sales and purchasing. Both Western interaction theory and Chinese post-Confucian dynamic theory use an extended horizon, with high relationship termination costs and a complex network of operational and social interdependence as well as the mutual convergence of business goals. These networks reflect a coalition of organizations cooperating in various areas, such as joint research and production. The comparison between Western and Chinese theories does not mean that they are exactly the same, but the principles behind the theories are, to some extent, similar. Guanxi is a "new" part of this relationship continuum. This relationship, which is the "gap" in the literature review, is the major theme of this research, as indicated in Table 3.3.

Summary

The Western TCA and Chinese defense theories were pioneering research with an emphasis on economic discussion. During the past decade, other theories have been developed, from the "intermediate" theories, such as social exchange and renqing theories, to the more complex, dynamic, and sophisticated post-Confucian dynamic theory and interaction theory. In the past, the "psychic distance" in the buyer-seller relationship was always regarded as a confrontational form of exchange, with conflicting or mutually exclusive interests, as illustrated in Figure 3.5. This figure illustrates the theoretical development of relationship and research questions. In recent studies, psychic distance has become smaller and gradually more "blurred," even nonexistent, probably leading eventually to the mutual-interest domains overlapping. The relationship may result in the "marriage" of buyer and seller.

Part A of Figure 3.5 reflects the "depth" of various theoretical developments during the last two decades. Note that Figure 3.5 does not show that TCA or defensive theories are inferior in quality but indicates the historical accumulation of knowledge.

The interaction and post-Confucian dynamic theories provide a very good framework for this research. The key research questions are part B of Figure 3.5. The adaptation process of the relationship is shown in part C of Figure 3.5. The outsider-insider dichotomy of guanxi development is represented by Q in Figure 3.5. These questions are explained in detail in Chapter 4.

Hall (1979) suggested classifying cultures into low-context and high-context types. China is regarded as a high-context culture, as relational bonding tends to be strong, with great distinctions between those outside and inside the culture.

CONTRAST BETWEEN WESTERN
AND CHINESE VIEWS

Wee's (1994) framework is adapted to contrast Western and Chinese views. Table 3.4 summarizes the contrasting emphasis of Western and Chinese theories. For example, the Chinese emphasize friendship more than their Western counterparts and treat a relationship as a means to competitive advantage. On the contrary, Westerners focus on profits and other business dimensions such as return on invest-

FIGURE 3.5. Comparison of Western and Chinese Theories and Research Gaps in the Literature Review

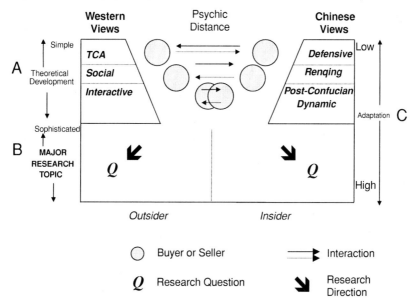

Note: This figure shows various psychic distances ranging from TCA to the post-Confucian dynamic and guanxi outsider-insider perception (interpersonal or inter-organizational adaptation in the dichotomy of outsider and insider perspectives). The major research question aims to reveal the inner workings of relationships in the PRC context.

ment. Moreover, Western TCA theory emphasizes fragmented societal values while the post-Confucian dynamic approach focuses more on disciplined and cohesive values. Also, in the Western world, gift giving (particularly gifts of significant economic value) may often be viewed as illegal, but, in the PRC, gift giving is often regarded as the major part of building guanxi. In addition, Western societal values operate more on a basis of legality while Chinese values rely more on morality (Wee 1994).

In short, the contrasts show a major difference in management philosophy: there is a preference in the West for "mind" management while in China more emphasis is placed on the "heart" approach (see Table 3.5).

TABLE 3.4. Contrast Between Western and Chinese Views

Western View	Chinese View
Societal Values and Practices	
Fragmented	Disciplined and cohesive
Encourage differing views	Instill discipline and order
Emphasize legality	Emphasize morality
Laws can be exploited	Laws to be enforced
Tolerance of failure	Intolerance of failure
Sense of sufficiency and invulnerability	Sense of survivability
Individual rights and freedom	Societal values and interest
Self over society	Society over self
New culture	Very established culture
Flexible	Inflexible
Loose friendship	Thrive on guanxi
Rely on government for welfare	Rely on self/family assistance
Business Practices	
Mechanistic	More organic than mechanistic
Short payback period and high return on investment	Long-term payback and investment approach
Major gift-giving viewed as illegal	Gift-giving part of building guanxi
More focus on profits	More focus on market share
Public relations more of a chore	Guanxi provides competitive advantages

Source: Adapted from Wee (1994).

Note: The contrasts between Western and Chinese views on management can be traced back to basic societal values and practices (such as the Western emphasis on the individual's rights and freedom versus the Chinese emphasis on society over the individual). In the context of different societal values, business operations generally focus more on short-term profit in the West and on securing a bigger market share in Chinese countries.

TABLE 3.5. The Heart and Mind of Management

The Mind (Logic and Reason)	The Heart (Feeling and Emotion)
1. Task orientation	1. Social orientation
2. Impersonal and systems driven	2. Personal and people centered
3. Breeds short-term mentality	3. Takes a long-term perspective
4. Develops self-interest and individualism	4. Builds group loyalty and group values
5. One's worth depends on economic value	5. Contributions assessed over one's lifetime
6. Focus on tangible benefits	6. Reliance on psychic rewards
7. Expertise can be bought and sold	7. Expertise not vulnerable to external exploitation
8. Management more a science	8. Management more an art

Source: Wee (1994).

Note: Under different societal values and practices of Western versus Chinese management, the "feeling" and "emotion" of the Chinese "heart" approach account for the defense, empathic, and favor-exchange elements of the guanxi model in Chapter 5, while the Western "mind" approach represents the stages from association through bonding to final commitment in the model.

Western theories have been regarded as a scientific discipline, which encourages the development of a common response to different situations and problems. The ultimate objective of Chinese management is to win the hearts of the people (employees, workers, suppliers, and business partners), and it is considered an art to find various solutions to different situations, because no two situations are the same (Wee 1994).

HOLISTIC CONCEPTUALIZATION OF RELATIONSHIP AND RESEARCH QUESTIONS

This section presents a holistic conceptualization of relationships. The conceptualization of Western and Chinese theories and the research questions is illustrated in Figure 3.6.

Based on the foundation of earlier research, two major research questions are established within the boundary of relationship marketing:

1. What are the determinants of guanxi? How can our guanxi model conceptually link all of these determinants in such a way that a businessperson can apply the model to relationship marketing?
2. How do we construct a valid and reliable concept to measure the performance of relationships in terms of adaptability and relationship-building quality?

FIGURE 3.6. Holistic Perception of Research Questions and Framework Integrating Research Questions in Marketing and Chinese and Western Relationship Literature

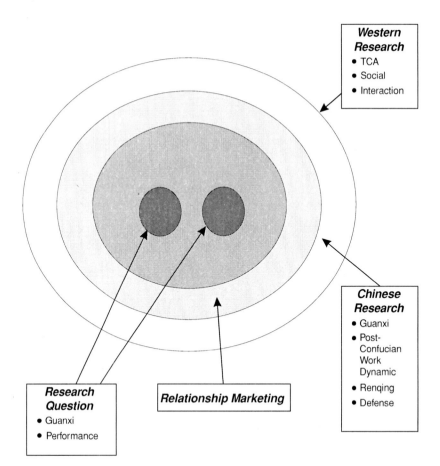

SUMMARY AND CONCLUSION

This chapter aims to justify the general characteristics and major ideas of Chinese relationship studies, theories, or approaches. The comparisons and contrasts between Western and Chinese views reveal the different management approaches of Western and Chinese research (i.e., the mind approach versus the heart approach). Heart approaches are concerned more with social orientation, are personal and people-centered, emphasize group values, and consider management more of an art than a science. Western "mind management" seems to be more concerned with task-orientation, is more impersonal and system-driven, emphasizes the development of self-interest and individualism, and considers management a science.

The Chinese have their own perceptions of relationship marketing. Guanxi has been regarded as an important variable in business dealing in the Chinese context. Renqing and face are used to describe the sociopsychological aspects of guanxi. The concepts of defense, mistrust and networks, lack of confrontation, trust, and risk management are explored as part of defense theory. In addition, another important interpretation of guanxi is the post-Confucian work dynamic.

To attempt to describe how Western and Chinese views differ, TCA and defense theory have been examined and compared, as have social exchange and renqing. Also, it is noted that in the interaction and post-Confucian work dynamic approaches, buyer-seller relationships have less psychic distance. The major difference lies in fundamental management approaches. Westerners appear to apply mind management whereas the Chinese focus on heart management. This difference motivated research to study guanxi constructs and the relationship between constructs and performance.

Chapter 4

Guanxi Context and Constructs

INTRODUCTION

Appendix A states that there is a gap in existing studies on the subject of guanxi. There is no study of the constructs of guanxi and the interactions among them, and of how guanxi may affect the development of relationships. This research aims to fill that gap. The primary objective is to investigate the constructs of guanxi and how these constructs affect relationship performance. A theoretical model has been developed to explain the constructs and the interactions between constructs and relationship quality, sales performance, relationship termination costs, and formalization.

Objectives and Organization

The objectives of this chapter are:

1. To propose an environmental context analysis as the background of the guanxi model
2. To construct a guanxi model and describe the variables affecting guanxi

The guanxi environmental context model builds on the comparison and contrast between Western and Chinese views presented in Chapter 3. There are significant differences between Chinese and Western societal values and business practices as well as managerial philosophy, such as the mind and heart approaches.

To understand these differences, it is important that a review of the environmental context is achieved by proposing a comprehensive model to incorporate political, legal, social, business, and individual psychology systems into a dynamic context model. The various components or constructs of the model are described later in this chapter.

Chapter Structure

This chapter starts with an analysis of the environmental context in the PRC by reviewing both traditional equilibrium-oriented and non-equilibrium-oriented perspectives. The second section includes a description of the post-Confucian work dynamic. The final section describes each component of the guanxi model: compromise, favor, trust, and adaptation, and their interactions.

ANALYSIS OF THE ENVIRONMENTAL CONTEXT IN THE PRC

Conceptual Context Framework

The literature review in Chapters 2 and 3 has helped explain relationships, with an emphasis on the need to do more cultural "context-laden" studies. A conceptual framework of the Chinese cultural context is proposed here. The framework includes five subsystems designated S, P, A, C, and E:

Subsystem	Components
S = System (macro)	Legal and political environment
P = Personalism system	Family and kin relationships
A = Adaptation system	Business and organizational adaptation
C = Changing social system	Social network
E = Egocentric system	Individual self

The subsystems are illustrated in Figure 4.1.

Two approaches are proposed to integrate the complex environmental, social, and individual context variables:

1. A traditional equilibrium-oriented approach
2. A new "dynamic" or non-equilibrium-oriented approach

The next section discusses the model according to the traditional equilibrium-oriented approach.

FIGURE 4.1. Guanxi Environmental Context Analysis (SPACE Perspective)

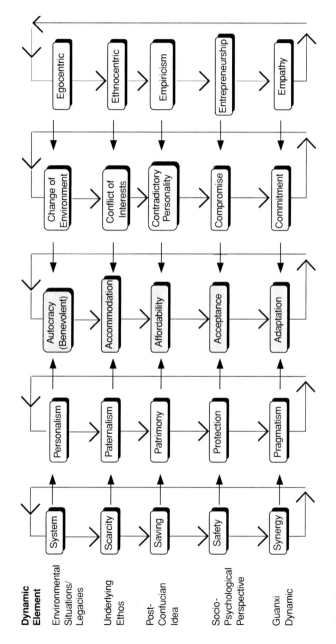

Note: Each subsystem indicates the probable logic leading from environmental legacies/situation to guanxi dynamic: S (System), P (Personalism), C (Changing Social System), and E (Egocentric system) affecting A (Adaptation processes from Autocracy phase to Adaptation phase).

SPACE Context Analysis

System. This subsystem reflects the legal and political macro-environment, in which there is a potential causal link between the variables of system, scarcity, saving, security, and success.

Owing to the poor institutional legal system in China and the unstable political systems of the present PRC government, most Chinese tend to feel the scarcity of individual personal economic resources. They may have a tendency to save more, perhaps in the form of social capital, such as guanxi and renqing. Their insecure psychology provides an incentive for them to work hard.

It is emphasized that the links in Figure 4.1 aim to provide some possible explanations for the context of the larger legal and political environment and do not mean to include all explanations. The sequence of each S variable may not be according to the same order absolutely.

Personalism. This generally refers to the personalism in a family and kin network. The major characteristic of Chinese society is personalism, emphasizing self-control and respect for authority. The major feature of personalism, which stresses the importance of a socially acceptable role, is obedience to the established order of relationships. This normative role has been institutionalized in Chinese law (Redding 1990). The underlying ethos of personalism is paternalism, which arises from the traditional inheritance system and Confucianism (Redding 1994). At the level of kin networks, paternalism is expressed particularly in aloofness and social distancing within a clear hierarchy with mutual vertical obligations. Paternalism tends to provide protection to key subordinates. One of the successful factors of the recent open policy of the PRC is the emphasis on pragmatism, which is demonstrated by the economic reform espoused by Deng Xiaoping as well as the broader context of East-West détente. The changes bear all the features of Deng's pragmatism, combining the wisdom of moderation and eclecticism. This pragmatic tendency may be the most important factor contributing to economic success in Confucian societies.

Adaptation. This refers generally to the adaptive processes of business organization. Basically, the political environment of China has been autocratic but with an emphasis on personalism and a benevolent ruling or managerial style. The Confucian emphasis on civilized conduct, paternalism, and hierarchical organization conflicts with the feeling of insecurity generated within society.

Changing social environment. This refers to the ever-changing Chinese environment; Huang (1994) described the period 1880-1990 as five generations of conflict and modernization. Each generation possessed different individual values, role norms, moral behavior, and expectations.

Table 4.1 presents the unstable course of Chinese history since 1880. The period from 1970 to the present includes the conflict between hard-line communist ideology and more moderate modern beliefs (Huang 1994). Huge conflicts occurred among different generations and regions (e.g., more open coastal cities were criticized by inland city officials as benefiting from special economic treatment and concessions). The Chinese tend to have a contradictory personality (reasoning versus feeling) (Huang 1994). The Chinese may try to reach a compromise between conflicting interests. In social networks, commitment is important for any successful long-term cooperation. Commitment is defined as "an implicit or explicit pledge of relational continuity between exchange partners" (Dwyer, Schurr, and Oh 1987, p. 19). Commitment indicates a willingness to make short-term sacrifices to realize longer-term benefits (Dwyer, Schurr, and Oh 1987).

TABLE 4.1. Five Generations of Conflict and Modernization

Generation	Historical Events
1880 - 1911	The Xinhai Revolution; the May Fourth Movement
1912 - 1930	The period of warfare among warlords
1930 - 1945	The war of resistance against Japan and civil war
1945 - 1960	The civil war; the founding of the PRC; the land-reform movement; the Korean War; the "struggle against the bourgeois rightists"; the Great Leap Forward
1960 - 1990	The Cultural Revolution; opening to the outside world; the Tiananmen Square crackdown

Source: Huang (1994).

Note: The period from the Xinhai Revolution to the Great Leap Forward and Cultural Revolution covers many decades of painful and messy environmental changes in China.

Unlike the economic view of rationality and discrete transactions, commitment is more closely related to the concerns of mutuality and loyalty. Commitment, in Chinese strategy, may not be proportionally shared between buyer and seller in the short term, and it may occasionally even involve irrational elements in the short term. For example, a buyer may ignore short-term gains to favor an old partner, who may possibly provide benefits over the long term. The emotional aspects tend to provide the shared goals and values for the parties, who tend to act instinctively for the long-term benefits of the partnership. Such commitment has the following benefits:

1. It minimizes the searching and start-up costs of dealing with new partners.
2. It economizes on the learning curve.
3. It may provide higher efficiency as a result of the adaptability and flexibility implicit in reduced role ambiguity.

This sort of commitment behavior tends to support a self-reinforcing cycle.

Ego. This means the individual's ego subsystem. In an ever-changing environment, the Chinese have tended toward egocentric attitudes. Ethnocentric behavior may originate from these attitudes. This behavior is a result of the isolation of Chinese society from the outside world for several hundred years during the Ching dynasty. The Ching dynasty lasted more than 200 years (A.D. 1644-1912), during which period China was ruled by Mongols. Most Chinese were not encouraged to express their feelings freely. This history of restrictive rule may have influenced the Chinese to develop ethnocentric attitudes. Also, the Chinese tried to escape from political involvement and at the same time directed their efforts to business involving a high degree of empiricism. This ego variable has encouraged strong entrepreneurship. The characteristics of Chinese entrepreneurship include a high centralization of authority and the ability to enjoy a high degree of flexible empathy with other members of a given guanxi network (Redding 1990).

Implications. In summary, the adaptation (A) of business organizations reflects the S (Synergy), P (Pragmatism), C (Commitment of each party), and E (Empathy of Chinese entrepreneurship) among inside members of a given network, as illustrated in Figure 4.1. The figure does not attempt to provide all explanations for all variables or all causal links but tries to provide a theoretical framework to enable an analysis of context in a more systematic way. Another contextual approach is non-equilibrium oriented.

Non-Equilibrium-Oriented Approach

The non-equilibrium-oriented approach is depicted in Figure 4.2. The key features of this approach are:

1. A stress on different subsystems to show the complex interplays among them
2. An emphasis on "changing" or "dynamic" elements within and among the subsystems as well as their interactions

Each system, S, P, A, C, and E, is assumed to consist of a complex set of mutually interacting components or forces that produces observed system changes. Each system interacts with or has influence on all other systems. The probable causality link is multiply determined and mutually reciprocal. The system is fluid, representing a flow of changes.

Symbolically, the forces of S, P, C, and E fuse to form what could be called a "Chinese harmony" through the adaptation (A) process. Both parts (S-P and C-E) still retain their own integrity and identity.

Importance of the contextual model. The importance of this environmental model is to provide an alternative view of interpreting the guanxi concept. The interpretations are as follows.

- An emphasis on the interaction among various political, legal, business, social, and individual subsystems shows a complex interplay with relationship performance, the focus of this research. This research attempts to identify the key constructs of guanxi because the interplay of various subsystems expresses how players or partners perceive the relationships among them. The understanding of the key constructs of guanxi provides insight, which may help businesspeople formulate strategic plans in customer services, partner relationships, and other business relationships.
- An emphasis on dynamic changes within the subsystems and how these dynamic changes are related to sales performance and

the perception of each relationship. The interacting subsystems S, P, C, and E are regarded as important variables affecting the central adaptation behavior of business organizations (i.e., subsystem A). The business adaptation behavior is analyzed and elaborated in a later section. One of the measurements of adaptation behavior is relationship outcome performance, which is defined as consisting of these indicators:

1. Overall relationship quality
2. Sales performance
3. Relationship termination costs
4. Relationship formalization

Summary. Each of the subsystems incorporates a complex set of mutually interacting components or forces to produce observed changes in the subsystem or the whole system. Each subsystem influences all other subsystems and the relationship performance outcomes. Relationship performance also interacts with and influences the five subsystems. The whole system is in a constant state of flux. The adaptation process is discussed in detail in Chapter 6.

GUANXI MODEL

Conceptual Model and Explanation

Coming to grips with interpersonal relationships is a significant topic for practicing managers and academics. One of the limitations of existing writing on relationships is its simplicity; this limitation, together with a lack of empirical evidence, probably leads to overgeneralization. For example, guanxi has been described as one of the most important culture-bound concepts that a businessperson faces (Huang 1994). However, neither the exact meaning of the term "guanxi" in the international marketing context nor research evidence supporting this assertion have been discussed.

A theoretical model has been developed to explain the dynamic of guanxi. The constructs are:

- Favor
- Trust
- Adaptation
- Dependence

FIGURE 4.2. SPACE Context Dynamic—Interacting Systems: How does each SPACE subsystem interact with the others to create a business dynamic?

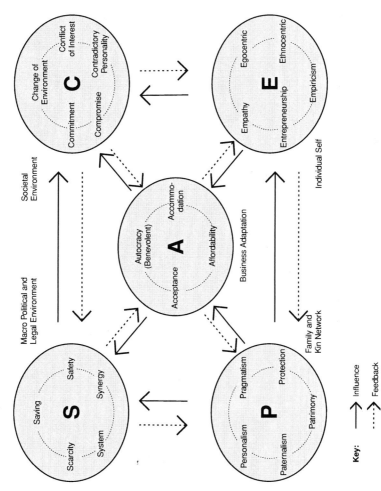

The constructs are independent variables, and guanxi performance is a dependent variable. Performance has three indicators: (1) termination risks or costs, (2) sales performance, and (3) relationship formalization. The conceptual model is shown in Figure 4.3. The arrows in Figure 4.3 show the postulated direction of influence. The model assumes that there is only a one-way flow of influence. The figure indicates a small number of the potential links. This empirical study is not an attempt to deal with all the variables or the combination of all variables; instead it focuses on the key constructs and the interaction of constructs and performance indicators.

System Dynamics Approach

Before going into the details of the model, a system dynamics approach is used to describe the mechanism of the model. The system dynamics approach is defined as a method of analyzing problems in which feedback is an important variable, and which involves the study of how a system can be made to benefit from shocks in the outside world. This approach helps us understand that:

1. Human behavior is complex and dynamic.
2. Although behavior is different in various areas, sometimes it displays a surprisingly similar pattern.
3. Occasionally, the dynamics of the system (e.g., SPACE organizational behavior as a whole system) raise a wide range of problems, such as, why is there a conflict between the constructs of trust and favor?

In general, this dynamic approach will help us to:

1. Explain behavior in terms of perceptual concepts, structures, and interacting results
2. Suggest ways to improve business structures and policies

There are three levels in Figure 4.3:

1. Input attributes
2. Guanxi indicator
3. Performance outcome

The constructs (input attributes) are linked to show the causality between guanxi performance indicators.

FIGURE 4.3. A Conceptual Structural Model of Guanxi and Relationship Performance—Dynamic Approach: Constructs As Input Affecting Performance of Guanxi Quality, Relationship Outcomes of Sales Performance, Termination Costs, and Formalization

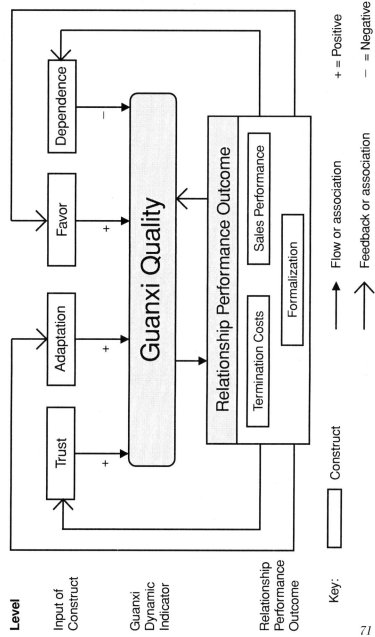

71

Among the three levels, feedback loops indicate whether the feedback behavior is positive or negative. The loop reinforces each level. The higher the trust input, the better the guanxi outcome is.

Another way of understanding Figure 4.3 is to imagine that the outcome (i.e., relationship performance level) is the end result of all input. Elements of the system are:

1. Constructs: trust, adaptation, favor, and dependence
2. Guanxi quality level: The level will be high or low according to the interactions of all input.
3. Relationship performance outcome: Three indicators are used to reflect the overall quality of relationships:

   • Termination risks or costs
   • Sales performance
   • Relationship formalization

Implications

In Figure 4.3, it is assumed that trust, adaptation, and favor affect guanxi quality positively and dependence influences guanxi quality negatively. In this study, the constructs are empirically identified or theoretically operationalized. The relationships between constructs and performance indicators are statistically tested in Chapter 5.

CONSTRUCTS

Trust

Chinese people usually employ defense mechanisms in the development of relationships. Particularly in the early stages of development, reciprocal trust is weak. Chinese people will keep a certain psychic distance from the other party. Therefore, this defense mechanism may have a negative effect on guanxi. Defensiveness may be due to worries about potential relationship termination costs and opportunistic reactions. Relationship termination costs include all expected losses resulting from a perceived switch to a potential alternative new partner. For example, a supplier who fails to obtain business from a customer may threaten to pass on confidential information to one of the customer's competitors (Morgan and Hunt 1994). This defensive strategy is one of the reactions to opportunistic behavior, which has been defined as self-interest seeking with guile (Williamson 1975). An individual may generally divide people into two categories: fiancé and fencer. An individual has more trust in a partner in the fiancé category.

Tong Wah Enterprises Ltd. imported raw plant oil from Brazil and reexported the raw plant oil in bulk to a reputable state-owned factory in Wuhan, China, starting in 1987. They established a joint venture in China and got an advantage from the friendship between John Lai, the director of Tong Wah, and a factory manager, their Chinese partner. This friendship has changed their relationship from business associates to old friends. Moreover, these two parties have established trust that was very important when Lai lent Rmb $3 million to this factory manager. The two parties trusted each other even before they started their project.

Anthony Ko, Managing Director of Hitech Investment (Group) Ltd., said, "the Chinese are relatively inexperienced in conducting business as compared with their foreign counterparts. They logically put more emphasis on trust rather than contract. So they are more willing to do business with friends." Therefore, when Hitech invested in some projects, including software manufacturing, motorcycle manufacturing, computer manufacturing, property development, and mobile phone battery manufacturing, in China in the early 1980s, they established trust through guanxi building, face giving, and mutual understanding exchange.

Favor

The Chinese word for favor is renqing, which means a resource that an individual can present to another person as a gift in the course of social exchange in order to strengthen the relationship between the parties. Thus, the more favor that is received by the resource petitioners, the more they will have to repay. Conceptually, if more favors are exchanged, the relationship between the parties, or the guanxi of the parties, may well be enhanced.

Refer to the case of Tong Wah Enterprises Ltd. When the factory manager, their partner, borrowed money from Tong Wah without any collateral, the manager owed Lai a renqing, which must be repaid at a later time. In addition, when the factory manager asked all the Chinese officials concerned to work in his factory for three days as part of the approval process, he owed them renqing which also has to be paid back later.

To generalize, Westerners usually employ the equity rule, which encourages individuals to allocate resources in proportion to their contributions. However, the Chinese generally employ the need rule, which dictates that dividends, profits, or other benefits should be distributed to satisfy recipients' legitimate needs, regardless of their relative contributions (Hwang 1987). Thus, they would likely give preference to allocating resources to someone whose need is urgent. If there is a discrepancy between these two rules, renqing may be adopted according to the degree of relationship with the party.

Favor and Compromise

In Chinese relationship building, when an individual owes someone renqing, he or she should be ready to pay back the debt once circumstances permit. In Chinese ethics, the obligation of reciprocity is quite important.

When the director of Tong Wah Enterprises Ltd. lent money to the factory manager, he had offered renqing to him. This manager, then, has to repay Lai's renqing by working hard. This reciprocity dynamic encouraged Lai to give a 5 percent bonus on profit to the manager to repay him for his management. As Lai admitted: "Because this factory manager has been performing well, we have promised to give him a 5 percent year-end bonus based on the profit generated by this joint venture. . . . This is the gentlemen's agreement between us. We did not put it on paper because it is not allowed in the PRC by law!" Without the norm of reciprocity, guanxi would no longer be a "weapon" in the power game.

However, the personality of the resource allocator is a variable that may influence the norm of reciprocity. For instance, a resource allocator who is a "heart-oriented" person tends to take a long-term perspective regarding the building of group loyalty and group values (Wee 1994). Guanxi and renqing may be the major factors influencing decision making. On the other hand, if the resource allocator is a "mind-oriented" (logical and reasonable) person, he or she is likely to be task-oriented (Wee 1994). The obligation of reciprocity may be considered less important by mind-oriented people than by heart-oriented people in the decision-making process.

The Chinese tend to be cautious in dealing with outsiders and to seek compromise (Yang 1981). Thus the Chinese do not like confrontation. When there was a conflict, Tong Wah Enterprises would not confront the other party but rather would endeavor to solve the problem. Hitech Investment would not confront their Chinese partners in a formal meeting when disagreement arose, either. They talked to their counterparts in some private meetings and attempted to understand the reasons for the disagreement. The understanding helped them resolve the problem, present their solutions in subsequent formal meetings, and maintain mutual guanxi.

The tendency toward compromise can be traced back to the Confucian "mean," which was defined by Confucius as having "no inclination to either side." This does not mean the absence of passion and the suppression of impulses but a tendency to regulate aggressive behavior to achieve internal harmony. Confucius said:

> While there are no stirrings of pleasure, anger, sorrow, or joy, the mind may be said to be in the state of equilibrium. When those feelings have been stirred, and they act in their due degree, there ensues what may be called the state of harmony. This equilibrium is the great root from which grow all the human actions in the world, and this harmony is the universal path which they all should pursue. (*The Doctrine of the Mean,* I, Legge 1960)

The social norms of restraining primitive passions and impulses have been taught in schools for hundreds of years. The definition of the mean is:

> The gentleman does what is proper to the station in which he is; he does not desire to go beyond this. In a position of wealth and honor, he does what is proper to a position of wealth and honor. In a poor and low position, he does what is proper to a poor and low position. . . . In a low situation, he does not court the favor of his superiors. He rectifies himself, and seeks for nothing from others so that he has no dissatisfactions. He does not murmur against Heaven, nor grumble against it. (*The Doctrine of the Mean,* XV, Legge 1960)

In public, individual Chinese are expected to have a high degree of self-control. Normally, inner feelings are channeled through family or intimate friends. This is why Chinese always emphasize the importance of friendships.

The doctrine of the mean implies minimization of complaining behavior, less litigation, the minimization of extreme behavior, and resistance to new fashion or technology.

Continuity

Continuity is one of the determinants of compromise, favor, and trust. Continuity means the continuity of relationships in the future. If Chinese network members expect a relationship to continue in the long term, they will conduct more interactions and social exchanges to maintain and improve the relationship. However, continuity must be built up through a process of interactions in which reciprocal trust can successively be deepened. Therefore, Hitech Investment visited their Chinese partners' offices after inviting their potential Chinese partners to come to Hong Kong and inspect their business offices. The long-term relationship was emphasized during these visits.

On the other hand, if the participants feel any insecurity about the first transaction, because of lack of mutual trust, they may test the partner through a trial order initially, and then move to repeat orders. As a result, security and trust in the relationship are enhanced over time, so that the relationship can continue.

Another element of continuity is an interrelationship with other people that most Chinese believe to be continuous. The Chinese saying "If you teach me for one day, I will regard you like my father forever" reflects this continuity in relationships. One of the major elements of continuity is time orientation, such as orientation to the past.

Concern for History

Chinese people tend to hold reverence for an imagined shared past. Van Oort (1970) pointed out that the principle of respect for the past or veneration of history is a second cultural value for the Chinese; if anyone in the world cares about history, it is the Chinese.

The Chinese are very proud of what they see as their cultural heritage. There is a Chinese proverb, "Among the three unfilial duties, the greatest one is to have no heir." The reasons are:

1. A family needs an heir to continue biologically.
2. To pass on the Chinese culture to the next generation.
3. To fulfill the hopes of their parents (Yang 1979).

Adaptation

Chinese culture has developed a great inertia and resistance to change. However, in an ever-changing environment, swift action is achieved by the ability to be adaptable.

There are three principles of adaptability:

1. Flexibility
2. Innovation
3. Initiative

Flexibility

One of the dynamics of Asian business is that, in some cases, there are no fixed rules and regulations. Strategies are fluid enough to react and to change instantaneously according to fast-moving events and situations.

The negative aspects of not following regulations or laws include bribery and unscrupulous business practices. The former may take the form of substantial gift giving, which may be regarded as unacceptable and, in extreme cases, illegal in Western culture, but may be viewed as acceptable behavior in some Asian countries. The latter practice may likely encourage some producers to supply products of inferior quality at very competitive prices.

The positive aspects of flexibility are demonstrated by subcontracting systems with high flexibility in production schedules. First, this flexibility provides cushioning against any fluctuations in demand. Second, multiple suppliers give more choices. Third, the competition among subcontractors may push up quality and push down costs. The low-price penetration strategies adopted by most Asian countries are another example of high flexibility in marketing. This flexibility even applies to some high-technology products, such as computers and vehicles.

Innovation

Unpredictable marketing and product changes require innovative tactics in the search for new and creative solutions. Particularly in Asian countries, where most businesses are small to medium size, a creative strategic entrepreneurship network can survive.

Initiative

Initiative differs from innovation in that innovation is a proactive and systematic approach while initiative uses both proactive and re-active approaches, requiring an individual to be highly adaptable and able to respond promptly. For example, most Hong Kong companies have reduced costs by moving manufacturing operations to the PRC. They are willing to accept a short-term reduction in profits rather than opting for the retrenchment of their managerial staff, to mini-mize the impact on staff morale.

Friendship

Friendship is another important variable affecting the process of adaptation. Friendship can be divided into two dimensions: outsider and insider. Generally, "insider" refers to a relationship that is rela-tively permanent and stable. The members of such primary groups as family, close friends, and other congenial groups are often regarded as insiders. On the other hand, "outsider" means a relationship that is basically unstable and temporary, e.g., the relationship between a new supplier and customer. The resource allocator may tend to allo-cate more resources to insiders, and less to outsiders.

However, there may be a situation where one party has a relation-ship with the resource allocator in a marginal case, and as a result, renqing or favor may play a more important role in strengthening guanxi with the resource allocator. Asia Link Ltd., a subsidiary of a highly profitable company, Toptele Ltd., maintains guanxi with their potential Chinese partners at two levels, negotiation and top manage-ment, to resolve their disagreements.

There are three types of friendships:

1. Natural friendship—Friendship for its own sake, e.g., when someone visits China, a hospitable stranger invites him or her for dinner just for friendship.
2. Friendship to keep righteousness—There is a Confucian philosophy that "gentlemen stress righteousness; mediocre men seek profit." Righteousness means a variety of things, such as justice and equity. This sort of friendship implies behavior based on justice.
3. Self-interest friendship—Friendship that is maintained for the sake of survival or furthering mutual self-interest.

In reality, Chinese friendship means a combination of two or three of these types of friendship. PRC sports propaganda includes the slogan: "Friendship first, competition second." The logic is that victory and defeat are short-lived but friendship continues on a long-term basis.

With the opening of China to the West, some Chinese people may open the back door to link with Westerners through the development of self-interest friendships because market mechanisms are limited and inefficient. Chemtech Ltd., one of the largest chemical and pharmaceutical companies in the world and the largest in Germany, attempted to satisfy the private goals of the Chinese, such as granting consultancy contracts to individual Chinese members of established joint ventures.

Characteristics of Chinese Friendship and Trust

Benevolence, righteousness, propriety, wisdom, and fidelity are the five constant virtues for the Chinese. Fidelity denotes loyalty, the repayment of debts of gratitude and honesty. Without self-interest, a person can help a friend, who should be obliged to pay back favors. The Chinese expect that the repayment value of a favor should be greater than the value of the original favor. Nonrepayment is regarded as immoral. The Chinese judge others by evaluating the extent to which they keep their promises. There is a Chinese saying: "A word once spoken cannot be taken back even by a team of four horses." A contract in Chinese is often regarded as tacit in accordance with individual reliability. Occasionally, the request for a written contract may create a dilemma of friendship versus trust because a written contract may imply no or weak trust in another party.

Timing for Friendship

"Don't embrace Buddha's feet only at a time of urgent need." This is a common Chinese saying describing friendships developed only to secure a favor. Difficult times may not be the right time for developing a good friendship.

Hitech Investment (Group) Ltd. had good guanxi with the secretary of the Shenzhen city government. This secretary, in order to give mianzi, offered them help in finding other PRC partners. This kind of guanxi invited other potential PRC partners to have dinner with the foreign partners and exhange ideas. Doing business at banquets is obviously a popular mode of operation in China.

INTERACTION OF GUANXI CONSTRUCTS

Figure 4.3 shows the interaction among the major factors affecting guanxi building. Favor and trust are the major variables of interaction.

The major characteristic of Chinese culture is the maintenance of internal harmony, which is most likely to be achieved by compromising individual interests and choosing social conformity, nonoffensive strategies, and submission to social expectations (Hwang 1987). Compromise and favor are interrelated to a certain extent. Guanxi networks provide two basic areas for interaction:

1. A petition always involves the resource allocator in the guanxi network as the first step.
2. The petitioner may use a third party to arrange a formal introduction and to influence the resource allocator's decision. This emphasis is reflected by the Chinese saying, "Before turning down your request, one should have a look at the Buddha's face." This saying means that one needs to show respect to the face of the resource allocator.

Adaptation, Compromise, and Favor

Renqing is not an objective variable. It is a blend of social cost, quality, and relationships, and is subject to different interpretations. Therefore the repayment of a renqing debt can be more difficult than the repayment of a financial debt. The way to evade entanglement in renqing is adaptive behavior. There are four main adaptative types.

First, as more Chinese people have been educated abroad, they tend to form a subculture in which they have been socialized according to equity norms, instead of the traditions of renqing. Therefore, modern Chinese attitudes can be said to include more of an individual orientation. The dilemma of renqing and equity needs have been adapted to each other.

Mega Elevator International, Inc. has faced this kind of dilemma. Established guanxi allowed them to identify their PRC counterparts' private goals. For example, the Chinese may want some important positions in the factory. Luckily, Mega prefers to employ capable local personnel in their joint venture instead of sending senior management from the United States. Thus, the dilemma resolved itself.

Second, another form of adaptation is the adoption of a clear-cut rule of social interaction, such as the practice of modern management rules in Chinese business organizations. Typical business organizations in Hong Kong, Taiwan, and Asia in general are family businesses, employing family or extended-family members as key managers. Some of the business owners use the renqing rule in their interaction with employees. With the adoption of Western management procedures, the functions of an organization tend to develop more clear-cut rules with a more open organizational climate and fair interaction.

Third, another way is to adapt a new interaction network rather than staying within the existing guanxi network. For example, someone leaves his birthplace and moves to a distant province to establish new instrumental ties with persons there.

The fourth way is to maintain different domains for equity rule and renqing needs. For example, when faced with limited resources, a resource allocator may follow the equity rule, and when resources are more plentiful or directly controlled, the resource allocator may follow the renqing rule.

Friendship, Trust, and Continuity

Levels of relationship building in the form of friendship are affected by the rate of interaction of trust and continuity. Why is trust so important in Chinese networks?

Trust

Trust, as defined by Morgan and Hunt (1994), exists "when one party has confidence in an exchange partner's reliability and integrity" (p. 23). Confidence is associated with consistency, competence, fairness, responsibility, helpfulness, and benevolence (Altman and Taylor 1973; Dwyer and LaGace 1986; Larzelere and Huston 1980; Rotter 1971). Trust promotes a willingness to rely on a trustworthy party and to take actions involving potential risk or actual risk (Morgan and Hunt 1994).

Trust has been studied widely in different contexts, such as:

- Social exchange—the norm of trust is regarded as a major characteristic in management theory (Barney 1990).
- Service marketing—Berry and Parasuraman (1991) noted that business-to-business relationships require trust. They also pointed out that the management of trust affects the effectiveness of service marketing because most of the customers purchase services before experiencing them.
- Strategic alliance—Regarding strategic alliances, Sherman (1992) indicated that lack of trust is the largest barrier to the success of alliances.
- Business-to-business market—In buyer-seller bargaining situations, Schurr and Ozanne (1985) found trust to be important to the process of achieving cooperative problem solving and constructive dialogue, leading to higher levels of loyalty (commitment) to the bargaining partner.
- IMP group—Trust is regarded as of fundamental importance in the studies conducted by Ford (1980) and Hakansson (1982).

All of this research confirms the importance of trust in business.

Relationship Quality

There is a major marketing directional change from transaction marketing to relationship marketing. "The cooperative aspect of economic behavior has been relatively neglected. Economists speak of competitive theory, of pure and perfect competition. There is no corresponding development of cooperative theory, of pure and perfect cooperation" (Alderson 1965).

Some authors (Parvatiyar, Sheth, and Whittington 1992) acknowledge the general paradigm shift toward relationship marketing and examine major elements such as relational contracting (MacNeil 1980), working partnerships (Anderson and Narus 1990), symbiotic marketing (Varadarajan and Rajaratnam 1986), and internal marketing (Arndt 1983; Berry and Parasuraman 1991).

The difference between relationship marketing and transaction marketing is that a transaction has a distinct beginning, short duration, and definite ending and relational exchange traces to previous agreements and is longer in duration (Dwyer, Schurr, and Oh 1987).

Summary

The guanxi model shows that the constructs of adaptation, favor, trust, and dependence contribute to relationship quality. Through interaction, a positive or negative flow determines whether the relationship moves up, down, or laterally. The constructs affect the level of relationship building; for example, adaptation and trust determine guanxi performance. Figure 4.3 illustrates the guanxi performance indicator as the end result of the dynamic level of guanxi and relationship quality.

SUMMARY AND CONCLUSION

This chapter describes a model of guanxi constructs and performance. It presents the environmental context in the PRC. A "SPACE" contextual framework is proposed to provide an integrated system of political, social, business, organizational, and individual sociopsychological frameworks for analysis purposes. Following the environmental contextual (SPACE) model, a guanxi model is proposed. The model has constructs, performance indicators, and their interactions are linked by flows and feedback loops. Each component or variable in the model has been discussed with a brief reference to literature.

Chapter 5

Theoretical and Practical Aspects

INTRODUCTION

This chapter discusses the theoretical and practical aspects of guanxi. First, the chapter provides implications for theoretical development. Second, a summary of theoretical framework development is given. Third, conclusions about the research questions are discussed in the form of various perspectives and perceptions. Finally, a summary of theoretical and practical implications for business practice is presented. The chapter organization is illustrated in Figure 5.1.

IMPLICATIONS FOR THEORETICAL FRAMEWORK DEVELOPMENT

This section elaborates on and reviews guanxi from social, cultural, and economic perspectives. From the economic perspective, the relationships between contracting, corruption, and guanxi are discussed in detail. In addition, the positive roles and benefits of guanxi are explored. Also, the framework of the adaptation process, position map, interaction dynamic, and guanxi outcome are presented. Finally, the implications of guanxi are critically reviewed by interpreting different processes using both mind and heart approaches. The concluding part of this section discusses the balance between mind and heart management.

The following are the elements involved in building a theoretical model:

1. Description
2. Explanation
3. Testability
4. Empirical support for research questions

FIGURE 5.1. Organization of Chapters 5 and 6, Plus Appendixes

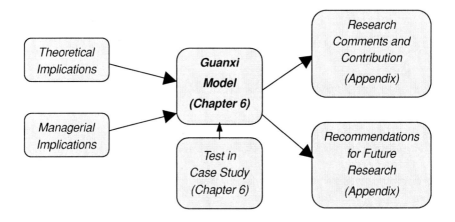

With descriptive theory building, four major constructs were identified: trust, adaptation, favor, and dependence. A measurement tool in the form of a questionnaire was devised to identify them.

The key questions of the explanatory aspect of theory building are "how" and "why." Relationships are found between guanxi quality and the constructs of trust and adaptation, while trust, adaptation, and opportunism also have relationships with the performance indicators of contract formalization, sale pattern development, and relationship termination costs.

To supplement existing theories in the West and China, three new major theoretical explanations of guanxi have been developed:

1. Guanxi as the product of Chinese favoritism and a dichotomy of conflict and harmony, or a dilemma arising from institutional weakness
2. Guanxi as an efficient network mechanism arising from poor development of property rights and contract law
3. Guanxi as the pursuit of individual personal gain in a tightly controlled society

Explanation 1 deals with social aspects while explanation 2 is concerned with economic questions. Explanation 3 is more concerned with individual interests.

The next chapter discusses a comprehensive model. Each part of the model provides a basic understanding of guanxi perspectives and applicable suggestions. Also, Chapter 6 describes the testability and empirical support for the development of the constructs, which constitute the major framework of the model.

Cultural and Social Context in China

Numerous authorities address cultural and social aspects of joint venture negotiation in China (Pye 1982, 1986; Leung and Yeung 1995; Wong 1997; Buttery and Leung 1998). Buttery and Leung (1998) indicate that China's cultural and social system reflects Confucian thought, which emphasizes harmony and hierarchy.

Harmony and Hierarchy

The principle of harmony implies aspirations toward conflict-free group-based systems of social relations (Shenkar and Ronen 1987). Confucius used the terms *jen* and *lun* to signify social ideals (Kam 1993). Jen means moral excellence in interpersonal relationships. Jen emphasizes self-education and analysis. It advocates the relative importance of knowing others and the relative unimportance of being known (Lin 1939). This explains why the Chinese are so interested in learning about the interests and personalities of visiting negotiators, and indeed their myriad questions, which are considered frustrating by overseas visitors. It also explains why Chinese negotiators are defensive about freely disseminating information about themselves.

Lun is the proper positioning of people within the social and political hierarchy (Lin 1939). Generally, there are five lun or relationships in a classical Confucian society: ruler and subject, father and son, husband and wife, elder brother and younger brother, friend and friend. A Confucian gentleman is a man who keeps these five fundamental relationships in perfect order (Deverge 1986). Confucius' idea was to create a harmonized society in which every person knows and stays in the proper position. The practice of paternalism is the highest ideal in the Chinese political system (Pye 1992).

Guanxi in Sociocultural Development

Harmony and hierarchy are also important in guanxi. The instrumental, expressive, and mixed relationships, as proposed by Hwang (1987), are one of the best explanations of guanxi and face. Expressive ties exist among extended family members and close friends, and social exchange is affected by the need rule, which means the allocation of limited resources is determined by individual need rather than individual contribution. Instrumental relationships involve the allocation of resources among outsiders or strangers according to individual contribution. Guanxi is very important in mixed relationships, which are ties between expressive and instrumental ties. In an instrumental relationship, a resource allocator faces a dilemma in attempting to satisfy all resource petitioners because direct refusal may mean losing face to the petitioner who requests the resources. However, the findings of our research indicate:

1. Favor is not related to guanxi quality.
2. Favor is not a major determinant of sale stability.

These results show that although favor is popular, the survey respondents may not have wanted to express this attitude openly or were not willing to answer directly because of the sensitive nature of some questions.

Westerners are often puzzled by a lengthy negotiation process. The findings indicate that overall quality of guanxi is the end product of trust and adaptation and both trust and adaptation need a long time to develop.

Economic Context in China

Since 1974, Communist Party leaders have been directing China toward its long-term national goal with its "four modernizations" program, the modernization up to world standards of agriculture, industry, science, and national defense by the year 2000. Its level of achievement has yet to be determined. At the Third Plenary Session of the Eleventh Central Committee of the Communist Party in December 1987, Deng Xiaoping restated that the primary national objective of China was to complete this economic reform program (Kaiser, Kirby, and Fan 1996). Chinese authorities also recognized that the only way to pursue this ambitious goal was to attract foreign direct investment (FDI), which would provide the capital, management skills, and technology that was lacking. The Chinese government attempts to use an economic model that actively integrates market mechanisms while maintaining overall control of the economy (Luo 1988). How does guanxi relate to the four modernizations?

Explanation of Guanxi from an Economic Perspective

The traditional transaction cost analysis proposed by economists suggests that guanxi tends to reduce transaction costs, which in turn makes business more effective and efficient. It also means that the progress of the four modernizations program can be more effective and efficient. As China lacks a formal legal system and a proper system of distribution, guanxi networks provide an informal and efficient system. In this study, guanxi quality correlates with relationship termination costs, contract formalization, and sales stability. Before explaining the importance of guanxi in economic development, Western concepts of contracts are discussed. There are two types of contracts (Davies 1995):

1. Classical contracting
2. Relationship contracting

Classical Contracting

Contract includes nonwritten, written, or verbal contracts or other forms of understanding. The classical contract is common in simple market transactions in which contract law covers all future contingencies. Most transactions governed by classical contracts tend to be self-liquidating. Most such contracts are on a medium to long-term basis. Sometimes, if there is any disagreement between two parties, there may be a need for arbitration.

Relationship Contracting

In the real world, classical contracting is difficult to achieve, as normal transactions are executed continuously and involve long-term relationships combined with the complexity of human interaction. In

China, most contracts are mainly used for points of reference and are subject to individual interpretation. Two parties are bound together because both want to keep the relationship going or to avoid or minimize the impact of losing the partner. For example, dealing with a new supplier occasionally requires changes of specifications and involves the risk that the supplier will not be able to fulfill all requirements. It takes a long time for the parties in a relationship to adapt to each other.

In addition, the relationship contract has two major forms (Davies 1995): obligation contract and unified governance. The former covers interactions between different firms. The latter refers to transactions coordinated by the managerial staff of a single firm. Relevant questions about guanxi are:

1. What are the relationships between guanxi constructs, particularly favor, and these forms of contracts?
2. What roles do the constructs of dependence and opportunism play in the development of relationships?

To answer the above questions, economists proposed the following variables:

1. Uncertainty—The key element that contracts aim to minimize.
2. Threat of opportunism—The potential loss of a customer as a result of opportunistic behavior on the part of the customer, for example, switching to a lower-priced supplier regardless of the long-term relationship.
3. Extent of asset specific investment—Asset specific investment refers to a supplier investing in new equipment (new assets) especially to meet the transaction requirements of a particular buyer. In other words, the asset is specific to the transaction.
4. The degree of connectedness and the frequency of transactions—The closer the buyer-seller relationship, the higher the transaction frequency or connectedness wll be.

The guanxi model is a useful tool for explaining these variables. Uncertainty indicates the tendency of each party to show opportunistic behavior. Adaptation is largely a measure of the degree of asset-specific investment. Favor is regarded as flexibility in transactions or contracting and is important in ensuring against unforseen contingencies. Even the most comprehensive contract will not cover all potential contingencies. Favor differs from Williamson's (1971, 1975) description of relationship contracting. The combination of people and organizations creates the favor element of a relationhip, which may imply unfair deals.

Davies (1995) described the guanxi network as "the social interactions within the network place and its members in the equivalent of an infinitely repeated game with a set of people they know" (p. 155). These repeated favor exchanges ensure some type of trust among the members of a guanxi network, which tends to minimize the risk of uncertainty and the inflexibility of asset specificity.

Legal Framework for Foreign Joint Venture Establishment

The Chinese political administrative system is bureaucratic in nature. This bureaucratic system and the centrally planned economy require a set of complicated procedures to establish foreign joint ventures in China. Sum (1996) has a thorough discussion on the legal framework for foreign joint venture establishment and its characteristics in China, which is summarized in Figure 5.2.

When a foreign firm determines to invest in China, it needs to identify a potential partner in the PRC. First, it can approach the market alone if the firm has existing business connections there. Second, it can go through a guanxi person who has ample business connections and can identify a potential partner. Finally, the foreign firm can contact some intermediary organizations. They are official Chinese agencies that help the Chinese government procure foreign capital. In any case, if this foreign firm wishes to operate in an industry that is driven by the four modernizations program, according to Chinese law it must contact the Ministry of Foreign Trade and Economic Cooperation (MOFTEC) because the business may affect the infrastructure of the country.

After the foreign firm identifies a potential partner, it normally signs a letter of intent, which signifies the intention of both parties to start negotiations. Meanwhile, they jointly draft the joint venture business proposal. It is the Chinese party's responsibility to submit the project proposal to secure a listing in the economic development plan and obtain initial approval from either local MOFTEC offices or central MOFTEC depending upon the size of the joint venture under PRC central planning policy.

FIGURE 5.2. Legal Procedures for Joint Venture Establishment

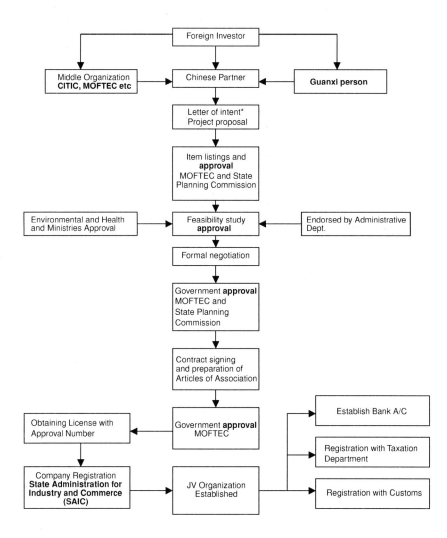

Source: Adapted from Sum (1996). *Practical Law Guide of Direct Foreign Investment in China.* Hong Kong: Commercial Press, p. 60.

*Some organizations prefer to sign the letter of intent after formal negotiation.

After the joint venture business proposal is approved, a feasibility study must be jointly conducted by the foreign and Chinese organizations to justify the project's economic contribution to the Chinese socialist economy. This feasibility study needs to be endorsed by the relevant ministry and the Ministry of Environment and Health. Approval of the joint venture formation is the first stage of government approval.

After all these procedures are carried out, formal negotiation can start on finer details of the joint venture. If both parties agree to proceed after negotiation, they must submit an amended project feasibility study to the relevant MOFTEC office and the State Planning Commission for initial approval of the recognition of the venture's economic contribution to the Chinese socialist economy. This is the second stage of official government approval.

After the feasibility study is approved by the government authorities and the structure of the joint venture is discussed between the two parties, the two parties will sign a contract. The number of contracts signed will increase when the joint venture becomes more complex. In a technology transfer joint venture, the joint venture partners will sign a technology transfer contract, an intellectual property rights transfer contract, and the business contract. These contracts, together with the articles of association, are submitted to the relevant MOFTEC office for final approval. This is the third stage of official government approval.

The decision to approve the joint venture will be made within forty-five days by the MOFTEC office. This second stage of formal approval will include a business license and number. The joint venture partners must register their business license with the State Administration for Industry and Commerce (ASIC) for administrative purposes. After the license is endorsed by ASIC, the joint venture is officially established. However, the joint venture needs to establish a bank account and register with the Taxation Department and the Customs Department before they can conduct business. This is the final stage of government approval.

The reader can see that the process of entering China to do business is complex. How can guanxi improve this situation?

Law and Guanxi

To some extent, guanxi helps to promote efficiency in transactions and even aids the process of entering China. China is a socialist state, which adopted Marxist theory regarding law as an offensive instrument used by capitalists against the working class. The Communist Party effectively dismantled the legal system after the Nationalists retreated to Taiwan in 1949 and installed a system of People's Courts. The People's Court consisted of individual judges selected on the basis of their personal political reliability and class background. Legal professionals were greatly affected. Under government central planning policy, the role of contract law diminished. Over the past twenty years, the Chinese government has gradually acknowledged the poor development of its country's legal systems and the need to rebuild the whole legal system. It was estimated by Vice Premier Zhu Rongzhi in 1994 that a fully effective legal system would require a minimum of 300,000 legal professionals; achieving this would be a long-term project. During this transitional period, guanxi has functioned in providing bonds of trust between insiders' expressive networks and the instrumental relationships of business circles.

In summary, guanxi works like a lubricant to "oil the wheels of a transaction" in the absence of well-developed legal systems. Most guanxi development comes in the form of dining together and gift giving, rather than in employing lawyers to protect the enforcement of a written contract. This research indicates that the Chinese, unlike Westerners, tend to create a formal contract at a later stage after building up some degree of mutual trust. This is in contrast to the Western philosophy that a contract should ideally be finalized before any formal cooperation or joint venture. In theory, if there is total trust, then the contract may be of less value.

Apart from the social, cultural, and economic interpretations of the role of guanxi, another perspective is the explanation of guanxi as the pursuit of individual personal gain in a tightly controlled society.

Guanxi and Corruption

The relationships between favor, guanxi, and corruption are explored in this section: Favor, which is defined as the special treatment of another party, may imply some unfair treatment. This treatment may be regarded as unethical and illegal. Nepotism is one of the reasons why the favor construct is so difficult to test empirically.

Lien (1990) discussed the relationship between guanxi and corruption:

> Moralists maintain that corruption is definitely detrimental while reformists argue that corruption provides some benefits to developing nations which in some may exceed the cost. . . . Despite some disagreement, it seems that the reformists' position is well established. (p. 153)

Favor, to a certain extent, refers to the use of an individual holding office to control resources or to provide special treatment regarding resource allocation of physical or invisible assets, such as the permission to import or export. Favor levels in guanxi networks appear to encourage this tendency to manifest in corrupt behavior.

Threshold's (1990) definition of corruption is the illegal use of public office for private gain. In his definition, a favor may be regarded as illegal behavior if any government official decides to award a government contract or permission and license to someone according to his personal self-interest instead of the government's intended criteria. Corruption arises when personal gain goes against the intended objective of the government, assuming that the government's objective is compatible with the social welfare of the nation. Another sort of corrupt behavior arises as the result of misallocation of limited social or public resources. An insider may not be able to offer the best combination of cost and quality to bid for the contract. The efficiency of the economy is affected.

Another consideration involved in corruption and favor is human subjectivity. Humans may unconsciously or consciously favor insiders. The extent of favor is determined by the degree of favor exchange. At one end of the scale, small gifts, dinner, and helping business friends are normally acceptable, because this behavior will not cause any misallocation of major resources. At the other extreme, a large bribe may distort the optimal allocation of public or social welfare resources. In real life, most favors lie between the two extremes. Sometimes it is difficult to draw the line between guanxi as lubricant and illegal behavior. In China, imperfect competition and ineffective mechanisms of preventing administrative abuse of, for example, the approval of government import permits, tend to enable individual officials to earn monopoly "rent," which is defined as the profits gained. This imperfect competitive climate tends to encourage the wide use of favor, for example, nepotism, which may be interpreted as corrupt behavior.

Summary

There are positive and negative aspects of guanxi. Viewed positively, guanxi networks offer an alternative means of facilitating business transactions. Negative aspects include the associated corrupt behavior, implying costs to national welfare. Chapter 3 described the empirical evidence that business executives perceive guanxi as a method of "maintaining a smooth flow of payments" or "smoothing transportation." These perceptions reflect business inefficiency. The considerations of "gaining access to electricity" or "gaining access to land" were not perceived as important lubricants. This interpretation is subject to further refinement because corrupt behavior is difficult to evaluate. Most people may have some kind of defense mechanism that allows them to rationalize, lie to themselves, or simply ignore the sensitive question of the benefits of guanxi. But, if there is overemphasis on favor or nepotism, will the future development of reform in China correct the detrimental forms of guanxi interaction? This depends on four things: first, the pace of economic change in various systems or to what extent the economy is open; second, progress in improving the legal system and anticorruption measures; third, the rate of improvement of government administrative control to minimize loopholes for unfair business practice; finally, the level of technological development of information systems, such as the Internet. Information exchange is one of the major factors in maintaining relationships.

POSITIVE FUNCTIONS OF GUANXI

According to empirical studies (Leung, Wong, and Tam 1995), guanxi has four major positive roles. The following were identified as key factors encouraging guanxi network members to work together:

1. Source of information—Market trends, government polices, import regulation, and business opportunities.
2. Source of resources—The approval of import license applications by provincial and central government is regarded as a bureaucratically controlled resource. Guanxi provides shortcuts to obtaining this resource and saving time.

3. Source of procurement/supply—For example, securing land, electricity, and raw materials for joint venture manufacturing.
4. Company image building, logistics, and payment—These are enhanced through the guanxi mechanism.

Chinese people probably have contradictory personalities. Guanxi reflects this contradictory feature. The relationship building process involves both cooperation and conflicts, which contradict each other. Anderson and Narus (1990) defined cooperation as complementary coordinated functions performed by firms in interdependent relationships to target mutual or singular outcomes for reciprocation over time. Dwyer, Schurr, and Oh (1987) indicated that a certain level of conflict is inevitable in business life. The development of good relationships shows the resolution of conflicts or confrontations to be constructively handled.

Adaptation and Guanxi

The findings of this research coincide with the research results of Jacobs (1982), Brunner and Taoka (1977), Lee and Lo (1988), Tse et al. (1988), Yang (1986), Hwang (1987), Brunner and Koh (1988), and Brunner et al. (1989). Information exchange and mutual expectation are the key variables affecting adaptation attributes of guanxi between the Hong Kong firms and their Chinese counterparts. Other factors may also influence the process of adaptation. A conceptual framework is proposed to indicate the complex relationship between guanxi and the process of adaptation.

Framework of Proposed Adaptation Processes and Guanxi

The underlying concept of an adaptation process is useful in the systematic analysis of the guanxi-building process. The conceptual framework is that guanxi elements are perceived to be determined by outsider/organization and insider/individual dichotomies. Even in the same adaptation process, an outsider and an insider will make different levels of effort and face various degrees of difficulty. For example, when the outsider tries very hard to establish a closer guanxi connection with another who owns resources, the insider may enjoy the benefits of information exchange and mutual understanding in his or her own network.

The process of adaptation is understood as a series of eight stages (see Table 5.1). A1 through A8 describe the processes of guanxi building between parties.

A1, Availability. Available sources for appropriate connection: the key exercise is searching for the right "source" or "gatekeeper" for a guanxi network entrance. The difficulty lies in selecting the right network members to associate with. If the Chinese party regards the other as an outsider, tough bargaining takes place. If they regard each other as belonging to the same network, negotiation is easier.

A2, Association. After searching for the starting point or initial contact person, through association, each party will try to accept the other if both have passed the testing period. For example, the potential buyer may not reveal his annual quantity requirement in the price quotation request. Instead, he asks for a quotation based on a minimum quantity. If the seller quotes on a minimum quantity, the price most likely will not be very attractive. So no business deal is concluded. Should each party regard the other as an insider, then they will work together by revealing more information, by being more willing to accept a below minimum order, or by revealing annual or monthly requirement schedules for an exact quotation.

A3, Acceptance. This is a crucial stage. In the outsider dimension, both parties clarify their positions and expect each other to under-

TABLE 5.1. Guanxi and Outsider-Insider Dichotomy—Perceptual Positioning

Process		Outsider	Insider
A1	Availability	Bargaining	Belonging
A2	Association	Testing	Teaming
A3	Acceptance	Clarifying	Compromise
A4	Affective	Fitting	Fine-tuning
A5	Affordability	Accommodation	Assimilation
A6	Affirmation	Trial	Trust
A7	Assurance	Convergence	Commitment
A8	Adaptation	Fiancé	Old Friend

Note: The adaptation processes all start with the letter A. Each outsider-insider dichotomy is represented by two words beginning with the same letter. For example, in the availability process, relationship situations are represented by bargaining perceptions for the outsider versus belonging perceptions for the insider.

stand their limitations and strong points. Sometimes, the weaker party is accepted because of the predominance of the strong party in negotiation. For example, the suppliers may be willing to accept a lower price in return for the potential of long-term business. They will compromise by accommodating their mutually beneficial cooperation if they are working in the insider perspective.

A4, Affective. At this stage, in the insider dimension, both parties are assured of the potential increasing confidence in each other by fitting into the requirements of the other party. In the outsider dimension they may prefer to have a minimum asset-specific investment. If they share an insider relationship, they may ensure the possibility of fine tuning, or the consolidation of each party's resources to optimize the effective pooling of expertise and experience. This affective stage means that individual decision-making has some elements of an expressive relationship.

A5, Affordability. It is also important for each party to determine how to afford the risk of going further and developing stronger relationship ties. Both parties face the dilemma of whether to accommodate the stability of working together or to keep on searching for an alternative standby supplier at lowest cost. If they are in an insider's circle, both parties will probably assimilate their resources or give up self-interest for mutual benefit.

A6, Affirmation. For an outsider, affirmation is a "go-ahead" signal. This stage involves feedback. Throughout the process from stages A1 to A5, if the parties are in an outsider dimension, they will not be so willing to have a closer relationship because they are in a trial period. On the other hand, if they are in an insider dimension, they may now enter the stage of mutual trust.

A7, Assurance. Once again, each party receives a signal reassuring it of the possibility of enhancing the long-term relationship. The difference in the mode of cooperation between outsider and insider is that the former expects a convergence of conflicting interests. The latter meanwhile is able to achieve mutual commitment. For example, a supplier is willing to invest in a special model for a new buyer who requests a new specification. This reflects a mutual commitment.

A8, Adaptation. This is the final stage. In the outsider dimension, both parties are now in the "fiancé" stage. They work closely, but psychologically they still prefer to keep their distance. On the other hand, when the insider reaches the "old friend" stage, they can actualize their relationship with higher commitment and mutual trust; they prefer to work together. A closer relationship is then established.

Summary

Stages A1 to A3 are perceived to be the mutual searching, familiarization, and reciprocity stages; each party scrutinizes the emotional aspects of the other. Stages A4 and A5 involve the art of achieving the balance of emotional versus instrumental elements of relationship building. The cautious handling of stages A4 and A5 may decide whether the partners are "friends" (insiders) or "partners" (outsiders).

The key functions of stages A7 and A8 are to achieve reconfirmation and to appreciate the values of adaptation to each other. The dilemma at this stage is confirmation versus conformity. Confirmation implies that one party is required to work closely and to adapt to the other party's requirements. During the process of conformity, conflicts of interests occasionally exist, concerning, for example, the allocation of advertising or research costs in a joint project. One party may be forced to conform to the other party's requests if the party does not want to break the relationship.

GUANXI PERSPECTIVES

The process and interactions just described are not a norm but rather a guideline or checklist for the understanding of relationship building. How can stages A1 through A8 be regrouped for easy understanding? A1 through A8 can be synthesized into four positioning frameworks.

Guanxi Positioning

The combinations of these interactions with the insider/outsider dichotomy form the framework of the perceptual map (Figure 5.3). To analyze the complex interactive behavior of guanxi, four outsider-

FIGURE 5.3. Guanxi Positioning Classification Map

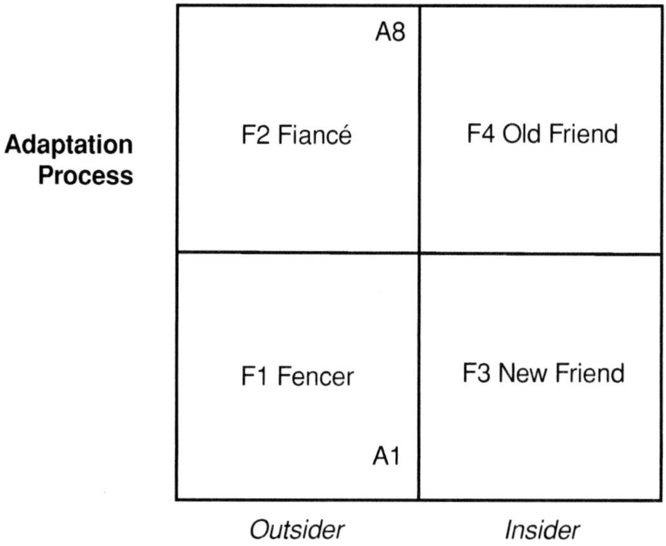

Adaptation Process	A8

insider psychological concepts are proposed: fencer, fiancé, new friend, and old friend.

Fencer

At the fencer stage, both parties are testing the intentions or reactions of the other (in the range of A1 through A4 or A5). Each party regards the other as an outsider. If they accept each other as friends, then they are in a "new friend" situation positioned in an insider quadrant. If a strong guanxi relationship has been established after the parties enter the new friend quadrant, they may enter the old friend stage with substantial relationship-specific investment. Otherwise, the parties may become "fiancés" with limited informal information exchanges.

Fiancé

In the F2 quadrant (fiancé), during the affirmative stage, both parties bargain with their power, which depends on how each party evaluates its dependence on the other party. This dependence has many forms, including two major forms: just or unjust. An unjust form of dependence means that one party may exercise power over the other without consent. A just form involves voluntary compliance or joint effort to promote collective goals. Whether the relationship is maintained depends on the exercise of power. At the adaptation stage, both parties trust each other. Trust is an important variable that greatly influences interpersonal and intergroup behavior.

Trust affects relational expectations regarding the solution of conflicts of interest and the enhancement or diminution of solidarity. Rotter (1967) defines trust as a belief that a word or promise of a party is reliable and can be actualized in an exchange relationship. A party will tend to take greater risks if he or she trusts his or her partner. For example, high-risk cooperative behavior includes the following:

1. Making a large concession to seek reciprocation
2. Compromise
3. Openness regarding individual motives and priorities
4. The unilateral initiation of tension-reduction actions

In short, the processes of association, acceptance, affordability, affirmation, and assurance in the form of bargaining power, expectation development, and mutual trust enable both parties to test their mutual compatibility, integrity, and interdependence.

Old Friend and New Friend

The new friend quadrant differs in approach from the fiancé quadrant. The Chinese approach tends to be more organic than the Western approach; cultivating guanxi as a competitive advantage and taking a long-term perspective on the investment in building a relationship; for example, regarding gift-giving as a part of enhancing the guanxi network. At the old friend level, each party tends to favor a heart perspective over the Western mind perspective. The former perspective views management as an art of dealing with people by understanding their feelings and emotions. All psychic rewards or costs are subject to ever-changing situations. In such an environment, continuity and consistency in maintaining the relationship in order to win the heart is of great importance.

Summary

In summary, the development of fencer and fiancé stages is similar to two people falling in love. The new friend stage is similar to a de facto relationship. The old friend position is like marriage, which implies the serious consequences of separation and divorce in the event of any major conflicts between parties. These positions may also be called "beware-beloved dimensions," as illustrated in Figure 5.4.

"Four Bs" Interaction Dynamic

The interaction dynamic means that fencer partners are wary of each other, as in the initial stages of a couple going out (box B1 in Figure 5.4). They will move to B2 (fiancé stage) by benefiting each other. B3 indicates that parties accept each other as belonging to the same network, while the B4 position is analogous to a couple in love who decide to get married. Figure 5.5 illustrates the outcome of the positions of each interaction stage.

FIGURE 5.4. Guanxi Interaction Dynamic: Various Stages from "Beware" to "Beloved"

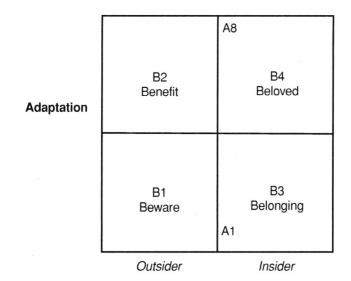

FIGURE 5.5. Guanxi Outcome Positioning, Following the Romance Analogy

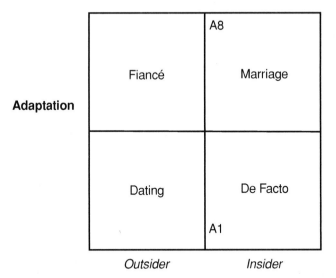

Guanxi Outcome Positioning

The dating and fiancé quadrants are grouped into the outsider category, as these two positions indicate that the parties are living separately in different psychological "houses." The de facto and marriage positions mean living together psychologically. A de facto relationship is informal and does not involve total trust. The couple are concerned about the potential impact of marriage termination costs, i.e., separation or divorce costs. They are not bound by any formal contract. Note that, in this research, trust needs to be tested over time. Normally, the Chinese want to have more interactions to prove mutual trust. Marriage, which is formally bound by written contract, is a type of socially and officially acceptable behavior. In Chinese society, a de facto couple is not legally recognized. In contrast, the de facto relationship has been accepted in some countries, such as Australia and Canada. In Western society, the son of a de facto couple is entitled to a share of the possessions if his father passes away. In China, a de facto son is not legally accepted. In addition, if someone is found to manipulate any favor in self-interest or for personal advantage and is given a prison sentence or the death penalty, then the associated de facto network members are likely to be associated with this sentence, which will bring shame to the individual, the family, or even the whole network. This sort of guanxi is summarized by the following comment (McDonald 1995):

> For many countries in the Asia Pacific Region there is a recognizable move from "under-developed" status to levels of greater economic security. These changes are being accompanied by moves away from systems of de facto patrimonialism where office holders are able to levy charges and override the formal prohibitions of office, to more equitable systems of ethical stewardship and accompanying social sanctions.
>
> One could surmise that in China ethical concerns will initially focus on corruption and bribery, for which the political and economic system provides numerous opportunities. It is under these circumstances that corruption is often endorsed as a useful mechanism by which the "wheels may be oiled." Viewed in this light, corruption is not seen as detrimental, but rather as a means of facilitating operational progress. When a rigidly centralised and state-planned economy fails to deliver, a parallel system becomes operative to provide needed goods and services as well as rewards or benefits to those that assist in the process. Similarly, unethical practices such as product piracy, counterfeit goods, and parallel imports are not seen as illegal procurement of another's profits, but an alternative means of providing goods at a price the local population can afford while also providing the means of achieving technological transfer. (p. 186)

Foreigners should take care to keep up with ever-changing normative standards in China. In China, the favoritism generated by guanxi has two major features: lubrication and subornation.

Lubrication and Subornation

Cateron (1993) pointed out that lubrication payments are made with requests for a person to perform a task faster or more efficiently, whereas subornation is an act of asking officials to neglect their duties or do something illegal.

Lubrication is generally acceptable behavior, but subornation is a very serious crime, as for example in the following report from the *Eastern Express* (Gilley 1994):

The arrest, announced in the mainland media last week, of Wang Jianye, a former department director of the Shenzhen planning commission, actually took place last September. Wang is charged with extorting HK$8.80m (10 million renminbi) in bribes and kickbacks from companies in the special economic zone. He was repatriated from Thailand . . .

In short, the general absence of business ethics, uneven income distribution, and a poor legal system are the general causes of corruption. The favoritism attributes of guanxi and the mutual reciprocation within guanxi networks result in the possibility of unethical behavior. Having reviewed the basic framework of the guanxi concept, the next question is: how to apply the guanxi concept to relationship marketing? The next section provides an integrated answer by using an "A-G" approach.

Implementation of Guanxi Management: A-G Approach

From a managerial angle, this research provides a useful and practical framework for managerial decision making. This section attempts to account for differences in Western and Chinese views and to provide a holistic perspective to balance or explain the apparently conflicting views.

The effectiveness of guanxi building lies in the different perceptions of relationships from Western and Eastern angles. Our advice to foreigners working in China is labeled the A, B, C, D, E, F, and G concerns, which stand for association, bonding, commitment, defensiveness, empathy, face and favor, and guanxi.

Association

Association with Chinese businesses starts with the problem of identifying access to the right decision makers. It can take time to find the right person. China's open-door policy has resulted in the rapid growth of different organizations and a higher staff turnover rate. The search for the right channel, the right decision maker, and contacts requires patience. The association will be effective if both parties accept each other by investing affective elements to affirm the relationship by assuring the other that the relationship is actualized. The old Chinese saying "A new ruler has a new court" reflects the close relationship between the ruler (the senior management) and the court (staff). If a new ruler takes over the court, the old team probably will be dismantled. This analogy reveals a dependence on the manager as the ruler who may intensify his or her power by reinforcing the loyalty of the staff.

Bonding

The Chinese saying "Taking a favor from another means a personal debt" implies that businesspeople should not expect immediate return within a short period. If a Chinese person is willing to accept a favor, this means that there will be probably a long-term beneficial bonding relationship.

Commitment

Commitment is one of the ultimate objectives for both buyer and seller. From initial contact with a potential buyer to the crucial stage of achieving mutual commitment, both parties normally go through several processes that can be labeled as "C words." Owing to the conflict of values of equity and equality norms or rules, compromise is usually the way to achieve a win/win situation. Misunderstanding can be avoided if more clarifying or coordinating functions are performed to encourage cooperation in converting conflicting ideas to mutually acceptable understanding or to reach the stage of concretization of guanxi. For example, pricing should normally not be the first topic for initial contact, as the Chinese do not want to hurt another's feelings by direct refusal. As a subtle way of refusing, the Chinese may ask for a quotation based on a minimum order. A quotation based on a minimum order may mean a higher price and will probably end with no business deal, because the Chinese buyer wants to turn down the offer by reluctance to reveal exact or estimated quantity requirements for quotation.

Defensiveness

Defensiveness is a major feature in dealing with the Chinese, who tend to mistrust foreigners if the foreigner is classified as outsider. Traditionally, the Chinese have emphasized the family or organization above the individual. With an accompanying lack of trust in institutions, the Chinese, stimulated by feelings of insecurity, have the tendency to overemphasize pragmatism and materialism in dealing with Western partners.

Empathy

Empathy represents the expressive tie of an interpersonal relationship. The Chinese tend to react in a subtle and indirect manner. Empathy helps Westerners to understand their partners' needs. For example, the need to save face is an extremely important element in business negotiation, because losing face is a major blow to the Chinese, which is described by the Chinese saying "like a tree without its bark."

Favor and Face

Favor has been discussed previously. The relationship between face and favor is elaborated here. Face refers to the projection of self-image. A good image is a very useful weapon to exert mutually coercive power on other parties. A Chinese social norm has always been to meet the expectations of others by the exchange of favors.

Guanxi

Guanxi has two major elements: instrumental and affective. The affective components consist of entertainment and social gathering, such as business dinners. Westerners often pursue affective approaches with overemphasis on treats or gift giving. The risk is that the Chinese may regard them as "meat and wine friends," who are not to be trusted. The Chinese always appreciate friendship built on hardship or developed in difficult situations.

Conclusion

In summary, B (bonding) is the way to convert basic A (association) to long-term mutual C (commitment). This approach is similar in Western or organizational behavior. D (defensiveness) and F (favor) are outstanding characteristics in Chinese business. To understand both D and F, we need to have effective understanding of the values and attitude of other persons by means of E (empathy) so as to achieve effective G (guanxi). These six concepts are illustrated in Figure 5.6.

Guanxi Dynamic

Generally speaking, association, bonding, and commitment variables are grouped into the mind approach. Defensiveness, empathy, and face (and favor) are regarded as the heart approach. The approaches may overlap, e.g., commitment may be regarded as a heart approach also. In addition, two major concepts, commitment and defensiveness, are "self-contradictory" because commitment implies responsibility but defensiveness implies responsibility avoidance. How can these self-contradictory issues be handled by the Chinese? Most issues surely are not just a matter of polar opposites. These two polar opposites are combined, and the combination creates a more productive "dynamism." The ancient Chinese yin and yang symbol consists of two self-sufficient elements that fuse to form a harmonious whole, while each element retains its own integrity and identity (Figure 5.7).

Self-Contradictory Issues and Guanxi Harmony

How can self-contradictory personality characteristics promote the work dynamic? In theory, A (association), through the adaptation process, and B (bonding) are integrated into C (commitment); i.e.,

FIGURE 5.6. Implementation of Guanxi (A-G Approach): The Interaction of Mind and Heart Approaches

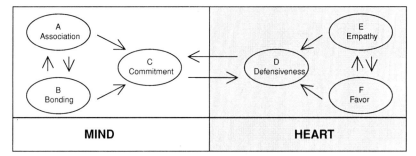

FIGURE 5.7. Guanxi "Yin-Yang" Harmony Integration

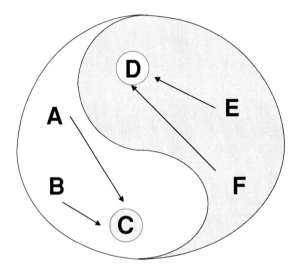

Note: C (Commitment) under the influence of A (Association) and B (Bonding) integrates or fuses with D (Defensiveness) motivated by F (Face and Favor) and E (Empathy) forces to form a work dynamic.

through association and bonding processes, each party eventually reaches commitment. Similarly, E (empathy) and F (face) integrate into D (defense); i.e., through empathy and face work, a defense mechanism is built up inside the guanxi network. Commitment (C) and defensiveness (D) are two polar opposites in the personality. The Chinese emphasize human feeling (heart). If they face a conflict between mind and heart, they will tend to retain feeling and surrender reason (Huang 1994). The importance of feeling is the root of Confucian benevolence. The Chinese character for the word "benevolence" means "two people." This implies the harmonious relationship of two people with human feeling.

How Can a Guanxi Dynamic Framework Help Business Executives Understand Relationship Marketing in the PRC?

Two further questions can be added to this question:

1. In today's competitive business world, how are the Chinese able to make friends while still maintaining their business interests?

2. Can a successful business deal include an intimate friendship? How are mind and heart approaches integrated to become the work dynamic? In short, how can the dilemma between rational reasoning and personal feeling be balanced?

Personal Friendship versus Business Interests— The Unity of Opposites

To exchange favors and to be loyal to your friends are the traditional ideals of Chinese friendship. In contemporary Chinese society, these traditional ideals are changing. The economic reforms during the last two decades have fanned the flames of high competitive profitability and efficiency. According to a slogan in the Shenzhen Special Economic Zone in Guangdong, "Time is money. Efficiency is life." However, it is important to note that Chinese society is a blend of old and new cultural values. Clan societies or associations are typical examples of how the Chinese combine friendship and business interests with the formation of clans based on a common surname or birthplace. Most networks are not well-structured organizations, having no external and limited organizational coercion. The networks consist of many small and medium-sized inner circles and groups. Instead of a strong central management core, the management may be a team of several powerful and capable individuals linking the common interests of various subgroups, because of their mutual confidence, tacit understanding and agreement, and the reciprocal benefits.

Summary

In short, guanxi networks involve taking advantage of official positions or informal power and thereby, to some extent, probably do damage to social or public benefits while favoring an individual or small circle of insiders. On the other hand, these networks play an important role in strengthening social synergy and communication by encouraging competition and development. For example, it may take many months to go through the normal bureaucratic procedure for obtaining a construction permit from the government; the use of guanxi provides a shortcut to approval for the project, which would mean more employment opportunities and growth.

Balance Between Mind and Heart: The Relationship Between Reason and Feeling

The major difference between Western and Chinese management practices seems to stem from basic management values. Sometimes, the Chinese may make their assessment of a potential partner's human feeling or considerate nature a priority, over concern for profits, because the Chinese believe that people must have feeling to be trusted to share profits or benefits. If a Chinese person faces the dilemma of feeling and reason, he will tend to prefer feeling and suppress reason, consciously or subconsciously.

MANAGERIAL IMPLICATIONS

This section includes the benefits of guanxi and flexibility in the establishment of guanxi strategies using a routing approach. The relationship between guanxi and sales activities is the first topic of this section. In analyzing the relationship between guanxi and sales activities, the following benefits, functions, and problems of guanxi are reviewed:

1. The activities involved in relationship building
2. The role of the relationship or guanxi in different business stages
3. The assistance available to a businessperson from a member of a guanxi network
4. The factors that affect the success of a business deal
5. Flexibility in business dealing

Guanxi and Business Development Activities in China

Our research (Leung, Wong, and Wong 1996) summarizes eleven important activities, which are broadly categorized as two major functions, communication tasks and daily operations:

1. **Communication tasks**
   Maintenance of a good connection/relationship network
   Identification of correct PRC contacts
   On-site visits to PRC contacts

Clarification of the communication gap with PRC contacts
Under-the-table methods

2. **Daily operations**
   Monitoring market trends
   Facilitating transportation into China
   Locating selling channel
   Arranging payment collection
   Obtaining import licenses
   Arranging storage

Generally, 88 percent of respondents agreed that maintaining a good connection or relationship is very important and 78 percent agreed that monitoring market trends is very important. All respondents agreed that most activities related to communication and daily operational activities are essential.

The term "under-the-table" implies illegal activities; hence, the respondents cannot admit to espousing these activities. The respondents show a tendency to deny the importance of this factor. However, the exploitation of guanxi to get things done is tolerated to some extent. Brunner et al. (1989) indicated that the Chinese cultivate some "backdoor" activities to bypass bureaucratic rules.

The figures in Table 5.2 show respondents' ratings of the value of guanxi in making deals. More than 76 percent of the respondents recognized that guanxi is an important variable when negotiating with the Chinese, and 87.8 percent agreed that it was significant throughout the whole process.

More than 50 percent of the respondents agreed that guanxi relationships have values relating to all the items listed, and their mean scores on six-point scales are all greater than or approximately equal to 3.5 except for recruitment of labor and approval of advertisements.

Also, respondents value networks for arranging smooth transportation. Mutual cooperation between Hong Kong and China improves the efficiency of channeling goods and services through highly complicated distribution systems. Large discrepancies exist in the scores for smooth collection of payment, smooth transportation arrangements, and application for import licenses. The respondents gave higher values to utilizing their contact network to cultivate and develop other business activities.

TABLE 5.2. Importance of Connection/Relationship Factors in the Negotiation Process

Important Activities	Percentage of Respondents That Agree with the Proposition
Importance of Relationship Factor in Negotiation Process	
• Significant for the whole process	87.8
• Significant in the negotiation stage	80.9
• Affect the preliminary stage	76.9
• Affect the final stage	76.9
Value of the Contact Network for:	
Source of Information	
• Government policies	83.4
• Import regulations and restrictions	82.0
• Business opportunity leads	79.4
• Market trends	61.3
Application for Resources	
• Application for import license	80.0
• Approval of application from provincial government	78.7
• Approval of application from central government	77.4
• Secure electricity for Joint Venture (JV)	60.7
• Secure land for JV	55.3
• Secure raw material for JV	53.3
• Recruitment of labor	48.0
• Approval of advertisements	47.3
Other Essential Areas	
• Smooth transport arrangements	84.0
• Smooth collection of payment	81.3
• Building up company reputation and image	72.2

Note: This table summarizes the importance of guanxi at different stages of negotiation and the value of guanxi in sourcing information and resources plus the impact of guanxi on transportation, payment collection activities, and reputation building.

In summary, guanxi may be useful in negotiating the acquisition of necessary resources. As shown in Table 5.3, a total of 90 percent of the respondents agreed that communication with PRC clients is important. But what factors cause business failure in the PRC? Lack of contact network, lack of updated market information, and change of key players are considered important. In comparison, price is only a minor factor accounting for business failures. Another important factor affecting failure in business deals is the flexibility of a company in its attempts to establish connections.

TABLE 5.3. Factors Leading to a Failed Business Deal in the PRC

Factors	Respondent %
Lack of communication with PRC clients	90.0
Lack of contact network	88.7
Lack of updated market information (e.g., policies, regulation, etc.)	83.4
Change of key players during negotiation	83.3
Misinterpretation of PRC client's needs	82.7
Lack of continuity in the negotiation team	80.0
Price competitiveness	75.3
Lack of public relations promotion	58.7
Too many taxes	58.0
Overstaffing in joint venture	54.7

Note: Most factors are personal rather than objective (e.g., price is regarded as the seventh most important factor while miscommunication with PRC clients is first).

Company Policy in Establishing PRC Connections

In our survey, 84.6 percent of respondents considered it important to entertain PRC clients, and 75.3 percent considered it important to take them on overseas trips. Less than 50 percent of the respondents indicated that they provided other forms of assistance to their clients, e.g., acting as guarantor for a client's children to study overseas and providing reduced rates of commission. Other factors contributing to flexibility are summarized in Table 5.4.

It is emphasized that reducing rates of commission is a sensitive question. The respondents might not be willing to answer honestly. Respondents preferred that such reductions not take place at a company level but hope that they are limited to a personal level at first.

These findings indicate that guanxi is a very important determinant in trading with China. In short, guanxi is another marketing variable that China trade executives need to manage, apart from the traditional four Ps. In China there may be a different attitude toward bribery and corruption. Gift giving or providing market investigation trips to clients in China may be considered normal rather than exceptional. The inconsistent policy regarding undercutting commissions at a personal level rather than at a company level tend to encourage firms to take a more flexible approach in trading with China.

TABLE 5.4. The Flexibility of Company Policy in Establishing PRC Connections

Factors	Respondent %
Entertaining PRC clients (e.g., gifts and hospitality)	84.6
Provide market investigation trips to PRC clients	75.3
Provide personal assistance to PRC clients (e.g., act as guarantor for client's children to study overseas)	46.0
Provide undercut commission	42.1

Note: Showing individual personal interest is the major factor contributing to flexibility in dealing with PRC clients.

Guanxi Strategies: Routing Approach

As described earlier in this chapter, the positioning classification map (Figure 5.3) summarizing the various relationships in the model of the adaptation process and insider-outsider dimensions is of practical value. This section includes another example of how to use this positioning map in implementing relationship marketing strategies. Most executives in China trade have the following questions:

1. Why do the Chinese take such a long time to negotiate with Westerners and conclude a business deal?
2. If a Chinese partner regards a Western partner as an outsider, will the Westerner be treated equally?

To answer question (1), a routing concept was developed (Figure 5.8). The shortcut route is from F1 to F4 (the "I" route) as the route is a straight diagonal fencer to old friend. This route often occurs when both parties have a mature friendship that was not built through business. Jimmy Leung, director of Tonken Enterprises Ltd., used this route to develop guanxi with his Chinese partner.

In the middle of 1992, after building a business relationship with a Wuhan factory, Leung lent the factory manager RMB 3 million without any collateral to set up another factory in Wuhan. At the end of that year, the factory manager repaid the debt and entered negotiations with Tonken. The guanxi between Leung and the factory manager was developed before their negotiations, so that it could develop quickly, from F1 directly to F4. As Leung recalled: "When he ap-

FIGURE 5.8. Routing of Guanxi Development: A Relationship Navigator Determining Various Positionings During the Interaction Process

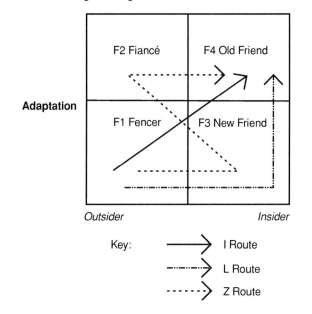

proached us, told us his plan, we supported him. I supposed the main reasons were that first, we knew his character; second, we trusted him; and finally, we have excellent guanxi with him!"

Another route is F1 through F3 to F4 or F1 through F2 to F4, i.e., fencer → new friend → old friend or fencer → fiancé → old friend. The route is called the "L" route because its shape resembles that of the letter.

The longest route is a Z-shaped route. There are two types of Z routes:

$$F1 \rightarrow F3 \rightarrow F2 \rightarrow F4$$
$$F1 \rightarrow F2 \rightarrow F3 \rightarrow F4$$

Figure 5.8 shows only three of the five possible routes for easy illustration. In terms of time spent, the I route is shorter than the Z route. If the Chinese regard the partner as an outsider, they will take a longer route. If the Chinese gradually accept the partner as an insider, then they will accommodate him or her as an old friend by investing feeling, affection, and trust. In addition to the route F1 → F2 → F3 → F4, the other route F1→ F3 → F2 → F4 indicates the possibility that both parties progress from outsider to insider, while the route F3 → F2 indicates the possibility of moving from an insider position back to outsider again. For example, the Chinese may initially want a foreign company to transfer advanced technology and thus will give many attractive concessions to the foreign investor. If the foreign investor is later found to be reluctant to share advanced technology, only backward and outdated technology, the Chinese may continue working with them, but instead of having a close relationship, the foreign investor will be treated as an outsider (as though it were a "forced marriage"). In the event of finding another good partner, the Chinese may abandon their initial Western partner after acquiring the limited technology that was offered.

Discrete Routing

There are some possibilities of discrete routes. For example, F1 → F2 is a vertical I route. Similarly, F1 → F3 is a horizontal I route, and F2 → F3 is a diagonal I route. These three routes are discrete, instead of one Z-type continuous route. An F1→ F2 route means the adaptation process takes place in the outsider quadrant only. The F2 → F4 route is impossible if both members do not regard each other as insiders. In theory, the longest route (or that which takes the longest time) is represented by the three discrete routes: (a) F1 → F2, (b) F2 → F3, and (c) F3 → F4, with time intervals between each quadrant as illustrated in Figure 5.9.

A case demonstrating Z routing is Mega Elevator International, Inc. In 1984, Mega began a joint venture with Tianjin Elevator Co., forming Mega Tianjin Elevator Company Ltd. They were in the fencer stage because both parties were testing whether the business could make a profit and cooperate happily. They spent over five years in this quadrant.

After they built more trust, they progressed to the fiancé stage. Mega started another joint venture in China in 1992. The following year, they established an additional joint venture and did more business with China. Their guanxi became closer. By 1997, they had five

FIGURE 5.9. Longest Guanxi Routing: Three Discrete Routes with Time Interval Between Each Quadrant

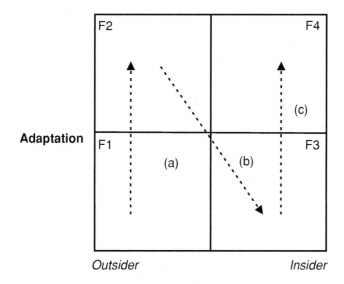

joint ventures in China and planned more in the future. This implies that they have reached the old friend stage and have mature trust; otherwise, they would not spend so much money in China.

Return Route

Sometimes, guanxi cannot be developed well or even goes backward, for example, from F2 to F1 or from F4 to F1. This is caused by many factors, such as misunderstanding each other. It may cause business lossses and bad relationships with others. Robertson Ltd. is a good example.

Robertson Ltd. set up a joint venture with their distributor in Hong Kong. Then they used this joint venture to negotiate for another joint venture at the beginning of 1993 and the joint venture was established at the end of 1994. Robertson never met their Chinese partner before the establishment of the Chinese joint venture, so they had not built up any guanxi. A lot of arguments occurred and Robertson is now talking about a total takeover of the Chinese joint venture. They are still arguing about the terms of the takeover at this writing.

Their guanxi started at F1, then moved to F2, but in the process, a lot of argument caused their guanxi to go backward to F1. Leslie Young, division manager of Torit Products, described the failure of this joint venture:

> I suppose the main reason for this unhappy marriage is that we have bad guanxi with our Chinese partner. In fact, we never met them before we established our factory in China. Second, we should not subcontract the negotiation to our Hong Kong distribution. Finally, we don't have mutual trust!

Summary

The routing of stages of guanxi reflects the fact that the Chinese take a long time to negotiate or to make their final decision. The Chinese may avoid discussing this perspective because insider positioning implies favoritism for individual personal gain. The guanxi development of each case is summarized in Figure 5.10.

Another explanation for the time used by the majority is the lengthy process of adaptation. In this study, 6.8 percent of respondents took more than five years to establish stable guanxi with their PRC partners. The possible explanation is that the route may be Z shaped in discrete stages. The objective of the routing concept is to provide a new vocabulary in relationship marketing to enhance the understanding of these complex and dynamic interactions.

FIGURE 5.10. Routing of Guanxi Development of Each Company

Company	F1 Fencer	F2 Fiancé	F3 New Friend	F4 Old Friend
Tonken Enterprises Ltd.	1			2
Mega Elevator International, Inc.	1	2	3	4
Robertson Ltd.	1 / 3	2		

CONCLUSION

The main objective of this chapter is to contribute to the understanding of guanxi constructs and relationship performance by developing a measurement tool to analyze the dynamic dimensions of adaptation process. This study, the first of its kind, provides a new vocabulary in terms of routing and position mapping for researchers who are interested in comparative studies of Chinese organizational behavior.

Chapter 6

A Comprehensive Model

This chapter discusses and summarizes the overall thoughts and comments of this study. It combines the elements and produces a comprehensive guanxi model. Then the model is tested with a case study.

GUANXI MODEL

This section elaborates the comprehensive guanxi model. One of the major objectives of this study is to present a managerial tool for business executives. The model has five basic components, which are typical elements of the strategic planning process (Figure 6.1). The comprehensive guanxi model is presented in Figure 6.2. Each stage of the model has been discussed earlier. The various components of the model are summarized in the following section.

Dimensions of the Guanxi Model

The dimensions of the model are:

- Detailed analysis of changing context (Box A as shown in Figure 6.2)
- Market intelligence in the form of perceptual positioning of guanxi or guanxi system dynamic (Box B)
- Choice of strategies (Box C)
- Swift implementation of guanxi (Box D) by:
    Adaptation in relationships
    Creation of strategies
    Competitive advantage through relationship-enhancing programs

FIGURE 6.1. The Art of Strategic Management in the Guanxi Model: Guanxi Strategic Process

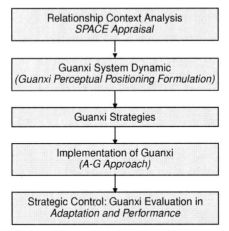

Note: The model starts with context (or situation analysis) and ends with strategic controls (or evaluations).

Detailed Analysis of Changing Context

Understanding the context to which the marketing strategies are applied is crucial, particularly in the ever-changing environment of the PRC. The SPACE approach described in Chapter 4 is a useful tool for incorporating the interactions of the dynamics of political and legal, sociopsychological, business organizational, family and personal, and self or psychological systems. These five systems encompass the dimensions from the micro to the macro levels, including both the controllable aspects (e.g., social capital saving in the form of guanxi networks in the "S" system) and uncontrollable aspects (e.g., the external political system), the internal variables (e.g., contradictory personality) and external variables (e.g., change of environment), the human component (e.g., personalism) and dynamic forces (e.g., empathy) of the "E" system.

Market Intelligence in the Form of Guanxi Perceptual Positioning

Detailed planning can be carried out effectively if there is a perceptual map for better understanding of the positioning of guanxi.

FIGURE 6.2. A Comprehensive Guanxi Model: The Links and Feedback Flows Between Various Components

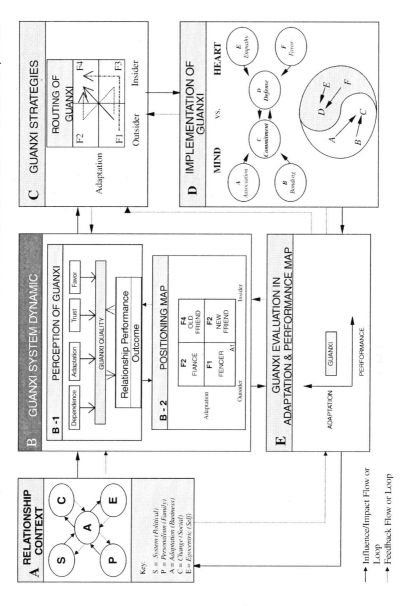

The constructs of trust, favor, dependence, and adaptation provide the major elements of initiating, maintaining, and enhancing a relationship, one of the most important roles of any human interaction.

For easy identification and digestion of the four constructs, the concept can be abbreviated "DFAT" (dependence, favor, adaptation, trust). The order of the letters represents the progression from dependence to trust. Owing to dependence on another party, one party may attempt to minimize the risk of uncertainty by exchanging favor with other members inside the guanxi network. If the exchange is productive, the members will continue adapting their behavior to accommodate the weakness of the other party. This adaptation process eventually leads to mutual trust. The DFAT concept does not require any absolute sequence or a causal link, because there are too many variables in the real world. However, DFAT provides a theoretical framework for determining the positioning of guanxi. A good position is most definitely an important navigator in the marketing mix.

The indicators of sales performance, termination costs, and relationship formalization are good analytic tools for understanding the correct use of the positioning map. Understanding which battleground is correct will ensure that an organization is able to exhibit its strengths and hopefully to camouflage its weaknesses. For example, in the F2 (new friend) position, the seller will exploit opportunities in the marketplace by revealing confidential information, such as knowledge of technology, to the buyer who has accommodated the seller as an insider, so as to build greater trust. This trust is particularly important for any joint product development. In addition, appreciating the characteristics of different positions will help decide the type of strategies that may be used effectively.

Choice of Strategies

Based on the understanding of the dynamic context through SPACE analysis and the position chosen, it is crucial for a plan to be executed in a swift and flexible way by adopting the I, L, or Z routes. Ideally, the continuous I route is used as it represents the shortest distance.

Swift Implementation of Guanxi

Swift routing has several benefits. First, it achieves a quick response, and hopefully a quick return, especially when the environment continues to change rapidly. Second, if the plan is implemented promptly, competitors will not have enough time to react. Competitors will not even have time to develop counterstrategies. Finally, swiftness in implementation minimizes the likelihood that the buyer will behave opportunistically. The buyer will have little time to maximize low-cost strategies, because of lack of trust in an outsider.

The environment is never static; the changing of key decision makers, competitors' aggressive pricing strategies, change in government policies, the improvement of technology, and adaptation in relationships all are incentives for quick response to innovation. To be competitive, a company should encourage the flow of innovative ideas at all points—from the conception of a new product idea to the actual implementation of relationship strategies. In other words, if both parties move successfully from the A1 stage (availability) to the A8 stage (actualization), they will enjoy the benefits of efficiency, especially within the insider network. Adaptation enables both parties to capitalize on any opportunities in the changing environment.

Summary of Dimensions of Guanxi

As shown in Box D, the A-G approaches in the implementation of guanxi provide new terminology to explain the contradictory personality of Chinese businesspeople. D (defense), E (empathy), and F (favor) can be difficult for foreigners to understand. These "heart" elements, particularly favor, imply unfair or even fraudulent practices, which may be regarded as unethical. Favoritism exists in most business transactions. The dilemma is that while one company may not practice favoritism, it cannot prevent its competitors from practicing favoritism or conducting unethical dealings, thereby gaining a competitive advantage. In the book *The Art of War,* Sun Tzu (Jomini 1971) highly recommended the use of deception, including such tactics as bait, illusion, and fakery in war planning. This book has greatly influenced the thinking of post-Confucian businesspeople (Wee, Lee, and Bambang 1993). To tackle these ethical issues, it is recommend that the issues be understood objectively, rather than pretending that they do not exist in the real world of the PRC where most business transactions or dealings are conducted within different sets of economic, legal, ethical, social, and political parameters.

Guanxi Evaluation: Adaptation and Performance

On the whole, the comprehensive model serves as a systematic analytical tool, providing various perspectives that are linked by flow and feedback loops to reflect the dynamic of the model. The guanxi evaluation in Box E of Figure 6.2 provides feedback for each stage of the whole process. For example, if government initiates a major policy change ("S" [system] of SPACE context analysis in Box A), adaptation may be needed through active intelligence flow among the various boxes of guanxi perceptual positioning (Box B1), formulation strategies (Box C), and implementation (Box D). This adaptation may be reflected by a performance indicator, for example, sales trends in the guanxi system dynamic (Box B). Conversely, if confidential information is leaked or a key player changes, one or more of the stages (boxes) will be affected, probably leading to either possible exercises of reassurance, readjustment, or modification or total changes in the original strategies in Boxes C and D. In short, the model is dynamic in the sense that feedback flows between boxes.

Condensed Dynamic Guanxi Model

In addition to Figure 6.2, a condensed integrated version of the guanxi model is presented in Figure 6.3. SPACE is the context in which A is the adaptation process of business organizations (A1-A8 process). The guanxi yin-yang dynamic (A-G approach) is represented by the yin-yang symbol. This symbol "moves" along the I, L, or Z routes from any F position to another F (e.g., F1 to F2), to produce an interactive dynamic labeled B1 through B4.

The movement of the yin-yang symbol is determined by the forces of A (association) and B (bonding) to push C (commitment) versus the force of D (defense) moved by E (empathy) and F (favor), as indicated by Box D of Figure 6.2. The speed of movement depends on the net outcome of the combined forces of C and D. Figure 6.3 illustrates the dynamic of the model to provide another conceptual tool to understand the complex relationship-building process.

FIGURE 6.3. Condensed Guanxi Dynamic Model

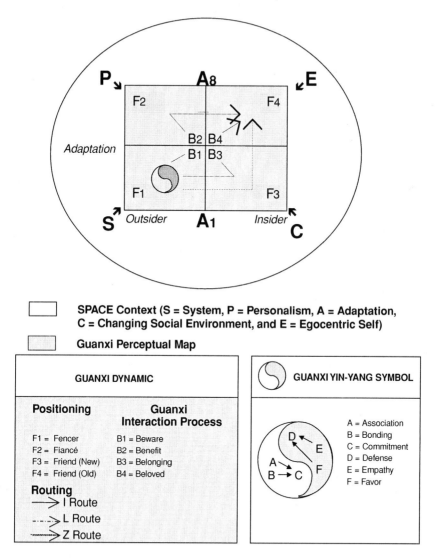

Note: Three types of routing with guanxi positions and outcomes, reflecting the end results of different interactions. The movements of the yin-yang symbol along the routes show the patterns of relationship development. The movement direction of the symbol is determined by the forces of A-F (association-favor) variables.

CASE STUDY: PATTERN DEVELOPMENT
ACCORDING TO PROPOSED GUANXI MODEL

This section aims to apply each component of the guanxi model to a real-life case. The design, methodology, research questions, and background of the company under study are discussed here. This section has six parts, namely:

1. Relationship context
2. Customer positions
3. Constructs and positioning
4. Routing
5. Implementation stages
6. Application of condensed guanxi model to case study

Relationship Context

Expert Ltd. has three major markets: the PRC, Hong Kong, and overseas. The Chinese market counts for approximately 70 percent of business turnover, Hong Kong 20 percent, and overseas 10 percent. The SPACE analytic tool shown in Box A of the guanxi model (Figure 6.2) is used to provide the contextual framework.

Expert Ltd. faces a constantly changing environment in its two major markets. The political and legal system (S) of China have been described by the management as "difficult to understand; it is difficult to predict the ever-changing and complex systems."

An example of going through the "back door" of the legal system was the use of different tax systems for different import customers. The rate of import tax was not standardized but was subject to the degree of guanxi between the importer and the customs officers. The company needed to use its associated agents in handling import processes. The personal (P) trust between them is very important because they are dealing with sensitive issues involving legal consequences. Owing to the lack of a formal legal system and the dense bureaucratic forest of PRC government regulations, management mentioned that the company's strategies and implementation plans were reviewed on a weekly basis. This demonstrates the sort of highly adaptive (A) behavior necessary to accommodate changes (C) of environment and conflicting interests in balancing the use of the formal systems or the "back door" of a guanxi network. The company has encountered the dilemma of how to achieve optimal strategies.

Also, most of Expert Ltd.'s PRC customers were mainly interested in pursuing self-interest and their own safety rather than maximizing their organizational interests. Some purchasing decisions were made because of under-the-table dealings or the incentives of sponsorship for overseas visits. Expert Ltd. spent considerable money sponsoring these visits. However, most buyers canceled the contracts after the visits. Expert Ltd. then faced the difficulty of taking legal action against the customers with no certainty of receiving a fair verdict.

Empathy (E) has been said to be a very effective means of achieving mutual understanding. The short-term and self-interested motives of some buyers showed a mistrust of legal and political systems, which have been "personalized" by the single ruling party over many years.

Customer Positions

Expert Ltd. had a total of nineteen customers in May 1996. Among them, fifteen were classified as Grade A customers and four as Grade B in accordance with the levels of sales turnover, potential sales growth, and profit. In addition, there were four new customers who could become long-term customers. The new or potential customers were also classified into grades A and B. The details are shown in Table 6.1. The company reviewed the grades every three months, allocating its resources to marketing and customer services accordingly.

The pattern-matching approach described by Campbell (1975) was used to link the data collected to the research propositions. In this design, the development of relationship patterns in the case study is related to the theoretical propositions of the guanxi model. The patterns were the I, L, and Z routes as well as the interactions of the guanxi constructs—dependence, adaptation, favor, and trust—with the outcome positions on the positioning map. These patterns are related to box C and boxes B1 and B2 of the guanxi model.

TABLE 6.1. Summary of Customer Classification

Grade		Customer
Grade A	1	Cullus*
	2	Superfood*
	3	Kong Dairy
	4	South Cement
	5	China Floor
	6	KHD
	7	Colla
	8	Boyma
	9	Café de Core
	10	Spain Soft Drink*
	11	Cooks
	12	PS
	13	Mead
	14	Yumyi*
	15	Tax HK
Grade B	1	Taste
	2	Kowloon Ham
	3	Avita
	4	Lee Food
		New Customer
Grade A	1	PCC/AHJ
	2	Lee Ho
Grade B	1	Juper
	2	Pacific Food

Note: Based on Expert Ltd.'s method of assessing sales volume, business potential, and profit levels.

*Company selected as unit of analysis in this case study.

Four Grade A customers were selected:

1. Cullus Ltd.—European-owned food giant in Hong Kong and South China.
2. Superfood Ltd.—Mainland Chinese-owned distilled water group, the third largest in Hong Kong.
3. Spain Soft Drink Ltd.—Owned by the Spain Pacific Group and Soft Drink USA group, the largest beverage company in Hong Kong with seven plants in China, with turnover of around US$1

billion in 1995. The Spain Pacific group is publicly listed on the Hong Kong and U.K. stock exchanges.
4. Yumyi (YY) Sauce Ltd.—Privately owned by a local Chinese family, it is said to be the "king" of oyster sauce, with exports to the whole world.

The criteria in selecting these four companies are:

1. They have different management styles because of their different ownership: Chinese, British, and American.
2. The relationship development in all four cases took place from early 1995 to May 1996. The period for all four relationships was the same to avoid any bias due to different time frames.
3. They all cover most of Expert Ltd.'s product ranges.
4. Their relationship development used different routes.

Constructs and Positioning

The four guanxi constructs—dependence, adaptation, favor, and trust—were used to measure relationship positioning.

Cullus Ltd.

Food processing is a sophisticated business. Cullus has depended on Expert Ltd. for the joint development of complex package specifications, as most specifications are tailor-made, depending on the requirements of shelf life, storage conditions, and refrigerating environments.

During the first year of the relationship, there was a very low level of trust. Cullus regarded Expert Ltd. as a standby supplier only. It would not place an order unless its primary supplier encountered a supply problem. Also, Cullus always placed small orders at short notice. After a year and a half, the customer showed adaptive behavior by starting to work with Expert Ltd. on a long-term planning basis. Sometimes, Cullus was willing to increase orders to minimum production runs, and eventually it favored Expert Ltd. by choosing to work with it on big new projects (e.g., fish sauce and microwave oven packaging for pizza) and agreed to accept new prices. This adaptation adjustment (a 15 percent higher price for microwave oven packaging) demonstrates the importance of guanxi in building mutual confidence.

Superfood Ltd.

Superfood's general manager, L. Chan, had attended a university with one of the directors of Expert Ltd. Insider favor was established even during the initial association period. Chan received help from Expert Ltd. in migrating to Australia. Superfood depended on Expert Ltd. for 100 percent of its plastic closures for more than two years. However, Expert had difficulty introducing new bag-in-box packaging to Superfood because of its high resistance to new packaging. Therefore, adaptation behavior is regarded as medium.

Spain Soft Drink Ltd.

Being one of the top multinational groups in Asia, Spain Soft Drink Ltd. always prefers low levels of dependence on any single supplier. It always insists that its suppliers adapt to its own requirements. It often dictates packaging specifications. Owing to an old relationship between Spain and one of the directors of Expert going back more than seventeen years, Spain still showed some favor by being willing to test new products, such as PET bottles, labels, caps, and other packaging. Normally, Spain would refuse to test new products because of the potential for decreased efficiency in its very tight production schedule. Trust was considered high, as there was no requirement to charge testing costs for new packaging trials. Spain was also willing to share some technical information to enable Expert to meet exact and crucial specifications.

Yumyi Sauce Ltd.

Yumyi Sauce Ltd. is a typical Chinese-owned family business. The owners are the sons of the founder, who invented oyster sauce. Expert spent a total of five years trying to sell to the company, which preferred to deal with an insider supplier only. The major problem was that the purchasing department had a gatekeeper attitude and was not willing to try any new packaging because they did not want to take any risks. There was a breakthrough two years before our study, when the managing director of Expert approached one of the directors of Yumyi though a mutual friend, a banker working for Yumyi. On the director's instructions, the purchasing department gradually started to show a positive attitude toward Expert. Indeed, the Yumyi purchasing department admitted having lost their file on Expert long before. The file was more than two inches thick. Yumyi requested Expert to photocopy all correspondence for its reference. Eventually, Yumyi placed bag-in-box packaging orders with Expert Ltd. for the export market. This involved a high degree of adaptation, because bag-in-box packaging is a high-tech system requiring nearly half a year to test. This case involved a 200-liter pack with crucial aseptic requirements.

The relationship positions of these four companies are shown in Figure 6.4, and the summary of guanxi perceptions is shown in Table 6.2. The study of these four companies highlights the dilemma of mind versus heart approaches as summarized in Table 6.3.

Routing

As shown in Figure 6.5, Cullus and Superfood both used I routes, while Spain took the L route and Yumyi followed the Z route.

FIGURE 6.4. Guanxi Positions of Four Companies in the Case Study: Perceptual Outcome Positions, May 1996

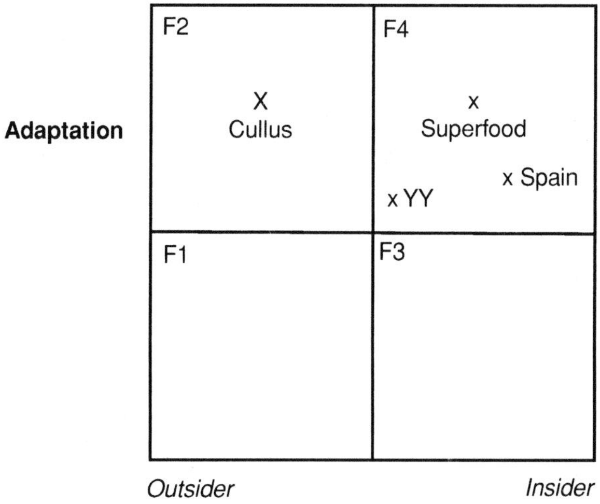

TABLE 6.2. Summary of Each Customer's Guanxi Constructs

Customer	Dependence	Adaptation	Favor	Trust
Cullus	H	M	M	M
Superfood	H	M	H	H
Spain	M	M	H	H
Yumyi	M	H	L	M

Note: The ranks were in accordance with the comments from the management of Expert Ltd.

Key: H = High; M = Medium; L = Low

TABLE 6.3. Implementation of Guanxi: Summary of Mind versus Heart Perspectives

Company	Ownership	Mind	vs.	Heart
Cullus	European	• Quality concern as the first priority in production • New product development as a long-term marketing strategy		• Less workload for workers • Disorganized management style
Superfood	PRC	• Minimum cost as the major criterion for purchasing decisions • New packaging as an important market penetration strategy in the PRC		• Friendship first as emphasized by top management in deals with its suppliers • Personal favor given to good friends
Spain Soft Drink	U.S./U.K.	• Criteria for selecting supplier: lowest costs and a minimum of two suppliers for every item • Under pressure from senior management to lower costs		• Minimize workload for employees' self-interest • Higher personal risk involved if there is a change to a new supplier • Tight production schedule encountered in qualifying a new supplier
Yumyi	Hong Kong	• The need to develop new packaging • Export needs		• Gatekeeper attitudes of some employees to avoid personal risk • Chinese managerial style (personalism) of top management

Note: The mind aspect represents reason, while the heart aspect represents personal and emotional behavior.

FIGURE 6.5. Development of Guanxi Routing

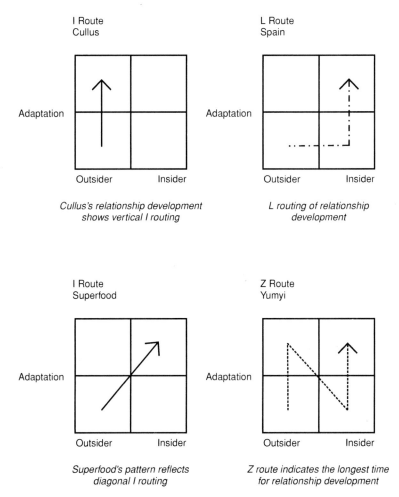

I Route
Cullus

Adaptation

Outsider   Insider

*Cullus's relationship development
shows vertical I routing*

L Route
Spain

Adaptation

Outsider   Insider

*L routing of relationship
development*

I Route
Superfood

Adaptation

Outsider   Insider

*Superfood's pattern reflects
diagonal I routing*

Z Route
Yumyi

Adaptation

Outsider   Insider

*Z route indicates the longest time
for relationship development*

I Route

Both Cullus and Superfood followed I routes. The former had a vertical I route while the latter used a diagonal I route. That is, Cullus's development was in the outsider dimension, in which the levels of trust and favor were said to be average. There had been changes in purchasing staff; within one year, there were three different purchasing managers. The existing purchasing manager was described as very unreasonable and just an order-processing person. To avoid working with the purchasing department, Expert often approached the production department as the user who could influence in purchasing decisions. However, most of the production personnel appeared to be more worried about tight production schedules than testing new and cost-saving packaging proposed by Expert.

On the other hand, Superfood displayed an insider's favor to Expert by being willing to source new caps from Europe, as its Australian cap supplier (represented by Expert) was unable to deliver one year before our study. The change of supply location from Australia to Europe indicates a high degree of both favor and trust, because it requires Superfood to allow for a longer lead-time.

L Route

The willingness of Spain to keep testing the new packaging seems to support the insider direction. Expert submitted several new packaging materials, such as shrink film and PET bottles, but some of them did not pass trial run tests. Spain was very patient in working with its PET technical experts from Expert Ltd.'s Canadian principal for more than two weeks. The tests were very demanding and required much fine-tuning of the machines. Testing means lower production efficiency. Spain even allowed Expert to carry out the trials in the peak summer season. The trials lasted for six months. Eventually, Spain placed multimillion U.S. dollar orders with Expert.

Z Route

Yumyi took the longest route, the Z route. It took Expert five years to secure the first order. The problem, according to one of Expert's directors, was the inability of its marketing team to follow a traditional Western sales approach in selling to a Chinese-owned company, because fighting between the founder's two sons appeared to create confusion in its purchasing strategies. Expert spent the first three years negotiating with one of the subordinates of the second son, who turned out not to be the right decision maker although he was senior director of Yumyi. Expert later reformulated its strategy to focus on a highly technical packaging system, the aseptic bag-in-box system, to consolidate the overall relationship between the two companies by developing a better relationship with the production department. Expert Ltd. provided a Yumyi production manager with a trip to Australia as a personal incentive.

Implementation Stages

Association

In summary, the four customers' relationships were different in the fencer position (F1) of Box B2 of the guanxi model during their initial associations (A in Box D of the model) because the buyers had various initial perceptions. For example, the relationships between the director of Expert and officials at Superfood and Spain were noted for renqing. The former had been classmates and the latter was a friendship going back over seventeen years.

Bonding

The bonding element appears in Box D of the model. The relationships between Expert Ltd. and Cullus as well as Yumyi indicated distant associations with no bonding involving renqing. The weaker bonding probably accounts for the longer period required to gain commitment, which is one of the crucial variables in determining the progress of cooperation.

Commitment

In an industrial buying situation, quality is mainly determined by the results of many trials and tests, and unless a buyer's production department is willing to work with the seller at the expense of production efficiency, most trials would most likely fail. The cooperation between Spain and Expert is typical commitment behavior (C in Box D).

Defense

Defense was noted to be strong in all cases except that of Superfood. There was clearly strong personal resistance from purchasing departments. The major obstacle facing Expert Ltd. was that it employed a market niche approach to introduce new packaging or technology to all of these four customers. The purchasing departments normally regarded the new packaging ideas as potential threats, as their performance is normally measured by whether they are able to order sufficient supplies to meet tight production schedules, not by the new ideas they introduce. The conclusion from Expert was that it needed to approach the senior managers of potential customers in order to avoid high resistance from the purchasing departments. If Expert failed to gain any assistance at a lower level, then it would approach key senior managers, such as the general manager. Sometimes, purchasing departments were upset with that approach because they thought Expert bypassed them and did not give them face. Expert always used its directors to approach the senior managers of the buyer. Its marketing team attempted to avoid defensive behavior on the part of the buyer's purchasing department by explaining occasionally that it had no control over the behavior of its directors. This excuse might well also convey the signal to the purchasing department that Expert's directors and supervisors might be good friends, which implies an insider relationship.

Empathy

Empathy was important for closing business deals. Expert's management needed to empathize with the hidden motives of the buyers to conclude deals. In the case of Yumyi, it was Expert's lack of awareness of the purchasing department's hidden objectives that prolonged the negotiating period.

Favor

As a packaging system is a highly sophisticated and technical product, its success depends on the cooperation of many departments. Favor is crucial in obtaining the full cooperation of various departments, such as production, quality control (QC), engineering, and marketing. For example, Yumyi used a faulty method of testing the strength of the bag-in-box packaging by dropping a full twenty-liter bag (without any box outside to protect it) from a height of three meters. The bag failed the test. Yumyi's inststance on developing its own test may be an example of a defense mechanism. However, after lengthy negotiations with the QC personnel, through empathy (E), Yumyi eventually showed favor to Expert by accepting a new standard test in which the filled bag was put inside a carton for the drop test. The test was eventually successful. In short, defense (D), empathy (E), and favor (F) were used in the implementation of guanxi.

Application of Condensed Guanxi Model to Case Study

The condensed guanxi model (see Figure 6.3) can be applied to the case study. The relationship patterns of three companies—Yumyi, Superfood, and Spain—are shown in Figure 6.6.

The guanxi positioning and interaction processes of the case study are summarized in Figure 6.6. The individual routing is shown on the position map. The final path of the relationship routing is determined by the forces of guanxi dynamic elements A-F.

Conclusion

On the whole, the guanxi model is acceptable to the top management of Expert Ltd. The logic of this case is to compare the four individual companies' patterns of positions, routes, and the outcomes of guanxi implementation interactions with the predicted theoretical patterns as suggested by the model. As the patterns coincide, the results enhance the internal validity of the model (Yin 1994).

The case study supports the propositions of the guanxi model. Three customers are regarded as insiders. Expert Ltd. found that selling efforts were more productive with insiders and that growth occurred on a long-term basis. Expert Ltd. thought that the traditional method of segmenting customers by product or business potential was not perfect. It was happy to adopt the guanxi model to help generate more quality business, and particularly, to help to convert outsider customers into insider customers.

RESEARCH SUMMARY AND CONCLUSION

Research Objectives and Scope

In the 1990s, there was increasing interest in understanding the importance of business relationships, particularly among the Chinese. The topic of guanxi attracted attention. Some businesspeople have

FIGURE 6.6. Guanxi Positioning—Routing of Three Companies

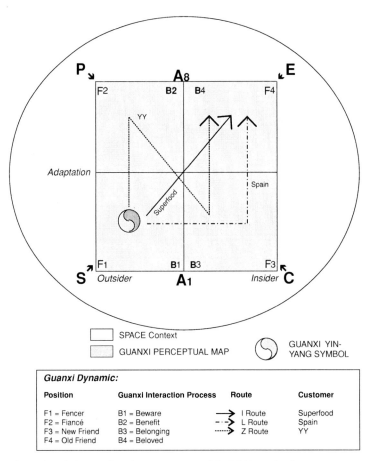

| | SPACE Context |
| | GUANXI PERCEPTUAL MAP |

GUANXI YIN-YANG SYMBOL

Guanxi Dynamic:

Position	Guanxi Interaction Process	Route	Customer
F1 = Fencer	B1 = Beware	→ I Route	Superfood
F2 = Fiancé	B2 = Benefit	--→ L Route	Spain
F3 = New Friend	B3 = Belonging	·····→ Z Route	YY
F4 = Old Friend	B4 = Beloved		

Note: Superfood shows the shortest route while YY has the longest route.

viewed guanxi as simply a desire for the pursuit of personal interest, or as a type of corruption. These views reflect some of the negative aspects of guanxi; some researchers have attributed the causes of corruption in guanxi networks to uneven income distribution, imperfect legal systems, and social change. A number of businesspeople and researchers have tried to understand and analyze guanxi from an exclusively Western point of view. Their interpretations may not unearth the root of guanxi behavior. The heart approach explanation, emphasized in the conclusion of Chapter 3, reveals the need to study guanxi in a Chinese context. As most literature on relationship studies has its roots in American and European cultures, it is not advisable to transplant Western theories and practices into a Chinese context without investigating the similarities and differences in the process of relationship building. Sheth (1985) gave evidence that generalization could be cross-cultural provided that there is a good contextualization of buyer behavior. Thus, this study attempts to contextualize guanxi by operationalizing guanxi constructs and investigating the effects of these constructs and other determinants on relationship development in a Chinese society.

The major research objectives and scope can be summarized as follows:

1. To draw together the different directions or approaches of Western and Chinese theories, views, and research in identifying the major research gaps, which are:
   - insufficient understanding of the major constructs of guanxi and their interaction with relationship performance; and
   - lack of any sophisticated research tool or systematic framework to measure guanxi and the absence of any comprehensive model to conceptualize guanxi.
2. To test the relationship between guanxi constructs and relationship performance indicators by (a) constructing a valid and reliable measurement scale to identify the constructs, relationship quality performance, and guanxi development mechanism; and (b) explaining the links between guanxi constructs and relationship performance.
3. To develop a comprehensive model that incorporates all the major determinants of relationship building: (a) environmental context, (b) guanxi perceptual positions, (c) choice of strategies (conceptualized as routes), (d) implementations of guanxi (in the form of the yin-yang dynamic), and (e) evaluation of guanxi (adaptation and performance).
4. To test the practical values of the guanxi model in a case study supplemented with in-depth interviews.
5. To provide a new vocabulary or framework of guanxi positions (four Fs), interaction dynamics (four Bs), and guanxi outcomes (dating-marriage) and routes (I, L, and Z) on a perceptual map

and to propose a guanxi dynamic implementation framework for explaining forces A-G.

Findings and Implications of the Model Framework

There are numerous studies on business-to-business exchange relationships between individuals who represent firms, but individual factors, such as cultural background, negotiation skills, and experience have been little explored (Dabholkar and Johnston 1994).

Summary of Results of Major Survey

The findings, drawn from the survey in Chapter 5, are new and important additions to existing behavioral constructs and norms. Adaptation, trust, dependence, and favor have been found to correlate with some relationship performance indicators. Adaptation correlates positively with past sales performance and relationship quality. Indeed, adaptation is the most important construct correlated with all performance indicators at significant levels. Favor, another important construct, correlates negatively with relationship termination costs. Adaptation is also negatively correlated with relationship termination costs. Trust has positive correlations with some performance indicators.

Implications of Guanxi Model

Traditionally, most studies in this field have examined business-to-business relationships either from an economic perspective (e.g., cost concerns) or a social perspective (e.g., social norms of relative power at the organizational level). This research is intended to fill the gap in dynamic sociopsychological and relationship marketing perspectives by allowing a deeper understanding of the dyadic relationship process and how it can lead to a quality relationship outcome. For example, favor is a major determinant, particularly in the situation of role conflict or ambiguity in the high-context culture of China (such as in the role conflict of self-interest versus organizational interest).

New Relationship Marketing Perspectives

Although many models and empirical studies have been produced on buyer-seller relationships, little research has attempted to understand the process of relationship building. This study offers a unique perspective on a dynamic process of routing, which can change both within and between specific exchange relationship positions. The case study provides support to the concept of guanxi routing from four F positions through four B interactions to outcome (dating-marriage). The framework of the yin-yang dynamic is particularly useful when negotiating parties, particularly Chinese and Western, interact with conflicting perceptions, expectations, and experience. These differences or conflicts may shift in relative power, competition, or switching costs, particularly when they occur in an unstable relationship. The mind approach, A-C (association-commitment), versus the heart approach, D-F (defense-favor), as demonstrated in the case study, integrates both economic and behavioral perspectives by taking into account the Chinese cultural background and various contradictory sociopsychological factors.

Implications of Research Findings

The Chinese are said to be very flexible in business dealings. The conceptual framework of the comprehensive guanxi model developed here helps companies to restructure their relationship marketing strategies so they can move efficiently and effectively along various routes on the condensed guanxi perceptual positioning/interaction/outcome map. The model assists businesspeople to gain a deeper understanding of the interplay among social, organizational, and individual variables (such as mind versus heart).

The model allows a businessperson, particularly a negotiator, to have greater flexibility in choosing optimal relationship behavior. In addition, by investigating how exchange relationships may change over time or through different routes, a company could proactively evaluate various relationship positions. It could then tailor its marketing strategies for each relationship. If it is in the fiancé quadrant of the guanxi model, it will need to formulate a new strategy in order to move on to a better quadrant, such as the old friend quadrant.

Contributions Made by This Study

Marketing Theory

Western interaction theory is one of few theories to provide a macro and dynamic framework, but few researchers have tested its conjectures. Most previous studies have been theoretical in the sense that most social or psychological processes were not tested or even hypothesized. Interaction theory proposes "dynamism" as an element but does not indicate how to apply the concept of dynamism.

Western TCA and social theories as well as Chinese renqing and defense theories limit discussion of the topic to relatively circumscribed and narrow aspects of behavior, attitude, and value. Most research has focused only on principles, or isolated behavioral aspects such as decision making, or demographic variables concerning problem-solving and background attributes. These research aspects have limited application value.

In contrast, the model and theoretical framework proposed here provide a more comprehensive concept and tool to create a relatively holistic view of guanxi. The guanxi constructs have been defined and operationalized, and the model was tested with a case study. This research, in general, gives new insight into relationship marketing.

Marketing Practices

The study makes a number of contributions to marketing practices. The model and findings give new directions and frameworks for developing marketing strategies:

1. SPACE environmental analysis
2. Guanxi positioning—a new vocabulary of various positions and the identification of major constructs
3. Positioning framework for strategic formulation and planning
4. Interaction of guanxi dynamic—yin-yang dynamic approach
5. Overall guanxi performance evaluation based on the relationship between guanxi adaptation and relationship performance indicators

All five of these frameworks provide tools for managers to analyze the ever-changing environment in China and the development of buyer-seller relationships, for example, the importance of personalism in guanxi development. Unless foreigners know the position of each relationship with a Chinese partner in a certain time frame, how can they formulate business strategies to work with Chinese partners effectively or smoothly? The dilemma of mind versus heart management can be easily understood with the yin-yang dynamic. The routing concepts help practitioners navigate the route to a quality relationship, which is a very important variable in achieving mutual trust.

In short, this research is intended to provide a more systematic and holistic framework for marketing managers to apply, and is intended to enable them to adapt their relationship marketing plans to the ever-changing environment of the Chinese market, which is potentially the world's largest market.

Appendix A

Literature Review

INTRODUCTION

The major objectives of this appendix are:

1. To identify the research gaps in the literature review in order to justify this research and to elaborate the link between the identified research gaps and the rest of the study
2. To formulate the research questions for this study

How does this study build on previous research? Two major questions are answered:

1. How do we explain the buyer-seller relationship?
2. What are the key variables in the literature regarding relationships and guanxi building and how do these variables affect the building processes?

The final section focuses on research problems and questions.

GAPS IN EXISTING LITERATURE

The motivation for this research is the increasing importance of relationship marketing. It is commonly believed that relationship marketing was the research focus of the 1990s (Christopher, Payne, and Ballantyne 1991). However, there is not enough empirical research literature on relationship marketing. Most literature has been written in the Western context. The interpretation of relationships is different in Asia and the West. Guanxi is one of the most controversial topics. Most research has been carried out using ambiguous terms and definitions of guanxi.

The review of literature on this subject reveals that Western interpretations have not yet managed to fully explain Chinese phenomena. There are gaps in the existing literature.

First, most research and theories are helpful for analysis, but they lack an overarching perspective. They tend to be fragmented, and some of them do not include any empirical tests. It is difficult to combine these piecemeal findings to form a new paradigm. Thus, there is a need to build a more comprehensive model, particularly a dynamic one, to incorporate more variables such as favor, friendship, reciprocity, and defense as well as extraneous variables, such as flexibility, adaptability, and relationship performance.

Second, there is a shortage of valid instruments or measurement tools. Old Western measurement instruments used in an Asian environment probably lead to unreliable research.

Third, relationship or guanxi building is very important for marketing managers in handling international marketing decisions. There is a gap between the behavioral construct of our proposed model and its application.

Fourth, cross-cultural research is the trend for modern international research, to prevent the problem of international managers making marketing decisions based on solely their own cultural reference criteria.

Finally, the importance of Asian markets and the competitiveness of the newly developed nations, such as the "four small dragons" in Asia (Hong Kong, Korea, Singapore, and Taiwan), justify this research, which enhances understanding of the topic.

HOW THE RESEARCH GAPS ARE LINKED
WITH THE REST OF THIS STUDY

In this section, the links between the research gaps identified in the literature review and the rest of this study are elaborated to cover two major areas, conceptual development and research methodology.

Conceptual Development

As there is no comprehensive guanxi model in the existing literature in this field, a conceptual model of guanxi and its interaction with relationship performance has been proposed in Chapter 5. The model has two major components: constructs (trust, adaptation, favor, and dependence) and guanxi performance indicators (relationship quality, termination costs, sales performance, and formalization). The operationalization of the constructs and the measurement of associations between the constructs and performance indicators are the two major objectives of this study.

The concepts of trust and power dependence identified in Western social exchange theory and the significance of adaptation emphasized in interaction theory provide a framework for the proposed model. The concept of favor originates in Chinese renqing theory. The dilemma of expressive versus instrumental guanxi relationships reveals the important role of the mixed relationship, but a mixed relationship is difficult to analyze without any new framework. An adaptation/outsider-insider positioning map (discussed in Chapter 5) is built on a perspective of both expressive (outsider-insider) and instrumental (adaptation) relationships. The Chinese post-Confucian work dynamic theory helps to explain the dynamic elements of Chinese guanxi networks as a means of security against ever-changing legal, political, and business environments. A new vocabulary of routing strategies (covered in Chapter 5) aims to provide further explanations for the "integration" principles behind the network members' relationships or bonding. How can the Western and Chinese perspectives be further refined?

Western Perspective

The TCA perspective, developed from the concepts of bounded rationality and opportunism, is able to give an economic dimension only because of its assumption of rational decision making (for minimizing transaction costs). This assumption is not realistic as the human mind involves subjective feeling, and human decisions may not be able to achieve optimal transaction costs.

A SPACE context analysis (system, personalism, adaptation, change, and ego) in Chapter 4 aims to offer a more dynamic contextual analysis to supplement social exchange theory. In addition, individual personal interests or needs proposed by Hakansson (1982) in interaction theory are further refined to incorporate an outsider-insider dimension.

Chinese Perspective

In renqing theory, the view of guanxi as social capital is a useful tool for understanding mixed relationships. To explore the concept of the mixed relationship is one of the challenges in this study. The correlations between guanxi constructs and performance indicators, particularly favor and trust, present empirical evidence for the significant role of guanxi in relationship development.

Defense theory explains the growth of guanxi security networks to protect against poor legal and political systems. The mind versus heart approach described in Chapter 3 helps to account for defensive behavior.

Apart from the Western and Chinese views, the relationship rules of collectivism, face, shame, and pragmatism are the key contributing elements to the proposed guanxi model. Commitment and defensive behavior (the A-F dynamic) are regarded as the forces behind the contradictory personality of the Chinese. Table A.1 is a summary of existing problems, limitations in existing literature, and the basis for further development.

TABLE A.1. Link Between Literature Review and Conceptual Development and Methodology of This Research

Theory/Studies	Perspective and Problems	Limitations	Basis for Further Development
Western Views			
TCA	Relationship formed because of bounded rationality and opportunism which tend to minimize transaction costs	Static dimension and rational behavior assumption	Underlying construct of adaptation (Ch. 2)
Social Exchange Theory	Trust and power dependence as basis for social exchanges	Highly culture specific	SPACE context analysis (Ch. 4)
Interaction Theory	Adaptation in dynamic interaction, regarding relationship as an investment	Most concepts vaguely defined	Positioning map of adaptation and outsider-insider dimensions (Ch. 6)
Chinese Views			
Renqing Theory	Face and social capital	Confusing mixed relationship	Favor and performance indicator correlations (Ch. 5)
Defense Theory	Mistrust of legal and political institutions leading to defense mechanisms	Focus on negative aspects of guanxi only	Mind versus heart approach (Ch. 3)
Post-Confucian Work Dynamic	Integrated network with insider members	Concentrates too much on macro context	Concept of I, L, and Z routes (Ch. 5)
Relationship Rules			
Collectivism, Face, and Shame	• Society over self • Face as social capital	Fragmented ideas	Condensed guanxi model (Ch. 6)
Work Ethics and Pragmatism	• More organic • Instills discipline and order	Lack of theoretical foundations	Yin-yang symbol (Ch. 6)
Favor	Rely on insider/family	Weak holistic conceptual dimensions	A-F dynamic (Ch. 6)

Research Methodology

There are extensive studies on some relationship marketing constructs, such as trust and adaptation, but some of the new underlying culture-bound constructs (e.g., favor) justify an empirical test to operationalize them. The correlation tests between constructs and performance indicators are attempts to provide a measurement tool to understand the interactions. In-depth interviews and a case study were carried out to supplement the quantitative research, so as to evaluate the relevance of the insider-outsider, defense mechanism, and routing concepts frameworks.

SUMMARY OF RESEARCH QUESTIONS

The research questions are summarized in Figure A.1. The figure shows each component or attribute of guanxi. The four constructs, trust, adaptation, favor, and dependence are independent variables. The perceived relationship quality, relationships termination costs, and formalization are dependent vari-

FIGURE A.1. Summary of Research Questions: How Are Guanxi Constructs Related to Relationship Outcome?

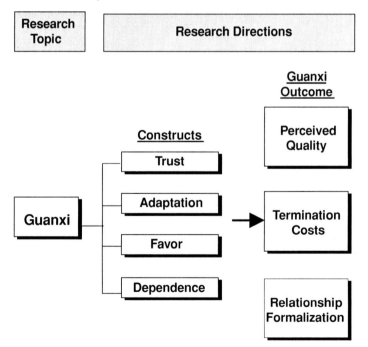

ables. The arrow indicates the relationships between the constructs and the outcome variables. Figure A.1 does not show any feedback flow or loops for the sake of simplicity.

The Major constructs can be regrouped as follows:

- Personal values (favor, opportunism, and trust)
- Attitude (dependence)
- Behavior (adaptation)

There are four major relationship performance indicators:

1. Perceived overall relationship quality
2. Sales performance
   - Past sales trends (over three years)
   - Past sales pattern stability
   - Perception of future sales trends (over three years)
3. Relationship termination costs
4. Relationship formalization (formalization is defined as cooperation in the form of a written agreement)

The key research topics, which concern the relationship between the major constructs and relationship performance indicators, are stated as follows:

A. Trust
   1. Trust is positively related to the overall quality of guanxi
   2. Trust is positively related to:
      - Past sales stability
      - Perceptions of future sales
   3. Trust is positively related to relationship formalization
   4. Trust is positively related to relationship termination costs
B. Favor—Favor is negatively related to overall relationship quality
C. Dependence—Dependence is positively related to overall relationship quality
D. Adaptation
   1. Adaptation is positively related to past sales performance
   2. Adaptation is positively related to perceived overall relationship
      quality
   3. Adaptation is negatively related to relationship termination costs

The summary of associations of constructs and relationship performance indicators is shown in Figure A.2.

FIGURE A.2. Summary of Research Questions: Operationalizing Constructs and Finding the Associations Between Constructs and Relationship Performance Indicators

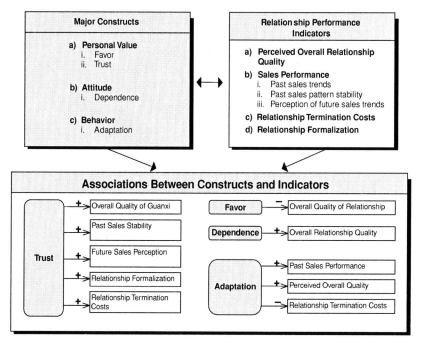

Key: − = negative
       + = positive

Appendix B

Research Design and Methodology

This appendix focuses on research design and methodology. It discusses the methodology of the survey by describing the design of focus groups and pilot studies, the procedures of purifying the questions and modifying the questionnaire, and the methodology of the in-depth interviews and case study.

MAJOR RESEARCH APPROACH

This research is both descriptive and exploratory. Descriptive research is defined as examining a phenomenon and defining it more fully, or differentiating it from other phenomena (Dane 1990). This research attempts to discover and to explain the relationships or correlations between guanxi constructs and relationship performance indicators.

Positivist Approach

One of the major paradigms adopted in the study is a logical positivist one. Rudner (1966) defines a positivist perspective as a systematically related set of statements, including an empirically testable generalization. This study aims to enhance scientific understanding through a systematized, structured study capable of explaining, proposing, and ideally predicting the patterns of guanxi phenomena. The validity of this approach is based on the method of checking the internal logic of the findings and then exposing them to empirical tests. As the proper foundation for theory development, logical positivism assists in developing a theoretical model for guanxi.

Hunt (1983) suggests that a logical positivist explanation remains one of the most viable approaches available for explaining a phenomenon. This does not mean that the positivist approach resolves all issues. The approach recognizes the fact that causality can never be conclusively verified, and it generally reflects the best explanation that science can provide at a given point in time.

Overcoming the Weakness of a Positivist Approach

The major weakness of a positivist approach lies in the problem of isolating the people under investigation from their social context and reducing human beings to a set of statistical variables. To overcome this weakness, a mixture of quantitative and qualitative approaches was employed. Qualitative data (from in-depth interviews and a case study) were used to clarify the quantitative findings. On the other hand, some quantitative data (from the questionnaire survey) were utilized to validate partially qualitative findings. In short, qualitative methods were adopted to understand what lies behind the phenomena, particularly the intricate details that are difficult to convey with quantitative methods.

To uncover the complexities of human reality, the authors followed Deising's (1972) holistic approach. First, assuming that context is closed to ordinary experience, a context analysis is the first component of the guanxi model. The emotive experience refers to an insider-outsider perspective, while subjective experience includes favoritism and defensive behavior. Second, the logic of each component of the proposed guanxi model dialectically includes various components, from a SPACE context analysis to an evaluation stage. Third, each component of the model is designed independently and subsequently linked. Finally, the model is tested by its power to explain the findings of a case study. This holistic approach aims to add a more human element to the method. In summary, the approach is a synthesis of ideas from both scientific approaches and a context perspective.

Mixed Approach: Soft Systems and Others

Another feature of the approach invovles Checkland's (1985) "soft systems" idea. Soft systems thinking assumes that problems can be explored by using a systems model. The development of the guanxi model partially follows the soft systems approach, particularly with emphasis on human experience. In the research, the relationship developments are:

- The readiness to note particular aspects of relationship building, namely guanxi
- To recognize guanxi in a particular way (or to identify the constructs of guanxi)
- To measure the effectiveness and reliability of guanxi constructs against particular standards of comparison, i.e., relationship performance indicators

Figure B.1 is a summary of different research methods and the perception and behavior of guanxi. The logic of different approaches and the link between the approaches and various research methods are summarized (see steps A-G in Figure B.1) as follows:

A. The research starts with the research gaps identified in the literature review. Various concepts of guanxi and its interactions with relationship quality performance were generated from focus groups.
B. Pilot studies were used to test the major research questions.
C. A questionnaire survey was undertaken to collect the data in a structured way.

FIGURE B.1. A Mixed Research Approach of Positivist, Holistic, and Soft Systems

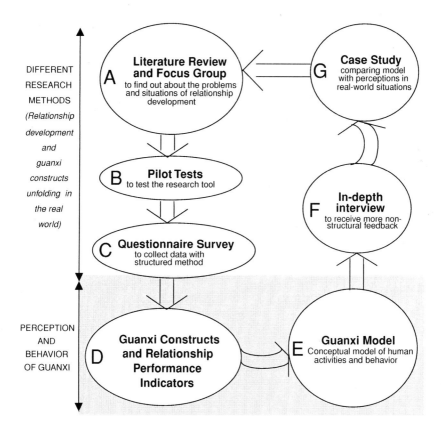

A through C are the major research methods, following a logical positivist approach.

    D. Through an understanding of the results of the research methods, guanxi constructs (values, attitudes, and behavior) and their related interactions with relationship performance indicators (including the relationship-building mechanism) were identified and analyzed.
    E. Based on the results and findings of D, a guanxi model is proposed.

D and E are concepts dealing with the real world by means of both positivist and holistic methods.

    F. The findings concerning guanxi constructs and their interaction activities were further "polished" through in-depth interviews in which additional psychological feedback was obtained.
    G. A case study was carried out to compare the conceptual guanxi model with perceptions and activities in real-life situations.

F and G were mainly used to test the reliability of the guanxi model by following a humanistic approach to consider the multiple realities of human behavior through in-depth interviews and the mutual interactions between interviewer and interviewees in the case study (Hirschman 1986).

The link with relationship building is structured by comparing the model with perceptions of the real world. The purpose of this comparison is to analyze business relationships. Such investigation may afford a more systematic understanding of relationship enhancement processes. In analyzing these enhancement processes or changes, a new problem or situation may arise, such as how to develop a closer relationship with a buyer, and the cyclic process can begin again; we return from G to A with more insight into guanxi.

METHODOLOGY

Three criteria are involved in considering a suitable methodology:

    1. The ability to demonstrate causality between the variables
    2. The avoidance of any bias in collecting data
    3. The ability to obtain an acceptable response rate in a reasonable time and cost

In this study, the major tool is a survey and the supplementary tools are in-depth interviews and a case study. With a well-designed and well-administered questionnaire, the above three criteria can be applied (Mum and Yau 1979).

Several criteria are involved in designing a survey (Tull and Hawkins, 1993):

1. Speed
2. The extent of information collection
3. Costs
4. The nonresponse rate

In 1992, a questionnaire survey was sent to the members of the Hong Kong Exporters' Association that taught us a lesson. One thousand questionnaires were sent out, and after three follow-up calls, the response rate was only 2.3 percent. This very poor response rate was the result of executives in Hong Kong being extremely busy. After four months, only twenty-three questionnaires were returned. For the following research, the survey was conducted not by mail but by personal contact to improve the response rate.

SURVEY DESIGN

After focus groups and pilot studies, a survey was undertaken. The survey is in the form of a questionnaire that uses various kinds of specific measurement scales.

Objectives of the Questionnaire

The objectives of the questionnaire are as follows:

1. To establish an understanding of the respondent's company, including details such as the size of the company in terms of staff, and individual personal data
2. To find out what the distribution activities of the respondent's organization are
3. To collect data concerning the respondent's perception of guanxi attributes
4. To evaluate relationship performance in terms of overall quality, past and future sales trends, and the impact of losing a partner (or relationship termination costs)
5. To gain an understanding of the mechanisms of building guanxi, for example, by tracking the number of visits paid to PRC customers

The next section discusses the focus group and the pilot study.

Focus Group

The purposes of our focus group discussions were:

1. To generate concepts of guanxi, or relationships. The concepts include processes, outcomes, factors, and expectations.
2. To understand the subjective perception of relationships and guanxi.
3. To provide flexibility to explore the opinions and behavior of respondents more fully (Dane 1990).

The design of group discussion follows Johnson's (1988) approach. The goal of the first nondirective focus group is to encourage the members to describe their general experience with limited guidance by the moderator. The analysis of findings aims to identity several main themes and their extent (Johnson 1988).

Eleven groups were assembled. The first three groups were mainly focused on nondirective discussions, meaning that the respondents were encouraged to discuss the topic with little or no guidance and very few direct questions. These groups consisted of practicing managers with international and China trade experience. The objective was to generate as many topics as possible and to receive some hints for the design of questions for later focus groups. It was found that most topics were overlapping and repetitive. Some of them were controversial and involved subjective bias, particularly concerning the confusion of process and terminal values. Process values refer to the behavior adopted to achieve an outcome. Terminal values refer to the terminal outcome of behavior. For example *la guanxi* (which literally means "to pull guanxi") is a process value, while the concept of *ho guanxi* (literally, "good relationship") is an outcome, or terminal value.

Based on the feedback of these three nondirective focus groups, eight focus groups were assembled. According to Johnson (1988), focus groups are intended to provide participants a chance to react to a concept still in a sketchy stage. The group discussion was partially structured or focused according to the following dimensions:

1. Time or process dimensions
2. "Issue" or "dichotomy" dimensions

The objective of these analyses was to find out the extent to which participants were able to comment on what makes up the dimensions of guanxi and to describe those essential elements in some typical relationship experience (Johnson 1988). For the process aspect, the dimensions are shown in Table B.1. For the dichotomy aspect, the dimensions are shown in Table B.2.

TABLE B.1. Process Dimensions of the Focus Groups

Approach	Process Dimension
1. Availability	Acquaintance
	Association
2. Affective	Acceptance
	Affordability
	Affirmation
3. Assertive	Assurance
	Actualization

Note: Each group was encouraged to express the process from initial acquaintance stage to final relationship actualization stage. If any group had difficulties in going through all processes, then only major approaches (availability, affective, and assertive) were discussed.

TABLE B.2. Dichotomy Dimensions of the Focus Groups

Group	Dichotomy		
1	Emotional	vs.	Instrumental
2	Insider	vs.	Outsider
3	Individual	vs.	Organizational
4	Chinese	vs.	Western
5	Formal	vs.	Informal
6	Investment	vs.	Consumption
7	Uncertainty	vs.	Safety
8	Distance	vs.	Commitment

Note: E.g., in the Group 1 discussion, emotional dimensions of guanxi (such as personal friendship) were compared with instrumental dimensions (such as company interest) in order to generate more ideas concerning the dynamic elements of guanxi.

The focus group facilitators were requested to the following guidelines.

Guidelines for Each Group

Following the principle of Mariampolski's (1988) technique, a probing exercise was used to validate focus group responses and to identify the facts behind the conversation. Each focus group was required to perform these activities:

1. Generate concepts—a minimum of forty concepts in each group
2. Group these concepts in categories according to the dichotomy or process dimensions

3. Explain how, what, why, why not, and when
4. Identify eighteen facets making up the domain of guanxi
5. Convert these eighteen facets into eighteen statements

All group facilitators then attended two meetings to identify a total of fifty-eight usable statements from the total of 144 statements. Most statements were similar in either meaning or ideas. Repetitive items were rejected. A questionnaire covering the fifty-eight items was finalized for the first pilot study.

Pilot Study and Major Survey

The purposes of the pilot study are as follows:

1. To discover any possible problems in the questionnaire and data collection procedure
2. To evaluate whether the findings are compatible with the research objectives
3. To evaluate and identify any possible errors and to check the reliability and validity of the findings for further refinement

In June 1995, the first formal pilot study was conducted.

Methodology of the Pilot Study

The first draft questionnaire includes fifty-eight statements or questions covering the attributes of guanxi, relationship performance, and working mechanisms, and eleven questions covering the demographic variables of company and personal profiles.

In the first round of the pilot study, seventy-eight questionnaires were sent out and fifty-eight valid questionnaires were collected. The data gathered were used to refine the questionnaire. In the second round of the pilot study, twenty-seven out of fifty questionnaires were valid for data analysis. The final draft of the questionnaire was based on the result of these two rounds.

Methodology of Data Analysis in the Pilot Study

There were two methods for the analysis of data. One approach uses factor analysis for all questions (the attributes of guanxi, relationship performance, and working mechanisms). The other approach groups the questions under the three concepts of the attributes of guanxi, performance, and working mechanisms. The latter method was selected since it gave a more meaningful and logical interpretation.

Purification of Questions

The final draft of the questionnaire was produced after two rounds of factor analysis. The questionnaire was eventually reduced to forty questions. The steps of this purification process are illustrated in Figure B.2.

Pilot Study Data Collection

The pilot study questionnaires were administered to business executives attending the training classes held in the Import/Export Training Center of the Hong Kong government's Vocational Training Council. Face-to-face interviews and personal survey methods were carried out in the form of proctored questionnaire, which means a proctor was available to answer

Figure B.2. Summary of the Questionnaire Purification Process

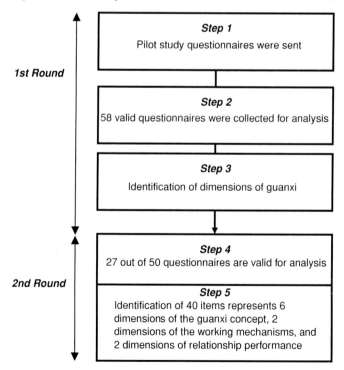

questions. This proctor collected the questionnaires from the respondents (Dane 1990).

The benefits of this proctored questionnaire are that, first, this approach allowed the respondents to complete the questionnaire privately and confidentially. Second, the proctor or interviewer was available to answer any questions to ensure understanding. The use of a captive audience raises the possibility of accidental sampling, meaning a selection based on the availability or ease of inclusion, which may limit the generalizability of this research. It is emphasized that the research is not predictive but exploratory.

After the survey, some respondents took part in in-depth interviews to comment on the quality of the questionnaire and any difficulties in answering the questions. These interviews were useful in eliminating any possible weaknesses. All feedback was taken into account in attempts to refine and improve the questionnaire design.

Factor Analysis

Factor analysis is used because a factor is a construct that is not directly observable. The analysis facilitates the grouping of variables and provides insights into the variables. It may identify underlying constructs that have practical and theoretical significance. The process reduces the number of questions to a manageable level. A large number of variables were reduced to several factors, allowing easier interpretation.

Determining the number of factors. To determine how many factors are needed, it is useful to examine the percentage of total variance explained by each. The total variance for each factor is listed in the second column, Eigenvalue, as shown in Table B.3. The third column contains the percentage of the total variance attributable to each factor. The fourth column, Cumulative Percentage, indicates the cumulative percentage of the total variance explained by the factors.

TABLE B.3. Summary of Major Factors

Factor	Eigenvalue	Percentage of Variance	Cumulative Percentage
1	8.29538	21.3	21.3
2	6.18092	15.8	37.1
3	4.85010	12.4	49.6
4	3.91700	10.0	59.6
5	3.38553	8.7	68.3
6	2.87080	7.4	75.6
7	2.59844	6.7	82.3
8	2.17370	5.6	88.9

The data in Table B.3 is extracted from attribute data. One criterion for inclusion is that those data should have values greater than two. The attributes of guanxi were grouped into eight factors, which explain the 88.9 percent (cumulative percentage) of variation in all statements.

Assignment of questions to factors. The assignment of a question is determined by the factor loading. Factor loading is the correlation between the factors and the original variables. The factor loading gives an indication of which variables are correlated with each factor and the extent of the correlation. The Varimax method (a rotation factor method) was used to identify the questions for each dimension. Table B.4 presents the results before factor rotation for some questions as an example.

After rotation, the factor loading (shown in Table B.5) is greater than that of the previous factor loading, so it is easy to identify the questions for various dimensions. For example, the rotated factor loadings of Q21, Q32, Q33, and Q38 are obviously greater than those of the previous factor loadings. So it is easier to assign Q21 to Factor 2, Q32 and Q33 to Factor 4, and Q38 to Factor 3. It is a rule of thumb for this research to set factor loading <0.4 to eliminate any irrelevant questions.

Reliability test. After grouping the factors, we carried out a reliability test to assess their internal consistency among the variables in each factor. Any variable that shows inconsistency with the majority of variables is eliminated.

TABLE B.4. Factor Loading Before Rotation

Factor	1	2	3	4	5	6	7	8
Q21	−.25941	.69933	−.23513	−.36319	.24601	.00319	−.12099	−.11053
Q32	.19554	.01990	−.49616	.22296	.16400	.16635	.45431	.52875
Q33	.26433	.51925	−.00786	.62596	−.28034	−.19597	.26279	.39582
Q38	.35944	.29390	.66299	−.09090	.35277	−.17794	.33379	.06998

TABLE B.5. Factor Loading After Rotation

Factor	1	2	3	4	5	6	7	8
Q21	.07256	.88652	−.11812	.15547	.14262	−.08057	−.20051	−.10710
Q32	.15318	−.04466	.35685	.82151	−.18996	.26294	−.00117	−.02626
Q33	−.02328	−.39502	.28752	.78673	−.20210	.13736	−.44617	−.05025
Q38	.26377	.11806	.83858	-.13457	.01125	−.04300	−.22012	−.28380

In Table B.6, the third column, Corrected Item (Total Correlation), is the correlation coefficient between the score on the individual question and the sum of the score on the remaining questions. The correlation between the score on Q42 and the sum of the scores on all questions is only 0.1854. Therefore, Q42 is rejected because of inconsistency. Questions that demonstrated consistency were selected.

After several rounds of factor analysis and reliability tests, the final draft of the questionnaire included thirty statements concerning the attributes of guanxi, six questions relevant to relationship performance, and four statements about the working mechanism.

After two rounds of the pilot study, which took four months to complete (June to September 1995), the questionnaire was finalized based on the modifications described in the next section.

Modification of Questionnaires After Completion of Pilot Studies

Based on a review of the data from the pilot study and the feedback from the respondents, the following modifications were made to ensure that the quality of the questionnaire was satisfactory.

Time. The time taken by respondents to complete the questionnaires in the first and second rounds was too long—from twenty-five to thirty-five minutes. The average time needed to complete the final draft was approximately ten to twenty-five minutes. This shorter time resulted in better response rates.

Question content. The number of attributes was reduced from forty-two to twenty. The deletions were made because the reliability of the items was low, because there was no response or a poor response to some items, or because questions were biased or leading questions.

TABLE B.6. Summary of Reliability Test

	Scale Variance if Item Deleted	Corrected Item (Total Correlation)
Q11	46.3263	.7117
Q16	54.6184	.4593
Q22	55.9868	.6722
Q23	50.4500	.7153
Q35	49.3158	.7500
Q37	50.8921	.7568
Q39	54.0000	.5529
Q42	62.9895	.1854 (rejected)

Some pilot study respondents complained that some attribute statements left them with no choice. Such statements were deleted. Some attribute statements, such as "The guest becomes the host," were deleted. This statement is one of the thirty-six famous Chinese war strategies, which have been used in the Chinese business world for more than 1,500 years (Chu 1991). However, some respondents found the statement to be unclear and unspecified.

Question phrasing. Pilot study respondents found that some parts of the questions were misleading and contradictory. Such questions were deleted or rephrased. The revised phrases were tested in the second round and were found to be acceptable.

Response format. The pilot study indicated that some respondents answered the questionnaire by using both ticks and circles. The final questionnaire include an example showing how to circle answers to avoid any misunderstanding. Also, the pilot questionnaire had two sections without any subheadings. The final questionnaire was subdivided into three sections with headings. All these amendments improved communication with the respondents. In order to develop more rapport, the most sensitive items concerning relationship performance and the mechanisms of guanxi were placed toward the end of the questionnaire.

Reduction of nonresponse errors. To increase the response rate and to reduce response bias, two measures were implemented. First, the researchers took time to explain the objectives of the research and to assure the respondents that all information was treated confidentially. The researchers were available for any questions and clarifications in the event that a respondent needed help. Second, the researchers and the interviewers were trained to persuade and to encourage respondents to answer and were briefed about the procedure and method of administering the survey.

Sampling

Two methods are generally employed in the design of a sample size. First, owing to a limited research budget and time, an arbitrary size was set. Second, with the desired level of precision and expenditure and based on the standard error formula, the optimal sample size was established (Yau 1994). Sudman (1976) proposed that the typical sample size for analyzing a limited marketing segment is in the range of 200 to 500. Tull and Hawkins (1984) discussed several methods for determining sample size. One method is based on the calculation of the sample size involving statistical means. The optimal sample size may be determined if the standard error, the relative allowable error, and the coefficient of variation can be found. In this research, the standard error is set at 2.58, which is equivalent to 99.5 percent of confidence, and the relative allowable error is 0.05 of the mean. One of the purposes of the pilot study was to find out the coefficient of variation. The formula to determine the optimal sample size is:

$$n = Z^2 \, C^2 / R^2$$

Where
n = optimal size
Z = standard error
C = coefficient of variation
R = coefficient of variation

in which

$$R = e/m^2 \ (e = \text{standard deviation}, \ m = \text{mean})$$

Based on the pilot study, the standard deviation and the mean score of the answer regarding the quality of relationship performance were calculated.

$$R \quad = 0.95/4.52^2$$
$$= 0.05$$

As the values of Z and R are fixed, the coefficient of variation is the variable to determine the sample size (Tull and Hawkins 1984):

$$n \ = Z^2 \, C^2 / R^2$$
$$= 2.58^2 \times 0.21^2 / 0.05^2$$
$$= 118$$

Therefore, the optimal sample size for this research is 118. The research methods mixed both interviews and proctored surveys of a captive audience (the adult executives who attended the short intensive courses at the Vocational Training Council's Import/Export Training Center). Some of our sample involved accidental sampling. To minimize the homogeneity of the sample, first, questionnaire collection was carried out from September 1995 to February 1996 and was spread throughout thirty-one classes ranging from the Basic Export Introduction Course to the Advanced Course in China Trade. The respondents differed widely in age, educational level, and working experience. Second, although the optimal sample size was calculated to be 118, the sample was increased to 272. Note that the purpose of this research is descriptive, not predictive. The possibility of overgeneralization owing to any sample bias is minimized.

In-Depth Interviews

The reliability and practical value of the proposed guanxi model (which is discussed in detail in Chapter 6) was further tested by in-depth interviews with business executives in thirteen companies. The objectives of these interviews were to:

- Obtain feedback from business executives regarding the meaning of guanxi and their experience of the recognition of its existence
- Ask whether they would be willing to accept or use the model, for example, in training their marketing staff

The in-depth interviews supplemented the questionnaire survey. The interviews pursued a sequence of topics by using a series of prompts to encourage free conversation.

Case Study

The methodology of the case study has three major parts: research design, validity and reliability, and method.

Research Design

The method of this case study follows the idea of pattern matching (Campbell 1975). In the pattern-matching method, various pieces of information in the case are related to the theoretical propositions. The findings of the case study support the theoretical propositions and provide real-life evidence for the perceptual values incorporated in the model as the criteria for interpreting the findings to match the real-life patterns with the theoretical pattern. It is hoped that the different patterns, such as the I and Z routes (discussed in detail in Chapter 5), are sufficiently different that the findings can be interpreted by comparing them.

Validity and Reliability

The tactics for achieving the construct validity of the case study are, first, to use multiple sources of evidence (from buyers, principals, sellers, and all related documents and correspondence); second, to establish a chain of evidence (e.g., to investigate the development of guanxi in the past three years); and third, to have the key informants review the draft case report. The company in this case study eventually adopted the new perceptual position map to allocate more of its marketing efforts to insider buyers or customers in order to improve the productivity of its selling efforts.

The reliability of the case study is enhanced by using a case study protocol proposed by Yin (1994). The protocol has three major parts:

I. Procedure
   A. Schedule of field visits
   B. Determination of persons to be interviewed
II. Case Study Protocol and Questions
   The question design mainly follows each component of the proposed guanxi model
III. Analysis Plan and Report
   A. Explanatory information (e.g., how the marketing managers in the case build up a relationship with the buyer)
   B. Outline of guanxi relationships (e.g., the development process from outsider to insider)
   C. Cross-guanxi analysis
      - Descriptive information (e.g., the background of each buyer)
      - Explanatory information (e.g., why each customer followed a different guanxi route)
      - Cross-guanxi information (e.g., how one company's perceptions of guanxi differed from those of other companies)

In summary, the case study design aims to reveal some insights into the causal processes, while the survey can give some indications of the prevalence of guanxi constructs and their interaction with relationship performance.

Method

The method included interviews with all managers of the studied company, its customers, and its suppliers in Hong Kong and Taiwan. The authors attended several staff meetings to observe the interactions between the company and visitors from its major principals (suppliers) during their regular visits to Hong Kong. Most documents and daily correspondence were made available to the authors except for confidential technical specifications and some sensitive price quotes.

Visiting associated companies confirmed the possibility of bending existing import regulations in China. The definitions of import items were not clear. It was defined by the end result of individual relationships between the exporter and exporter's importing agent and customs officers.

Appendix C

Analysis of Data and Results

DATA ANALYSIS

Survey Responses

This section deals with the responses to the pilot study and survey. In the main survey, a total of 1,000 questionnaires were sent out. The total number of questionnaires returned was 397, among which only 272 were usable because some respondents had not fully completed them. The response rates are summarized in Table C.1.

Characteristics of Sample

Profile of Respondents and Companies

Over 46.2 percent of the companies represented were involved in joint ventures, 39.5 percent of which were located in Guangzhou, 27.2 percent in Shenzhen, 16.7 percent in other Special Economic Zones, and 16.6 percent in other areas of China. Percentages of questionnaires returned were as follows: 17.8 percent from South China, 12.1 percent from Special Economic Zones, 10.6 percent from western China, and 8.3 percent from northern China. Regarding size distribution, the details of the companys' profiles and respondent profiles are summarized in Table C.2 and Table C.3 respectively.

In summary, 71 percent of head offices of companies in the survey are located in Hong Kong, while 13 percent are in Europe, the United States, or Canada. Also, 47.5 percent of the companies have joint ventures in the PRC. This high percentage demonstrates the close relationship between Hong Kong and China. A majority, 57 percent, employ less than 100 persons. This is typical of company size in Hong Kong.

TABLE C.1. Summary of Response Rate in Pilot Tests and Main Survey

Pilot Study (Including First and Second Rounds)	No.
Questionnaires sent out	128
Questionnaires received	88
Unusable	(3)
Usable questionnaires	85
Main Survey	**No.**
Questionnaires sent out	1,000
Questionnaires received	397
Unusable	(125)
Usable questionnaires	272
Total usable questionnaires	357

Regarding the personal profile of respondents, 87.4 percent are ages twenty to thirty-nine, 67.4 percent have a monthly income of HK$10,000-39,000 and an average of 5.8 years of experience in China trade. The profile can be regarded as typical of employees in the import/export sector, when compared with the figures of the 1994 Import/Export Manpower Survey (Hong Kong government Vocational Training Council 1994).

Working Mechanisms of Relationship Development

The dimensions of the relationship development mechanism are as follows:

1. The number of times per week that clients were entertained
2. The time taken to identify the "key" decision makers
3. The time normally taken to establish a stable relationship
4. The number of channels or persons involved in the relationship-building process

Entertainment

Only 15.5 percent of respondents indicated they entertained clients three to five times per week, while 7.3 percent said they did so six times or more. Both figures reflect the high weekly frequency of entertainment.

TABLE C.2. Profile of the Companies in the Main Survey

Characteristics	Number (N = 272)	(%)
1. Location of Head Office		
China	11	(3.9)
Hong Kong	193	(71.0)
Japan	9	(3.1)
Europe	20	(7.5)
Taiwan	3	(1.2)
USA and Canada	15	(5.5)
Others	21	(7.8)
		(100)
2. Existence of Joint Venture		
Yes	129	(47.5)
No	142	(52.1)
Other (e.g., other type of cooperation)	1	(0.4)
		(100)
3. Nature of the Company		
Trading	96	(35.4)
Manufacturing	61	(22.4)
Services	68	(25)
Utility	5	(1.8)
Others	42	(15.4)
		(100)
4. Export Channels Used		
Independent agent	97	(35.5)
Representative directly employed by company	94	(34.5)
Retail outlets (Agreement with related company, e.g., department store)	11	(4.1)
Sales plus production subsidiary	16	(5.9)
Foreign trade corporation	17	(6.4)
Local trading agents/distributors	10	(3.6)
PRC chambers of commerce	0	(0)
Special companies or persons with special import permits	7	(2.7)
Consignment	1	(0.5)
Others	19	(6.8)
		(100)
5. Number of Employees		
Less than 10	42	(15.6)
11-50	72	(26.4)
51-100	41	(15.2)
101-500	55	(20.0)
501-1,000	29	(10.8)
Above 1,000	33	(12.0)
		(100)

Note: In this summary, a typical company has its head office in Hong Kong and a joint venture in the PRC, is involved in the trading business, using an agent or direct representative, and is small to medium sized.

TABLE C.3. Profile of Respondents

Characteristics	Number (N=272)	(%)
1. Sex		
Male	131	(48)
Female	141	(52)
2. Age		
Below 20	5	(2.0)
20-29	163	(59.8)
30-39	75	(27.6)
40-49	19	(7.1)
50-59	8	(2.8)
60 and over	2	(0.8)
3. Education		
Primary or below	21	(7.9)
Secondary	74	(27.3)
Postsecondary	95	(34.8)
University or above	82	(30)
4. Monthly Salary (HK$)		
3,000 and under	8	(2.9)
3,000-5,999	9	(3.3)
6,000-9,999	56	(20.7)
10,000-19,999	133	(48.8)
20,000-39,999	51	(18.6)
40,000-59,999	12	(4.5)
60,000-89,999	2	(0.8)
90,000 and above	1	(0.4)
5. Years of Experience Working in China Trade		
1 year or less	98	(36.2)
2-5	115	(42.2)
6-10	38	(14.1)
11-15	12	(4.3)
16-20	6	(2.2)
20 years or above	3	(1.1)
6. Years of Experience Working in International Trade		
1 year or less	88	(33.3)
2-5	111	(41.9)
6-10	38	(14.5)
11-15	9	(3.4)
16-20	11	(4.3)
20 years or above	7	(2.6)

Note: Typical respondent characteristics: Age 20-39, secondary or post-secondary education, salary range of HK$10,000-39,999, 2-10 years work experience including 1-5 years in international trade.

Time Taken to Identify the Key Decision Makers

Generally, 71 percent of respondents said they required a minimum of three months to identify key decision makers, and 13 percent even said they needed over two years. This relatively high percentage reflects the difficulty of identifying key decision makers. Unlike in the West, in China, the managing director or general manager of a company may not be the key decision maker.

Time Taken to Establish a Stable Relationship

To establish a relationship, 29.7 percent of respondents required three to five months, and 27.9 percent took six months to a year. Another 6.8 percent even needed over five years. These time frames imply that a long period may be required to test a relationship.

Numbers of Channels and Persons Needed for Relationship Enhancement

In our survey, 41 percent of respondents indicated the need to go through two to four persons or channels, and 11 percent indicated a need for more than eight persons or channels. This demonstrates the complexity of channels and personal networks in the Chinese society.

Analysis and Discussion of Findings

This section discusses the importance of reliability and validity in measurement and provides analysis of the findings by focusing on, first, guanxi construct operationalization, and second, the relationship between the constructs and guanxi performance.

Cronbach (1970) defined the reliability of a scale as the extent to which a scale produces consistent and stable scores for a subject in repeated tests. According to Tull and Hawkins (1984), there are four major approaches for gauging reliability:

1. Test-retest reliability
2. Parallel form reliability
3. Scorer reliability
4. Internal comparison reliability

Test-retest reliability compares the results of the same scale in two or more similar situations by investigating the correlation coefficient on an item-by-item basis. Higher reliability is achieved if the difference between the items is smaller.

Parallel-form reliability is used to measure constructs on two parallel or comparable tests. The requirement is to construct two psychologically equivalent items to measure the same construct.

Score reliability is the measurement of correlation between the scores of different judges. This reliability was not required in our research, as scale instruments were mainly used.

Internal comparison reliability is used in the form of item-total correlation by employing an alpha coefficient, which is described by Bagozzi (1978) as having the lower bound for the reliability of a composite scale by providing the smallest reliability for a particular test scale. This item-to-total correlation analysis was performed to identify the degree of homogeneity in the scale and to confirm reliability.

Analysis of Questionnaire

This section has three parts. The first part is the analysis of means and standard deviations of each statement. The second part is guanxi construct operationalization, and the third part is the correlation between constructs and relationship performance indicators.

Summary of Scores for Each Statement

Guanxi constructs. The means and standard deviations of each statement are summarized in Table C.4.

In Table C.4, the first five statements with 5 points (5 out of the scale of 7 points, 70 percent) reflect the importance of networks. Two statements have a mean score of over 5.2 (74 percent). They are "Birds of a feather flock together" (mean score = 5.26) and "Timing is essential as the people in Chinese companies change and I don't know which person to contact" (mean = 5.24). The former reflects favoritism and the latter shows uncertainty. In addition, the worry caused by uncertainty about the future and trust and patience are important items. Also, the Chinese have a tendency to give a neutral score (i.e., 4 points) as a result of the influence of the Confucian mean norm. Our results show this tendency (half of the total of thirty statements have a mean of 4.3-3.7 points). All statements in the adaptation and continuity section result in consistent means of 4.27-4.41 (Table C.5). These statements reveal the significance of adaptation to relationship-building.

TABLE C.4. Guanxi Constructs Ranked by Mean Score

Statement Measuring Guanxi Values, Attitude, and Behavior	Mean	Std. Dev.
Birds of a feather flock together.	5.26	1.22
Timing is essential as the people in Chinese companies change and I don't know which person to contact.	5.24	1.39
Patience is a must in making money.	5.16	1.37
Don't suspect your subordinates. If you suspect them, don't deal with them.	5.11	1.56
It is difficult to enter the market unless we work together.	5.00	1.38
To pay back favor is more urgent than debts.	4.97	1.47
Organization of Chinese companies is not clear and I do not know where to start.	4.93	1.50
Try to make use of the principle of the mean.	4.75	1.39
Our business objectives are compatible with our partner's goals.	4.58	1.24
Making concessions to a Chinese counterpart is necessary.	4.55	1.29
We can reach consensus on the major issues.	4.53	1.10
The statement "Attack when near; befriend when distant" is very useful.	4.49	1.41
Lack of a business network.	4.45	1.52
The change made by you for your Chinese partners regarding technical features.	4.41	1.52
To be successful in negotiation, it is often necessary to compromise one's individual ethics.	4.40	1.50
Lack of continuity in the negotiation team.	4.35	1.32
Provide overseas market research trips to PRC representatives.	4.33	1.64
To achieve his or her own objectives, my partner often initially agrees to perform but fails to do so later.	4.32	1.33
Provide personal assistance to PRC contacts, e.g., to act as a guarantor for customer's child.	4.31	1.59
The change you made to adapt to your Chinese partners regarding production schedules.	4.27	1.53
It is easy to understand the partner's approach to doing business.	4.22	1.33
The change made by you to adapt to your Chinese partners regarding production capacity.	4.19	1.37
Brotherliness is an important way of promoting useful relations.	4.15	1.54
The statement "The golden cricket sheds its shell"* is very important.	3.89	1.40
Our partner attempts to exploit the advantage of our cooperation for his or her own benefit.	3.87	1.58

TABLE C.4 *(continued)*

Encourage others to owe you a favor.	3.85	1.55
Relationships with other companies have caused problems in building relationships with other customers.	3.78	1.48
The Chinese party is dependent on us.	3.74	1.36
The golden cricket sheds its shell.	3.72	1.38
Guanxi only affects the final stage of negotiation.	3.65	1.57

*This statement refers to when a cricket sheds its outer shell, then flies away and leaves the empty shell behind. The empty shell is often mistaken for the real cricket. In the Chinese business world, this phrase refers to a sneak or unsuspected attack behind a competitor's back.

TABLE C.5. Adaptation Statement Summary (Indicates the Significance of Adaptation)

Statement	Mean	Std. Dev.
The change made by you for your Chinese partners regarding technical features.	4.41	1.52
Lack of continuity in the negotiation team.	4.35	1.32
Provide overseas market research trips to PRC representatives.	4.33	1.64
The change you made to adapt to your Chinese partners regarding production schedules.	4.27	1.53
The change made by you to adapt to your Chinese partners regarding production capacity.	4.19	1.37

Guanxi outcome. The respondents were asked to describe their perception of guanxi outcome. They selected a score from on a scale of 1-7, as shown in Table C.6. Table C.7 indicates the mean and standard deviation scores of guanxi outcome indicators. The statement "The overall quality of a relationship" has a mean of 4.54. The sales performance questions (Questions 1, 2, and 4) reflect a higher average (4.19-4.76). On the other hand, the relationship termination costs question (Question 5) shows a lower mean score (3.84). The relationship formalization statement, "To what extent are your dealings with your partner formalized in written agreements?" has a mean score of 3.96 (56.7 percent) with a standard deviation of 1.62.

Factor analysis and varimax rotational factor analysis was used to estimate the properties of the latent constructs. Latent constructs cannot be measured directly but can be measured by indicators. For example, a person's attitude toward guanxi is difficult to measure precisely, but by asking various questions, it can be assessed. In combination, the answers to these questions may give a reasonably accurate measure of the latent construct. Then multiple regression was employed to estimate the model parameters.

TABLE C.6. Guanxi Outcome Measurement Questions

	Rapid decrease					Rapid increase	
Please describe the sales trends over last three years.	1	2	3	4	5	6	7
How about the stability of past sales patterns?	1	2	3	4	5	6	7
	Very bad					Very stable	
Describe the overall quality of relationship.	1	2	3	4	5	6	7
	Rapid decrease					Rapid increase	
What are your perceptions of future sales for the next three years?	1	2	3	4	5	6	7
	Disastrous					Negligible	
If you lose the partner, what would you regard the impact to be?	1	2	3	4	5	6	7
	None					Entirely	
To what extent are your dealings with your partner formalized in written agreement?	1	2	3	4	5	6	7

TABLE C.7. Statements Measuring Guanxi Outcome

Statement	Mean	Std. Dev.
Describe the sales trend over the last three years.	4.31	1.08
Describe the stability of your past sales pattern.	4.19	1.15
Describe the overall quality of your relationship.	4.54	1.02
What is your projection of future sales for the next three years?	4.76	1.14
If you lost your partner, what would you regard the impact to be?	3.84	1.29
To what extent are your dealings with your partner formalized in written agreements?	3.96	1.62

Guanxi Construct Operationalization

Principal component analysis was performed on thirteen items about guanxi personal values, eleven items measuring attitudes, and six items measuring guanxi behavior. The principal factors were extracted from each personal value, attitude, and aspect of behavior. The use of this method was based on the assumption that the dimensions of each construct are independent.

In the analysis of value factors, there are three principal factors with eigenvalues greater than one, which account for 39.2 percent of the total variance on thirteen items. Similarly, two factors are extracted from attitude statements, accounting for 32.1 percent of total variance on eleven items. For behavior, there are two factors accounting for 52.9 percent of total variance. The results are shown in Table C.8.

The factors were rotated by the varimax method. After inspection of the item loading on each factor, the labeling for each construct is as follows:

Value constructs:	Favor, opportunism, and trust
Attitude constructs:	Uncertainty and dependence
Behavior constructs:	Adaptation and continuity

The reliability of these constructs was examined with Cronbach's alpha coefficient. The reliability of all constructs except continuity is acceptable. The summary of results of factor analysis is shown in Table C.9.

The results indicate that opportunism and adaptation are highly reliable (all above 0.65), while other factors except continuity are marginally acceptable. Indeed, continuity is rejected because of its very low alpha coefficient.

Correlation Between the Constructs and Guanxi Performance

If any structural model is to hold, the individual relationship between variables must be statistically significantly in the predicted direction. The correlation test is used to assess the associations among empirical figures. No causality is intended to be measured. This measurement is used to form theoretical constructs. The relationship is tested by a Pearson correlation coefficient. Two-tail tests are used for all correlations.

TABLE C.8. Eigenvalue and Percentage of Variance of Each Factor

Factor	Eigenvalue	Percentage of Variance	Cumulative Percentage
Value			
1	1.89866	14.6	14.8
2	1.65744	12.7	27.4
3	1.53831	11.8	39.2
Attitude			
1	1.97343	17.9	17.9
2	1.55549	14.2	32.1
Behavior			
1	2.07506	34.6	34.6
2	1.10172	18.4	52.9

TABLE C.9. Results of Factor Analysis—To Identity Favor, Opportunism, and Trust as Value Constructs, Uncertainty and Dependence as Attitude Constructs, and Adaptation as a Behavior Construct

Item	Loading
Value	
Factor 1: Favor ($\alpha = 0.4940$)	
• To pay back favor is more urgent than debts.	0.48163
• The statement "Attack when near; befriend when distant" is very useful.	0.58159
• Birds of a feather flock together.	0.49060
• To be successful in negotiation, it is often necessary to compromise one's individual ethics.	0.57997
• Encourage others to owe you a favor.	0.58390
• Making concessions to a Chinese counterpart is a necessity.	0.48295
Factor 2: Opportunism ($\alpha = 0.7336$)	
• The statement "The golden cricket sheds its shell" is very important.	0.86004
• The golden cricket sheds its shell.	0.83542
Factor 3: Trust ($\alpha = 0.4729$)	
• Try to make use of the principle of the mean.	0.45961
• Patience is a must in making money.	0.41055
• Don't suspect your subordinates. If you suspect them, don't deal with them.	0.60724
• Brotherliness is an important way of promoting useful relations.	0.47722
• We can reach consensus on the major issues.	0.65650
Attitude	
Factor 1: Uncertainty ($\alpha = 0.5554$)	
• Timing is essential as the people in Chinese companies change and I don't know which person to contact.	0.69063
• Organization of Chinese companies is not clear and I do not know where to start.	0.75262
• It is difficult to enter the market unless we work together.	0.55816
• Relationships with other companies have caused problems in building relationships with other customers.	0.46961
• Lack of a business network.	0.40388
Factor 2: Dependence ($\alpha = 0.4070$)	
• The Chinese party is dependent on us.	0.70541
• Our business objectives are compatible with our partner's goals.	0.42275
• It is easy to understand the partner's approach to doing business.	0.62034
Behavior	
Factor 1: Adaptation ($\alpha = 0.6748$)	
• The change made by you to adapt to your Chinese partners regarding production capacity.	0.74708

TABLE C.9 *(continued)*

• Provide overseas market research trips to PRC representatives.	0.51214
• The change made by you for your Chinese partners regarding technical features.	0.82745
• The change you made to adapt to your Chinese partners regarding production schedules.	0.76096
Factor 2: Continuity ($\alpha = -0.0935$)—Rejected	
• Lack of continuity in the negotiation team.	0.74058

Chinese Personal Values

All of the three value constructs, favor, opportunism, and trust, were correlated with the guanxi performance indicators of sales performance (past and future sales trends and expectations), overall relationship quality, relationship termination costs, and formalization.

Trust

The key research question is about the relationship between values and guanxi performance. Each relationship is discussed here.

Trust is positively related to the overall quality of guanxi. As shown in column 4, Relationship Quality, of Table C.10, the correlation is in the predicted direction and significant at the level of 0.01. Therefore, it may be concluded that the higher the level of trust in the relationship is, the higher the quality of the overall relationship is.

Trust is positively related to sales performance. The above summary indicates the correlations between trust and guanxi performance, namely:

1. Trust and previous three years' sales stability
2. Trust and future sales perception
3. Trust and relationship formalization in the form of a written agreement
4. Trust and relationship termination costs

TABLE C.10. Summary of Correlations Between Trust and Guanxi Performance

Value	Past Sales	Sales Stability	Relationship Quality	Future Sales	Formalization	Relationship Termination Costs
Trust	0.0316 (P = 0.66)	0.1359 (P = 0.06)	0.1819 (P = 0.01)	0.1266 (P = 0.08)	0.0524 (P = 0.42)	0.2658 (P = 0.00)

P = Significant level.

As shown in Table C.10, the correlation between the trust level and the stability of past sales is positive but at an insignificant level of 0.66, and the correlation between future sales trends and trust is positively correlated at an insignificant level of 0.08.

A track record of cooperation is only a partial indication of trust, and, particularly in a Chinese context, the worry caused by the perception of an ever-changing environment accounts for an impulse to maintain quality relationships.

Note also that there is a positive relationship between trust and relationship formalization but not at a significant level (P > 0.42).

Another question concerns the correlation between trust and relationship termination costs. This correlation is positive at the significant level of 0.00. This indicates that the relationship termination costs are higher if the trust level is high. Also, in order to understand the complex relationship between trust and the above variables, multiple regression was used to find out more, as will be described later in this section.

Favor

Favor is positively related to overall relationship quality.

Favor is positively related to relationship termination costs.

These associations are found not in the proposed hypothetical direction at insignificant levels, as shown in Table C.11. Similarly, all correlations between favor and other guanxi performance indicators except relationship formalization are at insignificant levels. The only significant correlation is with formalization (at a significant level of P < 0.03). This correlation implies that the higher the favor, the greater the formalization. Favor is a controversial topic. All these variations in perspectives account for both the positive and negative impacts of favor on relationship development.

Dependence

Dependence is positively related to overall relationship quality. The correlation between dependence and overall relationship quality is not significant (P > 0.06). One of the reasons for cooperation may be mutual dependence, but dependence has many forms. Therefore, relationship quality may not be a good indicator of mutual dependence. The results are shown in Table C.12. The table indicates that all correlations are insignificant.

TABLE C.11. Favor and Guanxi Performance Correlations

Value Construct	Past Sales	Sales Stability	Relationship Quality	Future Sales	Relationship Termination Costs	Formalization
Favor	−0.0403 (P = 0.575)	−0.0747 (P = 0.297)	0.0328 (P = 0.648)	0.0767 (P = 0.285)	−0.1550 (P = 0.290)	0.0766 (P = 0.03)

TABLE C.12. Dependence and Guanxi Performance Correlations

Attitude Construct	Past Sales	Sales Stability	Relationship Quality	Future Sales	Relationship Termination Costs	Formalization
Dependence	0.0418 (P = 0.561)	0.1299 (P = 0.069)	0.1366 (P = 0.056)	0.0261 (P = 0.717)	0.0497 (P = 0.489)	−0.1049 (P = 0.145)

Adaptation

Adaptation is positively related to past sales performance. The associations between adaptation and past sales performance are positively correlated with past sales trends (P < 0.00) and past sales stability (P < 0.034), as shown in Table C.13. Adaptation is a mutual and substantial investment, which affects sales performance to a large extent. The same applies to other sales performance indicators except future sales trends, because the future is difficult to predict. This accounts for this insignificant correlation.

Adaptation is positively related to the perceived overall relationship quality. This correlation is positively related at a significant level (P > 0.00), as shown in Table C.13. Adaptation represents a durable commitment process in which the greater the extent of adaptation is, the greater the possibility of enhancing relationship quality will be.

Adaptation is negatively related to relationship termination costs. Adaptation is a type of investment, a particularly idiosyncratic one, that makes it difficult to switch to another relationship, especially if the switching costs are high and the partner perceives that there are no comparable alternative partners. The above correlation is in the proposed direction at a significant level of 0.001, reflecting the importance of adaptation in maintaining the relationship.

Summary

The constructs of favor, trust, dependence, and adaptation have been identified. The summary of all correlations between guanxi constructs and guanxi performance is shown in Table C.14 and significant correlations are shown in Table C.15.

TABLE C.13. Adaptation and Guanxi Performance

Behavior Construct	Past Sales	Sales Stability	Relationship Quality	Future Sales	Relationship Termination Costs	Formalization
Adaptation	0.2039 (P = 0.004)	0.1501 (P = 0.034)	0.2441 (P = 0.000)	0.0603 (P = 0.004)	−0.2357 (P = 0.001)	0.1321 (P = 0.044)

TABLE C.14. Summary of Correlations Between Guanxi Constructs and Guanxi Performance Indicators

	Guanxi Performance Indicator					
Construct	Past Sales	Sales Stability	Relationship Quality	Future Sales	Termination Costs	Formalization
Favor	−0.0403	−0.0747	0.0328	0.0767	−0.1550	0.0766[b]
Opportunism	−0.0647	−0.0639	−0.0174	−0.0846	−0.0823	−0.1330[c]
Trust	0.0316	0.1359[c]	0.1819[a]	0.1266[c]	0.2658[a]	0.0524
Uncertainty	0.0369	0.0857	0.0503	0.0926	0.0237	0.0588
Dependence	0.0418	0.1299[c]	0.1366[c]	0.0261	0.0497	−0.1049
Adaptation	0.2039[b]	0.1501[b]	0.2441[a]	0.0603[a]	−0.2357[a]	0.1321[b]

Note: Two-tailed significant, [a]significant at $P < 0.01$, [b]significant at $P < 0.05$, [c]significant at $P < 0.10$.

TABLE C.15. Significant Correlations of Guanxi Constructs and Performance

Attribute	Construct	Past Sales	Sales Stability	Future Sales	Rel. Quality	Termination Costs	Formalization
Value	Favor	–	–	–	–	–	✓(–)
	Trust	–	–	–	✓	✓	–
Behavior	Adaptation	✓	✓	✓	✓	✓(–)	✓

Note: Indicates the importance of trust and adaptation in performance; termination costs are negatively correlated with favor and adaptation.

✓ = Correlation (P < 0.05); (–) = Negative correlation

Table C.15 shows the summary of correlations between guanxi performance indicators, overall relationship quality, termination costs, sales development (past sales trends and stability as well as future sales perceptions), and formalization and the constructs of trust, favor, and adaptation. Note that overall relationship quality is positively correlated with trust and adaptation. Another angle to measure the role of guanxi constructs in relationship development is relationship termination costs. Trust is positively correlated with termination costs, while adaptation is negatively correlated with termination costs because adaptation is highly relationship-specific.

This negative correlation indicates the consequence of high termination costs if there is a broken relationship. Thus, the positive correlation between termination costs and trust is difficult to interpret. Here are three definitions of trust:

1. Trust is defined as a willingness to rely on an exchange partner in whom one has confidence (Moorman, Deshpande, and Zaltman 1993).
2. Trust is a general expectation that the words of an individual are reliable (Rotter 1967).
3. A trustworthy party is reliable and has high integrity, associated with qualities of being consistent, competent, honest, fair, responsible, helpful, and benevolent (Morgan and Hunt 1994).

The first and second definitions emphasize the importance of confidence, while the third highlights integrity. One of the projected outcomes of achieving trust is the formation of partnerships in which everyone shares risks and rewards. However, win-win situations are difficult to achieve.

Figure C.1 illustrates the complex correlations among all variables. In this figure, only adaptation, dependence, favor, and trust are shown as constructs; opportunism and uncertainty are not shown because their correlations are not significant at $P < 0.05$. The first four constructs are found to be positively correlated with overall relationship quality. Note that adaptation is positively correlated with all relationship indicators (i.e., sales performance and formalization) except termination costs. The same applies to trust, which correlates positively with all indicators except past sales trends. The figure has four parts: input (all-important constructs), output (guanxi quality and sales performance), perceived effectiveness (termination costs), and structural dimension (formalization).

Conclusion

There are two major conclusions:

1. Trust, dependence, and adaptation constructs are positively correlated with sales stability. Trust, dependence, and adaptation are positively correlated with relationship quality, but the correlation between adaptation and relationship termination costs is negative.
2. Adaptation and trust are important constructs, as indicated by positive correlations with relationship quality.

After the correlation tests, multiple regression analysis was used to further test the relationships.

FIGURE C.1. Summary of Correlations Between Constructs and Performance Indicators

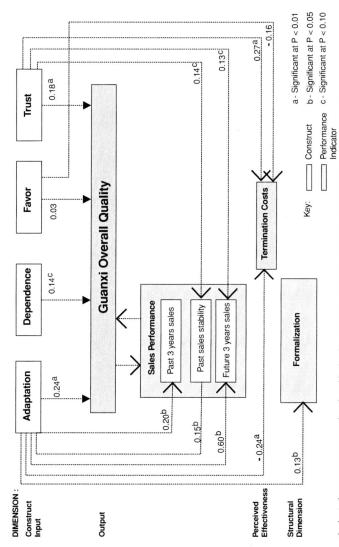

Note: Trust and adaptation constructs correlated positively with relationship quality and sales stability, but the correlation between favor and termination costs is negative. A negative correlation is also found between adaptation and termination costs.

Multiple Regression Analysis

Multiple regression was performed on the data to test the relationships between the constructs of favor, opportunism, adaptation, trust, uncertainty, and dependence as independent variables and sales performance, relationship quality, termination costs, and formalization as dependent variables. The purpose of this analysis is to construct an equation to estimate values for the criterion variables and to measure the closeness of the estimated relationships. The findings are summarized in Table C.16.

As in the previous correlation analysis, adaptation is an important variable affecting guanxi performance indicators of sales, relationship quality, termination costs, and formalization. Trust is related to termination costs at a significant level.

The overall summary of significant predictors in the multiple regression analysis is as follows (Table C.17):

1. The predictor of termination costs is trust.
2. The predictor of past sales trends, relationship quality, termination costs, and formalization is adaptation.

TABLE C.16. Multiple Regression Analysis

Independent Variable	B	Standard Error	Beta	T-Value	Sig. T
(1) Using Termination Costs As Dependent Variable					
Trust	0.44	0.13	0.26	3.38	0.00
Overall F = 3.93 R^2 = 0.11 Sig. = 0.0022					
(2) Using Past Sales Trends As Dependent Variable					
Adaptation	0.20	0.07	0.20	2.70	0.01
Overall F = 4.27 R^2 = 0.04 Sig. = 0.015					
(3) Using Overall Relationship Quality As Dependent Variable					
Adaptation	0.24	0.07	0.24	3.47	0.00
Overall F = 6.25 R^2 = 0.06 Sig. = 0.002					
(4) Using Termination Costs As Dependent Variable					
Adaptation	−0.30	0.09	−0.25	−3.44	0.00
Overall F = 5.79 R^2 = 0.06 Sig. = 0.0036					
(5) Using Formalization As Dependent Variable					
Adaptation	0.23	0.10	0.15	2.41	0.02
Overall F = 3.88 R^2 = 0.05 Sig. = 0.005					

TABLE C.17. Summary of Significant Predictors in the Multiple Regression

Independent Variable	Dependent Variable			
	Relationship Quality	Past Sales Trends	Relationship Termination Costs	Formalization
Value Trust	—	—	0.44	—
Attitude Adaptation	0.24	0.20	− 0.30	0.23

Comments on the Results of the Predictors

Trust. Trust is also a very important predictor for relationship termination costs. Trust is highly regarded by both parties, who desire to commit themselves to the relationship because commitment may entail less vulnerability.

Adaptation. The findings also demonstrate the importance of adaptation, which enhances the close cooperation of mutual understanding and the joint development of products and technical solutions. Thus, adaptation is negatively correlated with termination costs.

IN-DEPTH INTERVIEWS

A total of thirteen in-depth interviews were carried out. The distribution of the organizations interviewed is as follows:

Manufacturing companies	2
Computer companies	3
Engineering companies	2
Banks	2
Retailing	1
Other	3
Total	13

Company size ranged from 6 to 500 employees, with sales turnover from HK$2 million to $360 million. Only five out of thirteen companies were willing to be named. The rest preferred to keep their background confidential. Guanxi is a very sensitive topic, with possible implications of unethical behavior.

Summary of Findings

Guanxi

Examples were given in several cases of "smoothing" business activities. Guanxi works as a lubricant to help solve conflicts and to enhance efficiency, and thus creates value for business partners because it saves time.

Adaptation

Most examples of adaptation involve compromise. For example, one engineering company submitted an environmental impact assessment for the establishment of a factory to the local government three times but failed each time to receive approval. After they invited the relevant official to dinner, the report was accepted. In such cases, according to the interviewees, adaptation behavior includes "a change of mentality."

Trust

In the interviews, most respondents cited examples of trust that had the following major features:

1. A need for informality
2. A need for time to test the relationships
3. Confidence
4. Communication

Some examples included cash payment terms instead of letters of credit. In one case, the respondent indicated that he needed to open a personal account for a mainland Chinese company in Hong Kong to help the company evade taxes in the PRC.

Favor

Favor was a major topic in the in-depth interviews, because the data collected in the questionnaire survey provided limited information and insight into this sensitive topic. The summary of the findings is as follows:

1. To do a favor may be a two-way or one-way transaction.
2. Favor is regarded as a bait or treat and a quite natural element of a business friendship.

Continuity

The continuity and friendship demonstrated in respondents' interactions with their partners reflected the important role of favor and trust in the guanxi network. The conclusions of the in-depth interviews are:

1. All companies except one agreed on the understanding of guanxi as highly adaptable behavior to seek compromise through the exchange of favor and trust in the process of continuing relationships.
2. All thirteen companies were willing to adopt the ideas or to apply the concept of the guanxi model in their staff training. This confirms the practical value of the findings.

CASE STUDY

The case study involves a single case with embedded units (multiple units of analysis). The design provides opportunities to observe, understand, and analyze the phenomena that were not reflected in the statistical analysis of the survey.

In addition, this case study is used to test the model in a real-life situation and thus determine whether the model is correct or whether some alternative explanations might potentially be more relevant.

The potential vulnerability of this single case design is the possibility that the data may be biased. To avoid the chance of misrepresentation and to maximize data collection, multiple event analysis and a pattern-matching approach were used to ensure internal validity. During the data collection process, multiple sources and chains of evidence were established. Also, the involvement of the key interviewees in reviewing the draft case study reports also helped to ensure the construct validity (Yin 1994).

The case study, which is divided into two parts, is presented here and in Chapter 6:

1. Design and methodology: research design, research problems, study objective, major question, units of analysis, study propositions and criteria for interpreting findings, and the background and organization of the company in the case study are covered in this appendix.
2. Guanxi model: context, positions, constructs, positioning map, development patterns, and implementations of guanxi. These application elements are covered in Chapter 6, as it is necessary to explain the components of the guanxi model before going into the details of how to apply the model to the case study.

Design and Methodology

Research Design

The design follows the structure of Yin's (1994) research guidelines:

1. The study questions
2. The propositions
3. The unit of analysis
4. The logic linking the data and the propositions
5. The criteria for interpreting the findings

Research Problems

In this case study, Expert Ltd.* faced two major marketing problems:

1. The difficulty of obtaining long-term business contracts from big multinationals.
2. The difficulty, arising from product range diversity, of segmenting its customers and maintaining long-term relationships with key customers

Study Objective

The major objective is to test the guanxi model in a real situation.

Major Question and Purpose of Case Study

Facing the problems described, the company requested that the following question be addressed:

> Instead of employing conventional measurement criteria of business potential, sales volume, and market attraction as the basis for segmenting its customers, what is the method of using guanxi as an alternative type of segmentation?

The purpose of the study is to assist the organization to determine the positioning of its relationships in order to formulate relationship marketing strategies and implement them effectively in Hong Kong and China.

---

*This is an invented name, adopted to maintain confidentiality.

Study Question

The major study question is:

How and why does the guanxi model help the company to improve its relationship marketing strategies in order to build up the organization's long-term business with its major customers?

The subquestions were as follows:

1. How do guanxi constructs (dependence, adaptation, and trust) affect guanxi quality?
2. Why does the outcome of a relationship differ in various guanxi positions?
3. How are the guanxi routes followed? Why?
4. How do the different guanxi constructs interact?

Questions (1) and (2) are related to the guanxi system dynamic (Box B of Figure 6.2), while (3) and (4) refer to Box C (guanxi strategies) and Box D (guanxi implementation).

Units of Analysis

The main unit of analysis is the company as a whole, with individual members of the staff as the smallest units. The intermediary units are the company's principals and major existing and potential customers. Other subunits are the company's special import handling agents and associated companies. The summary of the types of data from different sources is shown in Table C.18. These multiple sources of evidence are required to ensure the reliability of the data and to avoid bias stemming from the use of only one source.

Criteria for Interpreting the Findings

The criteria are based on:

1. Guanxi constructs: dependence, adaptation, favor, and trust
2. Guanxi positioning map
3. Routing
4. Implementation of guanxi (A-G approach)

For further flexibility, the criteria were not applied indiscriminately but were selected on the basis of individual company cases.

TABLE C.18. Types of Data from Different Units of Analysis

Unit Source of Information	Total System Import/Export Regulations, Principal's Manuals and Specifications, Company Policy, and Strategic Documents	Intermediate Unit Products, Customer Markets, Trip Reports, Files, Market Research Reports, and Company Standard Forms (Visit Reports)	Intermediate Unit Daily Correspondence (e.g., Forms, Letters, and Faxes)	Individual Manager	Individual Principal	Individual Customer	Individual Associated Company
Company As a Whole (Head Office)	•	•	•	•	—	—	—
Branch Office	—	•	•	•	—	—	—
Customer's Office and Factory	—	•	•	—	—	•	—
Principal's Offices	•	•	•	—	•	—	—
Associated Company Offices	—	•	•	—	—	—	•

• = Focus of Study

Expert Ltd.

Background

The name of the company in this study and the names of all related principals (suppliers and customers) are invented. The name of the company is kept confidential at the request of the directors of Expert Ltd., who were concerned that some aspects of the study involved sensitive issues, such as the involvement of special import-facilitating activities and the confidential nature of products (as agreed with its principals regarding nondisclosure terms, as specified in exclusive sales agents' contracts). The directors were of course also worried about the disclosure of information to competitors.

Expert Ltd. is a trading company specializing in packaging systems. Its major product ranges are as follows:

- Beverage segment: bag-in-box packaging and filling systems, cans, caps, labels, labellers, and shrink film
- Food segment: bag-in-box packaging for ice cream, sauce, milk shakes, and oil, three-piece cans, can components, labels (sleeve and roll-fed) and label systems, flexible packs, and lipping
- Metal segment: metal cans, can components, laminated lids, and flexible packaging for dairy products
- Warehouse handling segment: plastic slip sheets for cement, beverage, and warehousing industries, reclosable boxes, paper sacks for flour and chemicals
- Special newly developed segment: PET plastic bottles and preformed bottles for soft drinks, special caps and fittings for beverage packaging, bulk containers for interplant transfer, and meat packing machines, such as skin packing, vacuum packing, and horizontal packing equipment

Organization

Expert Ltd. has two offices, its head office in Hong Kong and a sales liaison office in Beijing, with a total staff of twenty. The company was founded by two people in 1990. Both of them were classmates at the University of Hong Kong and both have extensive business experience in the packaging industry and in China trade going back more than eighteen years. All of the company's senior staff has at least undergraduate degrees. There are five senior members altogether.

The company represents several multinational packaging groups in Hong Kong and China. Its principals are market leaders in their own specialized fields, such as bag-in-box, PET, label, three-piece can, shrink film, and paper sacks.

Bibliography

Aaker, D., Kumar, V., and Day, G.S. 1995. *Marketing Research,* Singapore: John Wiley and Sons.

Abbot, K.A. 1970. *Harmony and Individualism,* Taipei: Taipei Orient Cultural Services.

Achrol, R., Scheer, L.K., and Stern, L.W. 1992. "Designing Successful Trans-organizational Marketing Alliances," Marketing Science Institute, Manuscript No. 92-101.

Ackoff, R.L. 1971. "Toward a System of Systems Concepts," *Management Science,* Vol. 17, 661-671.

Adams, G.B. and White, J.D. 1994. "Dissertation Research in Public Administration and Cognate Fields: An Assessment of Methods and Quality," *Public Administration Review,* Vol. 54, No. 6, 565-576.

Aiello, P. 1991. "Building a Joint Venture in China: The Case of Chrysler and the Beijing Jeep Corporation," *Journal of General Management,* Vol. 17, No. 2, 64.

Albrecht, M.A., Pagano, A.M., and Phoocharoon, P. 1996. "International Joint Ventures: An Integrated Conceptual Model for Human Resource and Business Strategies," in Baran, R., Pan, Y., and Kaynak, E. (eds.), *International Joint Ventures in East Asia,* New York: International Business Press, pp. 89-128.

Alder, N. 1991. *International Dimensions of Organisational Behaviour,* Boston: PWS-Kent.

Alder, N.J., Brahm, R., and Graham, J.L. 1992. "Strategy Implementation: A Comparison of Face-to-Face Negotiations in the People's Republic of China and the United States," *Strategic Management Journal,* Vol. 13 No. 6, 448-466.

Alderson, W. 1965. *Dynamic Marketing Behaviour,* Homewood, IL: Richard D. Irwin Inc., p. 239.

Allison, G.T. 1971. *Essence of Decision: Explaining the Cuban Missile Crisis,* Boston: Little, Brown and Co.

Alston, J.P. 1989. "Wa, Guanxi and Inhwa: Managerial Principles in Japan, China and Korea," *Business Horizon,* March-April, 26-31.

Altman, I. and Taylor, D.A. 1973. *Social Penetration: The Development of Interpersonal Relationships,* New York: Holt, Rinehart and Winston.

Ambler, T. 1994. "Marketing's Third Paradigm: Guanxi," *Business Strategy Review,* Vol. 5, No. 4, 69-80.

Anderson, J.A. and Narus, J.A. 1990. "A Model of Distribution Firm and Manufacturer Firm Working Partnerships," *Journal of Marketing,* Vol. 54, January, 42-58.

Anheier, H.K., Geshards, J., and Romo, F.P. 1995. "Forms of Capital and Social Structure in Cultural Fields: Examining Bourdieu's Social Topography," *The American Journal of Sociology,* Vol. 100, No. 4, 859-903.

Armstrong, W., Chan, C.F., Holbert, N.B., and Pecotich, T. 1991. "An Exploration of Ethical Perceptions of Hong Kong International Marketing Managers: Their Attitudes Towards the Organization, Industry and Country," *Hong Kong Journal of Business Management,* Vol. 9, 75-89.

Arndt, J. 1983. "The Political Economy Paradigm: Foundation for Theory Building in Marketing," *Journal of Marketing,* Vol. 47, Fall, 44-54.

Au, A.K.M. and Enderwick, P. 1994. "Small Firms in International Joint Ventures in China: The New Zealand Experience," *Journal of Small Business Management,* April, 88-94.

Austin, J.E. 1990. *Managing in Developing Countries,* New York: The Free Press.

Bagozzi, R.P. 1974. "Marketing As Exchange," *Journal of Marketing,* Vol. 39, Oct., 32-39.

Bagozzi, R.P. 1978. "Toward a General Theory for the Explanation of the Performance of Salespeople." Unpublished Ph.D. Dissertation, Northwestern University.

Bailey, M.T. 1992. "Do Physicists Use Case Studies? Thoughts on Public Administration Research," *Public Administration Review,* Vol. 52, No.1, 37.

Baird, L.S., Lyles, M.A., and Eharton, R. 1990. "Attitudinal Differences Between American and Chinese Managers Regarding Joint Venture Management," *Management International Review,* Vol. 30, Special Issue, 55-68.

Baker, M.J. 1976. *Marketing: Theory and Practice,* London: Macmillan Press.

Baker, M.J. 1991. *Marketing: An Introduction,* London: Macmillan Press.

Baran, R., Pan, Y., and Kaynak, E. 1996. *International Joint Venture in East Asia,* New York: International Business Press.

Barham, R. 1995. "United Kingdom," in Power, V. (ed.), *Setting Up a Business in . . . : An International Legal Survey,* London: Sweet and Maxwell.

Barney, J.B. 1990. "The Debate Between Traditional Management Theory and Organizational Economics," *Academy of Management Review,* Vol. 15, No. 3, 382-394.

Baugarten, S. and Rivard, R. 1991. "The Evolution of Conditions for Joint Ventures in China," *Journal of Global Marketing,* Vol. 5, No. 1/2, 183-199.

Beamish, P.W. and Wang, H.Y. 1989. "Investing in China via Joint Ventures," *Management International Review,* Vol. 29, No. 1, 57-64.

Beamish, P.W. and Wang, H.Y. 1993. "The Characteristics of Joint Ventures in the People's Republic of China," *Journal of International Marketing,* Vol. 1, No. 2, 29-48.

Bergere, M.C. 1984. "On the Historical Origins of Chinese Underdevelopment," *Theory and Society,* Vol. 13, No. 3, 327-337.

Berry, L.L. and Parasuraman, A. 1991. *Marketing Services,* New York: The Free Press.

Blackman, C. 1997. *Negotiating China—Case Studies and Strategies,* Sydney: Allen & Unwin.

Blau, P.M. 1964. *Exchange and Power in Social Life,* New York: John Wiley and Sons.

Bolton, G.E. 1991. "A Comparative Model of Bargaining: Theory and Evidence," *American Economic Review,* Vol. 81, No. 5, 1096-1136.

Bond, M.H. 1991. *Beyond the Chinese Face: Insights from Psychology,* Hong Kong: Oxford University Press.

Bonoma, T.V. 1985. "Case Research in Marketing: Opportunities, Problems, and a Process," *Journal of Marketing Research,* Vol. 22, May, 199-208.

Bourdieu, P. 1977. *Outline of a Theory of Practice,* Cambridge: Cambridge University Press, pp. 179-181.

Bourdieu, P. 1986. "The Forms of Capital," in J. Richardson (ed.), *Handbook of Theory and Research for the Sociology of Education,* New York: Greenwood Press, pp. 241-258.

Bradley, D.G. 1977. "Managing Against Expropriation," *Harvard Business Review,* July/August, 75-83.

Brahm, L.J. 1995. *Negotiating in China: 36 Strategies,* Singapore: Reed Academic Publishing Asia.

Brahm, L.J. and Li, D. 1996. *The Business Guide to China,* Singapore: Butterworth-Heinemann Asia.

Brown, R.H. 1992. *Writing the Social Text: Poetics and Politics in Social Scientific Discourse,* New York: Aldine.

Bruijin, E.J. de and Jia, X. 1993. "Managing Sino-Western Joint Ventures: Product Selection Strategy," *Management International Review,* Vol. 33, No. 4, 335-360.

Brunner, J.A., Chan, J., Sun, C., and Zhou, N. 1989. "The Role of Guanxi in Negotiations in the Pacific Basin," *Journal of Global Marketing,* Vol. 3, No. 2, 7-23.

Brunner, J.A. and Koh, A.C. 1988. "Negotiations in the People's Republic of China: An Empirical Study of American and Chinese Negotiators Perceptions and Practices," *Journal of Global Marketing,* Vol. 2, No. 1, 33-55.

Brunner, J.A., Koh, A., and Lou, X. 1992. "Chinese Perceptions of Issues and Obstacles Confronting Joint Ventures," *Journal of Global Marketing,* Vol. 1, No. 2, 29-48.

Brunner, J.A. and Taoka, G.M. 1977. "Marketing and Negotiating in the People's Republic of China: Perceptions of American Businessmen Who Attended the 1975 Canton Trade Fair," *Journal of International Business Studies,* Vol. 8, No. 2, 69-82.

Brunner, J.A. and Wang, Y. 1988. "Chinese Negotiation and the Concept of Face," *Journal of International Consumer Marketing,* Vol. 1, No. 1, 27-43.

Buttery, A.E. 1988. "New Paradigm Research Within Systems Development: An Exploratory Study of the Potential for Adopting New Paradigm Research As a Means of Developing a Short Term Operations System and Model for Stoddard

Holdings PLC." Unpublished PhD thesis, Glasgow: The University of Strathclyde.

Buttery, A.E. and Buttery, E. 1994. *Business Network: Reaching New Markets with Low-Cost Strategies,* Melbourne: Pitman Publishing.

Buttery, A.E. and Leung, T.K.P. 1998. "The Difference Between Chinese and Western Negotiations," *European Journal of Marketing,* Vol. 32, No. 3/4, 374-389.

Calhourn, C. 1992. "Culture, History, and the Problem of Specificity in Social Theory," in Seidman, S. and Wager, D. (eds.), *Postmodernism and Social Theory,* Oxford: Basil Blackwell, pp. 244-288.

Campbell, D.T. 1975. "Degree of Freedom and the Case Study," *Comparative Political Studies.* pp.178-193.

Campbell, N.C.G. 1989. *A Strategic Guide to Equity Joint Ventures in China,* Oxford: Pergamon Press.

Casson, M. and Zhang, J. 1992. "Western Joint Ventures in China," in Casson, M. (ed.), *International Business and Global Integration: Empiricial Studies,* London: Macmillan, pp. 25-62.

Cateron, P. 1993. *International Marketing,* Burr Ridge, IL: Irwin.

Chan, K.S. 1988. "Trade Negotiations in a Nash Bargaining Model," *Journal of International Economics,* Vol. 25, No. 22, 354-363.

Chandler, A.D. 1986. "The Evolution of Multiple Global Competition," in Porter, M.E. (ed.), *Competition in Global Industries,* Boston: Harvard Business School Press, pp. 405-448.

Checkland, P.B. 1981. *System Thinking, System Practice,* London: John Wiley and Sons.

Checkland, P.B. 1985. "From Optimizing to Learning: A Development of System Thinking for the 1990s," *Journal of Operation Research,* Vol. 36, No. 9, 757-767.

Chen, H.T. and Rossi, P.H. 1987. "The Theory-Driven Approach to Validity," *Evaluation and Program Planning,* Vol. 10, 95-103.

Chen, M. 1993. "Tricks of the China Trade," *China Business Review,* Vol. 20, No. 2, 12-16.

Cheng, P. 1995. *World Executive's Digest,* December, 12-14.

Child, J., Li, Z., and Watts, J. 1990. "Study of Management of Sino-Foreign Joint Ventures," in Li, Z. (ed.), *Managing Equity Joint Ventures in China,* Beijing: Enterprise Management Press (in Chinese).

Child, J., Li, Z., and Watts, J. 1991. "Managerial Adaptation in Reforming Economies: The Case of Joint Ventures," Paper presented at the annual meeting of the Academy of Management, Miami Beach.

Child, J., Li, Z., Watts, J., and Markoczy, L. 1993. "Host-Country Managerial Behaviour and Learning in Chinese and Hungarian Joint Ventures," *Journal of Management Studies,* Vol. 30, No. 4, 611-631.

Ching, F. 1997. "China: Problem of Succession," *Far East Economic Review,* October 16, 34-37.

Chiu, T., Dobinsin, D., and Findlay, M. 1991. *Legal Systems of the PRC,* Hong Kong: Longman.

Christopher, M., Payne, A., and Ballantyne, M. 1991. *Relationship Marketing,* London: Heinemann.

Chu, C.N. 1991. *The Asian Mind Game: Unlocking the Hidden Agenda of the Asian Business Culture: A Westerner's Survival Manual.* New York: Rawson Associates.

Churchill Jr., G.A. 1991. *Marketing Research, Methodological Foundations,* Orlando, FL: Dryden Press.

Clarke, A. 1976. *Experimenting with Organisational Life: The Action-Research Approach,* London: Plenum Press.

Clayton, D. 1995. "Red Tape Delays $ 38b in US Deals," *South China Morning Post,* October 19, B1.

Collier, J. 1945. "The US Indian Administration as a Laboratory of Ethnic Relations," *Social Research,* Vol. 12, No. 3, 265-303.

Cook, H.F. 1996. *The Commercial Environment in the PRC,* Hong Kong: Joint Publishing (in Chinese).

Cooksey, R.W. and Gates, G.R. 1995. "HRM: A Management Science in Need of Displine," *Journal of the Australia and New Zealand Academey of Management,* Vol. 1, November 1, 1-6.

Cory, S. 1953. *Action-Research to Improve School Practice,* New York: Teachers College Press.

Crocombe, G.T., Enright, M.T., and Porter, M.E. 1991. *Upgrading New Zealand's Competitive Advantage,* Auckland: Oxford University Press.

Croghan, L. 1995. "Don't Look Back," *Financial World,* July 18, 50.

Cronbach, L.J. 1970. *Essentials of Psychological Testing* (Third Edition). New York: Harper and Row.

Crowther, J. (ed.). 1995. *Oxford Advanced Learner's Dictionary,* Fifth Edition, Oxford: Oxford University Press.

Cullen, D.E. 1965. *Negotiating Labour-Management Contracts,* Ithaca, NY: New York State School of Industrial and Labour Relations, Cornell University.

Cunningham, M.T. 1980. "International Marketing and Purchasing of Industrial Goods: Features of a European Research Project," *European Journal of Marketing,* Vol. 14, 322-338.

Dabholkar, P.A. and Johnston, W.J. 1994. "The Dynamics of Long-Term Business-to-Business Exchange Relationships," *Journal of the Academy of Marketing Science,* Vol. 22, No. 2, 130-145.

Daft, R.L. 1983. "Learning the Craft of Organisational Research," *Academy of Management Review,* Vol. 8, No. 4, 539-546.

Dane, F.C. 1990. *Research Methods,* Pacific Grove, CA: Brooks/Cole Publishing Company.

Danniels, J.D., Krug, J., and Nigh, D. 1985. "U.S. Joint Ventures in China: Motivation and Management of Political Risk," *California Management Review,* Vol. 27, No. 4, 46-58.

Davidson, W.H. 1987. "Creating and Managing Joint Ventures in China," *California Management Review*, Vol. 39, No. 4, 77-94.

Davies, H. 1995. *China Business: Context and Issues*, Hong Kong: Longman Asia Ltd.

Davies, H.A., Leung, T.K.P., Luk, S., and Wong, Y.H. 1995. "The Benefits of 'Guanxi,' An Exploration of the Value of Relationships in Developing the Chinese Market," *Industrial Marketing Management*, Vol. 24, No. 3, 94-191.

Deamer, D.D. 1996. "Comparison of Key Features of Equity, Wholly Foreign-owned and Co-operatives in China," *East Asian Executive Reports*, February 15, 10-16.

Deising, P. 1972. *Patterns of Discovery in the Social Sciences*, London: Routlege and Kegan Paul.

DeKeijzer, A.J. 1986. *The China Business Handbook*, Weston, CT: Asia Business Communications.

Delfs, R. 1989. "Irony in Deng's 'Hear the People' Policy Idea," *Far Eastern Economic Review*, Vol. 146, October 5, 58-60.

Deng, L.P. 1997. "Understanding Japanese Investment in China," *American Journal of Economics and Sociology*, Vol. 56, No. 1, 115-127.

DePauw, J.W. 1981. *U.S.-Chinese Trade Negotiations*, New York: Praeger Publishers.

Deverge, M. 1983. "Understanding Confucianism," *Euro-Asia Business Review*, Vol. 2, No. 3, 50-53.

Deverge, M. 1986. "Negotiating with the Chinese," *Euro-Asia Business Review*, Vol. 5, No. 1, 34-36.

Douglas, J.D. 1976. *Investigative Social Research: Individual and Team Field Research*, Beverly Hills, CA: Sage.

Dubin, R. 1982. "Management: Meanings, Method and Moxie," *Academy of Management Review*, Vol. 7, No. 3, 372-379.

Dunning, J.H. 1980. "Toward an Eclectic Theory of International Production: Some Empirical Tests," *Journal of International Business Studies*, Vol. 11, 8-31.

Dutta, M. and Merva, M. 1990. "U.S.-China Joint Ventures: An Economic Appraisal," in Dutta, M., Chang, P.-K., and Lin, S.-K. (eds.), *Research in Asian Economic Studies*, 1990: *China's Modernization and Open Economic Policy*, Westport, CT: JAI Press, pp. 171-196.

Dwyer, F.R. and LaGace, R.R. 1986. "On the Nature and Role of Buyer-Seller Trust." T. Shimp (ed.), *AMA Summer Education Conference Proceedings*, Chicago: American Marketing Association, pp. 40-45.

Dwyer, F.R., Schurr, P.H., and Oh, S. 1987. "Developing Buyer-Seller Relationships," *Journal of Marketing*, Vol. 51, No. 2, 11-27.

Dwyer, F.R. and Walker, O.C. Jr. 1981. "Bargaining in an Asymmetrical Power Structure," *Journal of Marketing*, Vol. 45, winter, 109-115.

Eistenhardt, K.M. 1989. "Building Theories from Case Study Research," *Academy of Management Review*, Vol. 14, No. 4, 532-550.

Eiteman, D.K. 1990. "American Executives' Perceptions of Negotiating Joint Ventures with the People's Republic of China: Lessons Learned," *Columbia Journal of World Business,* Vol. 25, No. 4, 59-67.

Ekeh, P.P. 1974. *Social Exchange Theory: The Two Traditions,* Cambridge, MA: Harvard University Press.

Elashmawi, F. and Harris, P.R. 1993. *Multicultural Management: New Skills for Global Success,* Houston, TX: Gulf Publishing Company.

Elliott, J. 1981. "Action-Research: A Framework for Self-Evaluation in Schools," working paper no. 1 of Schools Council Programme Teacher-Pupil Interaction and the Quality of Learning, Schools Council, London.

Ellis, P.D. 1995. "Cosmopolitanism and the Marco Polo Effect: The Social Determinants of Exports in Western Australian Small to Medium Sized Enterprises," unpublished PhD thesis, University of Western Australia.

Emmerson, R.M. 1962. "Power-Dependence Relations." *American Sociological Review,* Vol. 27, pp. 31-34.

Fan, Y. 1996. "Research on Joint Ventures in China: Progress and Prognosis," in Roger, B., Pan,Y., and Kaynak, E. (eds.), *International Joint Ventures in East Asia,* New York: International Business Press, pp. 71-88.

Fisher, R. and Ury, W. 1981. *Getting to Yes,* New York: Penguin.

Foo, C.P. 1994. "China Is Renegotiating Foreign Joint Ventures," *South China Morning Post,* January 12, 1.

Ford, D. 1980. "The Development of Buyer-Seller Relationships in Industrial Market," *European Journal of Marketing,* Vol. 14, No. 56, 339-353.

Forrester, J.W. 1961. *Industrial Dynamics,* Cambridge, MA: MIT Press.

Frazier, G.L., Spekman, R.E., and O'Neal, C.R. 1988. "Just-in-Time Exchange Relationships in Industrial Markets." *Journal of Marketing,* Vol. 52, October, 52-67.

Fukuyama, F. 1995. *Trust: The Social Virtues and The Creation of Prosperity,* The Free Press.

Galbraith, J.K. 1974. *The New Industrial State,* London: Pelican.

Gatignon, H. and Anderson, E. 1988. "The Multinational Corporation's Degree of Control over Subsidiaries: An Empirical Test of a Transaction Cost Explanation," *Journal of Law Economics and Organisation,* Vol. 6, 2.

Giddens, A. 1982. *Sociology: A Brief but Critical Introduction,* Orlando, FL: Harcourt Brace Jovanovich.

Gilley, B. 1994. "Following the Trail of Corruption," *Eastern Express,* July 18.

Glaister, K.W. and Wang, Y. 1993. "UK Ventures in China: Motivation and Partner Selection," *Marketing Intelligence and Planning,* Vol. 11, No. 2, 9-15.

Goetz, C.J. and Scott, R.E. 1981. "Priciples of Relational Contracts," *Virginia Law Review,* Vol. 67, No. 6, 1089-1150.

Graham, J.L. 1986. "The Problem-Solving Approach to Negotiation in Industrial Marketing," *Journal of Business Research,* Vol. 14, No. 6, 546-566.

Graham, J.L., Kim, D.K., Lin, C.Y., and Robinson, M. 1988. "Buyer-Seller Negotiations Around the Pacific Rim: Differences in Fundamental Exchange Processes," *Journal of Consumer Research,* Vol. 15, June, 48-54.

Guba, Y. and Lincoln, E. 1981. *Effective Evaluation: Improving the Effectiveness of Evaluation Results Through Responsive and Naturalistic Approaches*, San Francisco: Jossey-Bass.

Gummesson, E. 1991. *Qualitative Methods in Management Research*, Newbury Park, CA: Sage Publications.

Gundlach, G.T. and Murphy, P.E. 1993. "Ethical and Legal Foundations of Relational Marketing Exchanges," *Journal of Marketing*, Vol. 57, October, 35-46.

Hakam, A.N. and Chan, K.Y. 1990. "Negotiation Between Singaporeans and Firms in China: The Case of a Singapore Electronic Firm Contemplating Investments in China," in Campbell, N. and Henley, J.S. (eds.), *Advances in Chinese Industrial Studies*, Vol. 1, part B, Westport, CT: JAI Press, pp. 249-261.

Hakansson, H. (ed.) 1982. *International Marketing and Purchasing of Industrial Goods: An Interaction Approach*. Chichester, England: John Wiley and Sons.

Hakansson, H. and Snehota, I. 1989. "No Business Is an Island: The Network Concept of Business Strategy," *Scandinavian Journal of Management*, Vol. 5, No. 3, 187-200.

Halbert, M. 1964. "The Requirements for Theory in Marketing," in Cox, R., Alderson, W., and Shapiro, S.J. (eds.), *Theory in Marketing*, Homewood, IL: Richard D. Irwin, Inc., pp. 17-36.

Hall, E.T. 1976. "How Cultures Collide," *Psychology Today*, July, 66-97.

Hall, E.T. 1977. *Beyond Culture*, New York: Doubleday Anchor.

Hall, E.T. 1979. "Learning the Arab's Silent Language," *Psychology Today*, August, 45-53.

Hallen, L., Johanson, J., and Seyed-Mohamed, N. 1991. "Interfirm Adaptation in Business Relationships," *Journal of Marketing*, Vol. 5, No. 2, 29-37.

Hamel, G. 1991. "Competition for Competence and Inter-Partner Learning Within International Strategic Alliance," *Strategic Management Journal*, Vol. 12, No. 1, 83-103.

Harris, P. and Moran, R.T. 1991. *Managing Cultural Differences: High Performance Strategies for a New World of Business*, Houston, TX: Gulf Publishing Company.

Harris, S.G. and Sutton, R.I. 1986. "Functions of Parting Ceremonies in Dying Organisations," *Academy of Management Journal*, Vol. 29, No. 1, 5-30.

Hemmings, S. and Parshall, M. 1995. "Australia," in Power, V. (ed.), *Setting Up a Business in . . . : An International Legal Survey*, London: Sweet and Maxwell.

Hendrex, R.S. 1986. "Implementation of a Technology Transfer Joint Venture in the People's Republic of China: A Management Perspective," *Columbia Journal of World Business*, Vol. 21, No. 1, 57-66.

Henley, J.S. and Nyaw, M.K. 1990. "The System of Management and Performance of Joint Ventures in China: Some Evidence from Shenzhen Special Economic Zone," *Advances in Chinese Industrial Studies*, Vol. 1, Part B, 277-295.

Hennart, J.F. 1988. "A Transaction Costs Theory of Equity Joint Ventures," *Strategic Management Journal*, Vol. 9, No. 4, 361-374.

Hennart, J.F. 1991. "The Transaction Costs Theory of Joint Ventures: An Empirical Study of Japanese Subsidiaries in the United States," *Management Science,* Vol. 37, No. 4, 483-497.

Heskett, J.L., Stern, L.W., and Beier, F.J. 1977. "Bases and Uses of Power in Inter-organizational Relations," in L.P. Buckling (ed.), *Vertical Marketing Systems,* Glenview, IL: Scott Foresman.

Hiltrop, J.-M. and Udall, S. 1995. *The Essence of Negotiation,* Hertfordshire, U.K.: Prentice-Hall.

Hirschman, E.C. 1986. "Humanistic Inquiry in Marketing Research: Philosophy, Method and Criteria," *Journal of Marketing Research,* Vol. 53, August, 237-249.

Ho, D.Y. 1976. "On the Concept of Face," *American Journal of Sociology,* Vol. 81, No. 4, 867-884.

Ho, S.C. 1986. "Entering the China Market—Via Hong Kong?" *Asia Pacific Community,* Vol. 36, Winter, 45-54.

Ho, Y.F. and Lee, L.Y. 1974. "Authoritarianism and Attitude Toward Filial Piety in Chinese Teachers," *The Journal of Social Psychology,* Vol. 92, 305-306.

Hodgetts, R. 1993. "A Conversation with Geert Hofstede," *Organizational Dynamics,* Vol. 21, No. 4, 53-61.

Hofstede, G. 1980. *Culture's Consequences: International Differences in Work-Related Values.* Beverly Hills, CA: Sage.

Hofstede, G. 1991. *Cultures and Organizations, Software of the Mind,* Berkshire, U.K.: McGraw-Hill Book.

Hofstede, G. 1999. "Problems Remain, But Theories Will Change: The Universal and the Specific in 21st-Century Global Management," *Organizational Dynamics,* Vol. 28, No. 1, 34-44.

Hofstede, G. and Bond, M.H. 1988. "Confucius and Economic Growth: New Trends into Culture's Consequences," *Organizational Dynamics,* Vol. 16, No. 4, 4-21.

Hogan, J. 1991. "Structure of Physical Performance in Occupational Tasks," *Journal of Applied Psychology,* Vol. 76, No. 4, 495-507.

Hollenson, S. 1998. *Global Marketing: A Market-Tesponsible Approach,* Herfordshire, U.K.: Prentice-Hall.

Hong, T. 1998. "Guanxi Between Mainland Network Operators and Their Partners," *Hong Kong Economic Journal,* March 20, 25 (in Chinese).

Hong Kong Government. 1995. *Annual Report.* Hong Kong: Author.

Hsu, F.L.K. 1971. "Psycho-Social Homeostasis: Conceptual Tools for Advancing Psychological Anthropology," *American Anthropologist,* Vol. 73, 23-44.

Hu, H.C. 1944. "The Chinese Concept of Face," *American Anthropologist,* Vol. 46, January-March, 45-64.

Hu, M.Y., Chen, H., and Shieh, J.C. 1992. "Impact of U.S.-China Joint Ventures on Stockholders' Wealth by Degree of International Involvement," *Management International Review,* Vol. 32, No. 2, 135-148.

Huang Quanyu, Andrulis, R.S., and Chen Tong. 1994. *A Guide to Successful Business Relations with the Chinese: Opening the Great Wall's Gate,* Binghamton, NY: International Business Press.

Hunger, J.D. and Wheelen, T.L. 1993. *Strategic Management* (Fourth Edition), Reading, MA: Addison-Wesley Publishing Company, Inc.

Hunt, N.J. and Shelby, D. 1977. "Positive vs Normative Theory in Marketing: The Three Dichotomies Model As a General Paradigm for Marketing." *Contemporary Thought in Marketing,* Chicago: AMA.

Hunt, S.D. 1983. *Marketing Theory: The Philosophy of Marketing Science,* Homewood, IL: Richard D Irwin Inc.

Hunter, A. 1990. *The Rhetoric of Social Research: Understood and Believed,* New Brunswick, NJ: Rutgers University Press.

Hwang, C.H. 1982. "Studies in Chinese Personality: A Critical Review," *Bulletin of Educational Psychology,* Vol. 15, 227-242.

Hwang, K.K. 1987. "Face and Favour: The Chinese Power Game," *American Journal of Sociology,* Vol. 92, No. 4, 944-974.

Iacobucci, D. and Hopkins, N. 1992. "Modeling Dyadic Interactions and Networks in Marketing," *Journal of Marketing Research,* Vol. 29, February, 5-17.

Ikle, F.C. 1964. *How Nations Negotiate,* New York: Harper and Row.

IMD (International Institute for Management Development). 1996. *The World Competitiveness Yearbook.* Lausanne, Switzerland: International Institute for Management Development.

Import/Export Manpower Survey. 1994. Hong Kong: Vocational Training Council.

Jackson, B.B. 1985. *Winning and Keeping Industrial Customers: The Dynamics of Customer Relationships,* Lexington, MA: Lexington Books.

Jacobs, J.B. 1980. *Local Politics in a Rural Chinese Cultural Setting: A Field Study of Mazu Township, Taiwan,* Canberra: Contemporary China Centre, Research School of Pacific Studies, Australian National University.

Jick, T.D. 1979. "Mixing Qualitative and Quantitative Methods: Triangulation in Action," *Administrative Science Quarterly,* Vol. 24, December, 602-611.

Johnson, R.R. 1988. *Marketing News,* Vol. 22, October 24, 21.

Jomini, A.H. 1971. *The Art of War,* New Edition, Westport, CT: Greenwood Press.

Kahn, H. 1979. *World Economic Development: 1979 and Beyond.* London: Croom Helm.

Kaiser, S., Kirby, D.A., and Fan, Y. 1996. "Foreign Direct Investment in China: An Examination of the Literature," *Asia Pacific Business Review,* Vol. 2, No. 3, 45-65.

Kam, Y.K. 1993. *The Chinese Society and Its Culture,* Hong Kong: Oxford University Press (in Chinese).

Kanter, R.M. 1977. *Men and Women of the Corporation,* New York: Basic Books.

Karass, C.L. 1970. *The Negotiation Game,* New York: Thomas Y. Crowell.

Kaynak, E. and Hudanah, B.I. 1987. "Operationalising the Relationship Between Marketing and Economic Development: Some Insights from Less-Developed Countries," *European Journal of Marketing,* Vol. 21, No. 1, 48-65.

Keegan, W. J. 1995. *Global Marketing Management* (Fifth Edition), Englewood Cliffs, NJ: Prentice-Hall.

Keenan, T. 1995. "Let's Clean the Air: Donaldson, Hoechst Celanese Develop New Filter," *Ward's Auto World,* September, 85.

Kelley, H.H. 1966. "A Classroom Study of the Dilemmas in Interpersonal Negotiations," in Archibald, K. (ed.), *Strategic Interaction and Conflict,* Berkeley, CA: Berkeley Institute of International Studies, University of California, pp. 49-73.

Killing, P.J. 1983. *Strategies for Joint Venture Success,* New York: Praeger.

King, A.U.C. and Myers, J.R. 1977. "Shame As an Incomplete Conception of Chinese Culture: A Study of Face." Research Monograph, Hong Kong: Social Research Institute, The Chinese University Press.

Kirkbride, P., Tang, S., and Westwood, R. 1991. "Chinese Conflict Preferences and Negotiating Behaviour: Cultural and Psychological Influences," *Organisation Studies,* Vol. 12, No. 3, 365-386.

Klein, B., Craqford, R.G., and Alchian, A.A. 1978. "Vertical Integration, Appropriable Rents and the Competition Contracting Process," *Journal of Law and Economics,* Vol. 21, 297-326.

Knowles, L.L., Mathur, I., and Chen, J. 1989. "Chinese Perspectives on Joint Ventures for Marketing in China," *Journal of Global Marketing,* Vol. 3, No. 1, 33-53.

Kogut, B. 1988. "Joint Ventures: Theoretical and Empirical Perspectives," *Strategic Management Journal,* Vol. 9, No. 4, 319-332.

Kotler, P. 1990. Presentation at the Trustees Meeting of the Marketing Science Institute, November, Boston.

Kotler, P. 1994. *Marketing Management: Analysis, Planning, Implementation, and Control,* Englewood Cliffs, NJ: Prentice-Hall.

Krantz, M. 1997. "Otis Gets a Lift by Using Locals in Foreign Posts," *Investor's Business Daily,* January 7, A4.

Krapfel, R.E., Salmond Jr., D., and Spekman, R. 1991. "A Strategic Approach to Managing Buyer-Seller Relationships," *European Journal of Marketing,* Vol. 25, No. 9, 22-37

Kublin, M. 1995. *International Negotiating: A Primer for American Business Professionals,* Binghamton, NY: International Business Press.

Kutschler, M. 1985. "The Multi-Organizational Interaction Approach to Industrial Marketing," *Journal of Business Research,* Vol. 13, No. 5, 383-403.

Kwan, D. 1998. "Zhu's Cabinet Focuses on Staff Cutbacks," *South China Morning Post,* March 23, 7.

Ladwig, J.G. 1996. *Academic Distinctions, Theory and Methodology in the Sociology of School Knowledge,* London: Routledge.

Lamb, C.W. Jr., Hair, J.F. Jr., and McDaniel, C. 1994. *Principle of Marketing* (Second Edition), Cincinnati, OH: South-Western Publishing.

Lan, P. 1996. "Role of International Joint Ventures (IJVs) in Transferring Technology to China," in Baran, R., Pan, Y., and Kaynak, E. (eds.), *International Joint Ventures in East Asia,* Binghamton, NY: International Business Press, pp. 129-153.

Larzelere, R.E. and Huston, T.L. 1980. "The Dyadic Trust Scale: Toward Understanding Interpersonal Trust in Close Relationships," *Journal of Marriage and the Family,* Vol. 42, August, 595-604.

Lather, P. 1991. *Getting Smart: Feminist Research and Pedagogy with/in the Post-Modern,* London: Routledge.

Leap, T. 1995. *Collective Bargaining and Labour Relations,* Englewood Cliffs, NJ: Prentice-Hall.

Lee, K.H. 1989. "Culture and Marketing Negotiation." In Kaynak, E. and Lee, K.H. (eds.), *Global Business Asia-Pacific Dimension,* London: Routledge.

Lee, K.H. and Lo, W.C. 1988. "American Businesspeople's Perceptions of Marketing and Negotiating in the People's Republic of China," *International Marketing Review,* Vol. 5, No. 2, 41-51.

Legge, J. 1960. *The Chinese Classics,* 1. Hong Kong: Hong Kong University Press.

Lengnick-Hall, C.A. and Lengnick-Hall, M.L. 1990. *Interactive Human Resource Management and Strategic Planning,* New York: Quorum Books.

Leung, T.K.P. 1997. "The Cultural Context of Business Negotiation in the PRC," in Rioni, S.G. (ed.), *Politics and Economics of Hong Kong,* New York: Nova Science Publishers, pp. 1-13.

Leung, T., Wong, Y.H., and Tam, J. 1995. "Adaptation and Relationship Building Process in the People's Republic of China (PRC)," *Journal of International Consumer Marketing,* Vol. 8, No. 2, 7-26.

Leung, T.K.P., Wong, YH., and Wong, S. 1996. "A Study of Hong Kong Businessmen's Perceptions of the Role 'Guanxi' in the People's Republic of China (PRC)," *Journal of Business Ethic,* Vol. 15, No. 7, 749-758.

Leung, T.K.P. and Yeung, L.L. 1995. "Negotiation in the People's Republic of China: Results of a Survey of Small Businesses in Hong Kong," *Journal of Small Business Management,* Vol. 33, No. 1, 70-77.

Levine, S. and White, P.E. 1961. "Exchange As a Conceptual Framework for the Study of Inter-Organizational Relationships," *Administrative Science Quarterly,* Vol. 5, 583-601.

Levy, S. and Zaltman, G. 1975. *Marketing, Society and Conflict.* Englewood Cliffs, NJ: Prentice-Hall.

Lewis, D. 1994. *China Trade and Marketing Manual,* Hong Kong: Asia Law and Practice Co.

Li, D.K.T., Walker, G.R., Fox, M.A., Lau, S.K., and Leung, T.K.P. 1996. "Foreign Direct Investment in the PRC: Foreign Exchange Reform and Business Risk," *International Company and Commercial Law Review,* Vol. 7, No. 7, 254-260.

Lien, D. 1990. "Corruption and Allocation Efficiency," *Journal of Development Economics,* Vol. 33, 153-164.

Lin, Y.H.L. 1939. "Confucius on Interpersonal Relations," *Psychiatry,* Vol. 5, 475-481.

Linda, D. M. 1991. "Affect and Social Exchange: Satisfaction in a Power-Dependence Relationship," *American Sociological Review,* Vol. 56, August, 475-493.

Lindsay, C.P. and Dempsey, B.L. 1983. "Ten Painfully Learned Lessons About Working in China: The Insights of Two American Behavioural Scientists," *Journal of Applied Behavioural Science,* Vol. 19, No. 3, 265-276.

Litwak, E. and Hylton, L.F. 1962. "Inter-Organizational Analysis: A Hypothesis on Coordinating Agencies," *Administrative Science Quarterly,* Vol. 6, 359-420.

Lu Xun. 1934. *On Face, Selected Works,* Vol. 4, Beijing: Foreign Languages Press, pp. 131-134.

Luo, C. 1988. "China's Economic Reforms Face Major Constraints," *Far East Economic Review,* Vol. 139, No. 4, 72-73.

MacInnes, P. 1993. "Guanxi or Contract: A Way to Understand and Predict Conflict Between Chinese and Western Senior Managers in China-Based Joint Ventures," in McCarty, D. and Hille, S. (eds.), *Research on Multinational Business Management and Internationalisation of Chinese Enterprises,* Nanjing: Nanjing University, pp. 345-351.

MacNeil, I.R. 1980. *The New Social Contract: An Inquiry Into Modern Contractual Relations.* New Haven, CT: Yale University Press.

Maddux, R. 1988. *Successful Negotiation,* London: Kogan Page.

Man, Y.H. 1997. "Foreign Investors Cry for High Cost," *Hong Kong Economic Times,* November 27, A7 (in Chinese).

Mariampolski, H. 1988. *Marketing News,* 22 (October 24), 22, 26.

Mattsson, L.G. 1988. "Interaction Strategies: A Network Approach," in *AMA Marketing Educator's Conference,* Summer, San Francisco, Calif.

Mayer, C.S., Han, J., and Lim, H. 1990. "Joint Venture Performances: Six Case Studies from Tianjin," in Campbell, N. and Henley, J.S. (eds.), *Advances in Chinese Industrial Studies,* Vol.1, part B, Westport, CT: JAI Press, pp. 263-275.

McCarthy, D.J. and Puffer, S.M. 1997. "Strategic Investment Flexibility for MNE Success in Russia: Evolving Beyond Entry Modes," *Journal of World Business,* Vol. 32, No. 4, 293-319.

McDonald, G. 1995. "Business Ethics in China." In Davies, H. (ed.), *China Business: Context and Issues,* Hong Kong: Longman Hong Kong, pp. 170-189.

Mente, B. 1992. *Chinese Etiquette and Ethics in Business,* New York: NTC Business Book.

Metcalf, L.E., Frear, C.R., and Krishnan, R. 1992. "Buyer-Seller Relationships: An Application of the IMP Interaction Model," *European Journal of Marketing,* Vol. 26, No. 2, 27-46.

Miles, M.B. and Huberman, M. 1984. *Qualitative Data Analysis: An Expanded Sourcebook,* Beverly Hills, CA: Sage.

Miles, M.B. and Huberman, M. 1994. *Qualitative Data Analysis: An Expanded Sourcebook* (Second Edition), Thousand Oaks, CA: Sage.

Miller, R.W. 1987. *Fact and Method, Explanation, Confirmation and Reality in the Natural and Social Sciences,* Princeton, NJ: Princeton University Press.

Mills, C.W. 1967. *The Sociological Imagination,* New York: Oxford University Press.

Mills, R.W. and Chen, G. 1996. "Evaluating International Joint Ventures Using Strategic Value Analysis," *Long Range Planning,* Vol. 29, No. 4, 552-561.

Mintzberg, H. 1979. "An Emerging Strategy of 'Direct' Research," *Administrative Science Quarterly,* 24, December, 582-589.

Mintzberg, H. and Walters, J.A. 1982. "Tracking strategy in an entrepreneurial firm," *Academy of Management Journal,* Vol. 25, 465-499.

Moore, R.L. 1988. "Face and Network in Urban Hong Kong," *City and Society,* Vol. 2, 50-59.

Moorman, C., Deshpande, R., and Zaltman, G. 1993. "Factors Affecting Trust in Market Research Relationships," *Journal of Marketing,* Vol. 57, January, 81-101.

Moran, R.T. and Stripp, W.G. 1991. *Successful International Business Negotiations,* Houston, TX: Gulf Publishing Company.

Morgan, R.M. and Hunt, S.D. 1994. "The Commitment-Trust Theory of Relationship Marketing," *Journal of Marketing,* Vol. 58, July, 20-38.

Morrow, R.A. and Brown, D.D. 1994. *Critical Theory and Methodology,* Thousand Oaks, CA: Sage Publications.

Mum, K.C. and Yau, O.H.M. 1979. *Marketing Research: Basic Methods,* Hong Kong, The Chinese University Press (In Chinese).

Mun, K.C. and Chan, T.S. 1986. "The Role of Hong Kong in US-China Trade," *Columbia Journal of World Business,* Vol. 21, No. 1, 67-73.

Murphy, I.P. 1996. "It Takes Guanxi to Do Business in China," *Marketing News,* October 21, 12.

Nash, J.F. 1950. "The Bargaining Problem," *Econometrica,* Vol. 18, April, 155-162.

Newman, W.H. 1992. "Launching a Viable Joint Venture," *California Management Review,* Vol. 35, No. 1, 68-80.

Nielsen, J.M. 1990. *Feminist Research Methods: Exemplary Readings in Social Sciences,* Boulder, CO: Westview.

Nyaw, M. 1990. "The Significant and Managerial Roles of Trade Unions in Joint Ventures in China," in Shenkar, O. (ed.), *Organisation and Management in China: 1979-1990,* Armonk, NY: M.E. Sharpe, pp. 108-123.

Ogden S. 1995. *China's Unresolved Issues,* Englewood Cliffs, NJ: Prentice-Hall.

O'Neil, M. and Miller, M. 1998. "Mainland Bans Direct Marketing," *South China Morning Post,* April 23, B1.

O'Reilly, A.J.F. 1988. "Establishing Successful Joint Ventures in Developing Nations: A CEO's Perspectives," *Columbia Journal of World Business,* Vol. 23, No. 1, 65-71.

Osland, G. 1989. "Doing Business in China: A Framework for Cross-Cultural Understanding," *Marketing Intelligence and Planning,* Vol. 8, 4.

Ouchi, W. 1980. "Markets, Bureaucracies and Clans," *Administrative Science Quarterly,* Vol. 25, pp. 129-62.

Palmer, A. and Bejou, D. 1994. "Buyer-Seller Relationships: A Conceptual Model and Empirical Investigation," *Journal of Marketing Management,* Vol. 10, October, 495-512.

Pan, Y., Vanhonacker, W., and Pitts, R.E. 1993. "International Equity Joint Ventures in China: Operations and Potential Close-Down," presented at the Second Conference on Joint Ventures in East Asia, December, Bangkok, Thailand.

Parkhe, A. 1993. "Messy Research, Methodological Predisposition, and Theory Development in International Joint Venture," *Academy of Management Review,* Vol. 18, No. 2, 227-268.

Parkin, M. (1994). *Economics,* Second Edition. Ontario: Addison-Wesley Publishing Company.

Parvatiyar, A., Sheth, J.N., and Whittington, F.B. Jr. 1992. "Paradigm Shift in Interfirm Marketing Relationships: Emerging Research Issues." Working Paper, Emory University.

Patton, M.Q. 1990. *Qualitative Evaluation and Research Methods,* London: Sage Publications.

Pawson, R. and Tilley, N. 1997. *Realistic Evaluation,* London: Sage Publications.

Pearson, M.M. 1991. *Joint Venture in the People's Republic of China: The Control of Foreign Direct Investment Under Socialism,* Princeton, NJ: Princeton University Press.

Perry, C. 1994. "A Structured Approach to Presenting PhD Thesis: Notes for Candidates and their Supervisors," Paper presented to the ANZ Doctoral Consortium, University of Sydney, April.

Perry, C., Riege, A., and Brown, L. 1998. "Realism Rules OK: Scientific Paradigms in Marketing Research About Networks," competitive paper, presented at Australia and New Zealand Marketing Academy Conference (ANZMAC98), University of Otago, Dunedin, New Zealand, December, 1955-1959.

Pettigrew, A.M. 1992. "The Character and Significance of Strategy Process Research," *Strategic Management Journal,* Vol. 13, winter special issue, 5-16.

Pettigrew, A.M., Ferlie, E., and McKee, L. 1992. *Shaping Strategic Change: Making Change in Large Organisations: The Case of the National Health Service,* London: Sage Publications.

Phatak, A., Muralidharan, R., and Chandran, R. 1996. "A Study of the Impact of Location Specific and Moderating Factors on the Choice of Entry Mode in Thailand, Malaysia, and Indonesia," in Baran, R., Pan, Y. and Kaynak, E. (eds.), *International Joint Ventures in East Asia,* Binghamton, NY: International Business Press, pp. 37-54.

Pomfret, R. 1989. *Equity Joint Ventures in Jiangsu Province,* Hong Kong: Longman.

Pomfret, R. 1991. *Investing in China: Ten Years of the Open Door Policy,* Hertfordshire: Harvester Wheatsheaf.

Popper, K. 1959. *The Logic of Scientific Discovery,* London: Hutchinson.

Population Reference Bureau. 2000. *2000 World Population Data Sheet,* <http://www.prb.org/wpds2000/>.

Porter, M.E. 1980. *Competitive Strategy, Techniques for Analysing Industries and Competitors,* New York: Free Press.

Porter, M.E. 1985. *Competitive Advantage,* New York: Free Press.

Porter, M.E. 1986. "The Changing Patterns of International Competition," *California Management Review*, Vol. 22, No. 4, 9-38.

Porter, M.E. 1990. *The Competitive Advantage of Nations*, New York: Free Press.

Pruitt, D.G. 1981. *Negotiation Behaviour*. New York: Academic Press, p. 101.

Putnam, L.L. 1990. "Re-Framing Integrative and Distribution Bargaining: A Process Perspective," *Research on Negotiation in Organisations*, Vol. 2, 3-30.

Pye, L. 1978. "Communications and Chinese Political Culture," *Asian Survey*, Vol. 14, 221-246.

Pye, L. 1982. *Chinese Commercial Negotiation Styles*, Cambridge, U.K.: Oelgeschlager, Gunn and Hain.

Pye, L. 1986. "The China Trade: Making the Deal," *Harvard Business Review*, No. 4, July-August, 74-80.

Pye, L. 1992. *The Spirit of Chinese Politics*, Boston, MA: Harvard University Press.

Ragin, C.C. 1987. *The Comparative Method: Moving Beyond Qualitative and Quantitative Strategies*, Berkeley, CA: University of California Press.

Raiffa, H. 1982. *The Art and Science of Negotiation*, Boston, MA: The Harvard University Press.

Redding, S.G. 1990. *The Spirit of Chinese Capitalism*, New York: Walter de Gruyter.

Redding, S.G. 1994. "Competitive Advantage in the Context of Hong Kong," *Journal of Far Eastern Business*, Vol. 6, No. 1, 71-89.

Redding, S.G. and Tam, S. "Networks and Molecular Organisation: An Exploratory View of Chinese Firms in Hong Kong," Unpublished paper, University of Hong Kong: Department of Management Studies.

Reuters. 2000. "GDP Rise Ends Dip in Growth," *South China Morgning Post*, Annual Review, December 31, p. 2.

Rinehart, L.M. and Page, T.J. Jr. 1992. "The Development and Test of a Model of Transaction Negotiation," *Journal of Marketing*, Vol. 56, No. 4, 18-32.

Root, F.R. 1987. *Entry Strategies for International Markets*, Lexington, MA: DC Heath.

Rosemont, H. Jr. 1991. *A Chinese Mirror*, La Selle, IL: Open Court.

Rotter, J.B. 1967. "A New Scale for the Measurement of Interpersonal Trust," *Journal of Personality*, Vol. 35, No. 4, 651-665.

Rotter, J.B. 1971. "Generalized Expectancies for Interpersonal Trust," *American Psychologist*, Vol. 26, May, 443-452.

Rubin, J.Z. and Brown, B.R. 1975. *The Social Psychology of Bargaining and Negotiation*, New York: Academic Press.

Rubin, P. and Carter, J. 1990. "Joint Optimality in Buyer-Supplier Negotiations," *Journal of Purchasing and Materials Management*, Spring, 20-26.

Rudner, R.S. 1966. *The Philosophy of Social Sciences*, Englewood Cliffs, NJ: Prentice-Hall.

Ruggles, R.L. Jr. 1983. "The Environment for American Business Ventures in the People's Republic of China," *Columbia Journal of World Business*, Vol. 18, No. 4, 67-73.

Sayer, A. 1992. *Method in Social Science: A Realist Approach* (Second Edition), London: Routledge.

Schelling, T.C. 1960. *The Strategy of Conflict,* Cambridge, MA: Harvard University Press.

Schermerhorn, J.R. Jr., Hunt, J.G., and Osborn, R.N. 1997. *Organisational Behaviour,* Singapore City: John Wiley and Sons.

Schoderbek, P., Schoderbek, C., and Kefalas, A.B. 1985. *Management Systems: Conception Consideration,* Plano, TX: Business Publications Inc.

Schurr, P.H. and Ozanne, J.L. 1985. "Influences on Exchange Processes: Buyers' Preconceptions of a Seller's Trustworthiness and Bargaining Toughness," *Journal of Consumer Research,* Vol. 11, March, 939-953.

Sebenius, J.K. 1992. "Negotiation Analysis: A Characterisation and Review," *Management Science,* Vol. 38, January, 18-38.

Shapiro, E. 1972. "Educational Evaluation: Rethinking the Criteria of Competence," *School Review,* Vol. 81, August, 523-549.

Shapiro, J.E., Behrman, J.N., Fischer, W.A., and Powell, S.G. 1991. *Direct Investment and Joint Ventures in China,* New York: Quorum Books.

Shenkar, O. 1990. "International Joint Ventures' Problems in China: Risks and Remedies," *Long Range Planning,* Vol. 23, No. 3, 82-90.

Shenkar, O. and Ronen, S. 1987. "The Cultural Context of Negotiations: The Implications of Chinese Interpersonal Norms," *The Journal of Applied Behavioural Science,* Vol. 23, No. 2, 263-275.

Sherman, S. 1992. "Are Strategic Alliances Working?" *Fortune,* September, 77-78.

Sheth, J.N. 1985. Keynote Address, Historical and International Perspectives of Consumer Research Conference, National University of Singapore and the Association for Consumer Research, Singapore.

Sheth, J.N., Gradner, D.M., David, M.E., and Carrett, D.D. 1988. *Marketing Theory: Evolution and Evaluation,* New York: John Wiley and Sons, pp. 29-32.

Simons, H.W., Berkowitz, B., and Moyer, R.J. 1970. "Similarity, Credibility, and Attitude Change: A Review and a Theory," *Psychology Bulletin,* Vol. 73, January, 1-16.

Sinlin, R.H. 1976. *Leadership and Values: The Organization of Large-Scale Taiwanese Enterprises,* Cambridge, MA: Harvard University Press.

Siu, W.S. 1992. "Corporate Entrepreneurs in the People's Republic of China: Problems Encountered and Respective Solutions," *International Small Business Journal,* Vol. 10, No. 4, 26-33.

Slind-Flor, V. 1998. "In Search of Punishment for Pirates," *National Law Journal,* Vol. 21, No. 3, A7.

Smart, A. 1993. "Gifts, Bribes, and Guanxi: A Reconsideration of Bourdieu's Social Capital," *Cultural Anthropology,* Vol. 8, No. 3, 388-408.

Smith, L.M. and Kleine, P.F. 1986. "Qualitative Research and Evaluation: Triangulation and Multimethods Reconsidered," in William, D.D. (ed.), *Naturalistic Evaluation.* Vol. 30, New Directions for Program Evaluation, Francisco: Jossey-Bass, 55-72.

Spagna, G.J. 1984. "Questionnaires: Which Approach Do You Use?" *Journal of Advertising Research,* Vol. 24, No. 1, 67-70.

Spector, B.I. 1978. "Negotiation As a Psychological Process," in Zartman, I.W. (ed.), *The Negotiation Process: Theories and Applications,* London: Sage Publications, pp. 55-66.

Stelzer, L., Ma, C., and Banthin, J. 1992. "Gauging Investor Satisfaction," *The China Business Review,* November-December, 54-56.

Stewart, D. and Mickunas, A. 1990. *Exploring Phenomenology: A Guide to the Field and Its Literature,* Athens, OH: Ohio University Press.

Stewart, S. and Keown, C. 1989. "Talking with the Dragon: Negotiating in the People's Republic of China," *Columbia Journal of World Business,* Fall, 68-72.

Sudman, S. 1976. *Applied Sampling.* New York: Academic Press.

Sullivan, J. and Peterson, R.B. 1982. "Factors Associated with Trust in Japanese-American Joint Ventures," *Management International Review,* Vol. 22, No. 4, 30-40.

Sum, L.P. 1996. *Practical Law Guide of Direct Foreign Investment in China,* Hong Kong: Commercial Press (in Chinese).

Sun, W.Y. 1994. "China's Experience in Absorbing Foreign Direct Investment for Its Economic Development," *The Brown Journal Journal of World Affairs,* Vol. 2, No. 1, 113-122.

Sundaram, A.K. and Black, J.S. 1992. "The Environment and Internal Organisation of Multinational Enterprises," *Academy of Management Review,* Vol. 17, No. 4, 729-757.

Tai, L.S.T. 1988. "Doing Business in the PRC: Some Keys to Success," *Management International Review,* Vol. 28, No. 1, 5-9.

Tanzer, A. 1993. "Guanxi Spoken Here," *Forbes,* Vol. 152, No. 11, 210-211.

Tanzer, A. 1995. "First Pacific's Pearls," *Forbes,* Vol. 155, No. 4, 48-50.

Tawney, R.H. 1931. *Equality.* London: Allen and Unwin, p. 229.

Teagarden, M.B. 1990. *Sino-U.S. Joint Venture Effectiveness,* Unpublished doctoral dissertation, Los Angeles: University of Southern California.

Teagarden, M.B. and Glinow, M.A.V. 1991. "Sino-Foreign Strategic Alliance Types and Related Operating Characteristics," in Shankar, O. (ed.), *Organisation and Management in China: 1979-1990,* New York: M.E. Sharpe, pp. 99-107.

Teece, D.J. 1986. "Transaction Cost Economics and Multinational Enterprise: An Assessment," *Journal of Economic Behaviour and Organisation,* Vol. 7, No. 2, 21-45.

Thomas, K. 1977. "Toward Multidimensional Values in Teaching: The Examples of Conflict Behaviours," *Academy of Management Review,* Vol. 2, No. 3, 487.

Thomas, K. and Kilmann, R. 1974. *Conflict Mode Instrument,* Tuxedo, NY: XICOM, Inc.

Thompson, L. 1995. "The Derivation of GUANXI," *Marketing Management,* Vol. 4, No.1, 27.

Threshold, R. 1990. *Corruption, Development and Underdevelopment.* Durham, NC: Duke University BUSS.

Tsang, E.W.K. 1993. "Strategies for Transferring Technology to China," *Long Range Planning,* Vol. 27, No. 3, 98-107.

Tsang, E.W.K. 1998. "Sustained Competitive Advantage for Doing Business in China," *Academy of Management Executive,* Vol. 12, No. 8, 64-72.

Tsang, H.S. 1991. "How to Market and Promote Brand Name Products," paper presented in a seminar organised by the Hong Kong Trade Development Council, June 25.

Tse, D., Lee, K.H., Vertinsky, H., and Wehrung, D.A. 1988. "Does Culture Matter? A Class Culture Study of Executives' Choice, Decisiveness, and Risk Adjustment in International Marketing," *Journal of Marketing,* Vol. 52, No. 4, 81-95.

Tsui, A.S., and Farh, J.-L.L. 1997. "Where Guanxi Matters: Relational Demography and Guanxi in the Chinese Context," *Work and Occupations,* Vol. 24, No. 1, 56-79.

Tull, D.S. and Hawkins, D.I. 1984. *Marketing Research: Measurement and Method* (Third Edition), New York: Macmillan.

Tull, D.S. and Hawkins, D.I. 1993. *Marketing Research: Measurement and Methods* (Eighth Edition). New York: Macmillan.

Tung, R.L. 1982a. "US-China Trade Negotiations: Practices, Procedures and Outcomes," *Journal of International Business Studies,* Vol. 13, Fall, 25-38.

Tung, R.L. 1982b. *US-China Trade Negotiations,* New York: Pergamon Press.

Turnbull, P.W. 1987. "Organisational Buying Behaviour," in Baker, M.J. (ed.), *The Marketing Book,* London: Heinemann, pp. 147-164.

Uhrynuk, M. and Sarles, S. 1995. "United States," in Power, V. (ed.), *Setting Up a Business in . . .: An International Legal Survey,* London: Sweet and Maxwell.

Usunier, J.C. 1993. *International Marketing: A Cultural Approach,* Hertfordshire, London: Prentice-Hall.

Van Oort, H.A. 1970. "Chinese Culture Values: Past and Present," *Chinese Culture, Taipei: The China Academy,* Vol. 11, March 1, 1-10.

Varadarajan, P. and Rajaratnam, D. 1986. "Symbolic Marketing Revisited," *Journal of Marketing,* Vol. 50, January, 7-17.

Vickers, G. 1972. *Freedom in a Rocking Boat: Changing Values in an Unstable Society,* Harmondsworth: Penguin.

Vickers, G. 1984. Letter to Guy Adams, in M. Blunden, "Geoffrey Vickers—An Intellectual Journey," in *The Vickers Papers,* London: Harper and Row.

von Hippel, E. 1978. "A Customer Active Paradigm with Evidence and Implications," *Journal of Marketing,* Vol. 42, No. 1, 39-49.

Wagner, C.L. 1990. "Influences on Sino-Western Joint Venture Negotiations," *Asia Pacific Journal of Management,* Vol. 7, No. 2, 79-100.

Wang, F. 1995. "Relying on Person with Strong Chinese Background to Penetrate the Chinese Market," *The China Times* magazine, March 5-11, 11-13.

Weber, M. 1947. *The Theory of Social and Economic Organization,* New York: Oxford University Press, p. 152.

Weber, M. 1951. *The Religion of China.* Glencoe, Il: Free Press, p. 244.

Webster, C. 1993. "Refinement of the Marketing Cultural Scale and the Relationship Between Marketing Culture and Profitability of a Service Firm," *Journal of Business Research,* Vol. 26, No. 2, 111-131.

Wee, C.H. 1994. "Research on Chinese Management: Some Issues and Challenges," in Yau, O. (ed.), *Proceedings of Symposium: Theorizing about Chinese Business and Management,* Hong Kong: City Polytechnic of Hong Kong.

Wee, C.H., Lee, K.S., and Bambang, W.H. 1993. *Sun Tzu's Art of War and Management,* Reading, MA: Addison-Wesley Publishing Company

Weitz, B.A. 1978. "The Relationship Between Salesperson Performance and Understanding of Customer Decision Making," *Journal of Marketing Research,* Vol. 15, November, 501-516.

Westlake, M. 1993. "Millions Calling," *Far East Economic Review,* April 8, 48-50.

Wilhelm, A.D. Jr. 1994. *The Chinese at the Negotiation Table: Style and Characteristics,* Washington, DC: National Defense University Press.

Wilkins, L. 1967. *Social Policy, Action, and Research,* London: Tavistock.

Williamson, O.E. 1971. "The Vertical Integration of Production: Market Failure Consideration," *American Economic Review,* Vol. 61, No. 2, 112-127.

Williamson, O.E. 1975. *Markets and Hierarchies, Analysis and Antitrust Implications.* New York: Free Press.

Williamson, O.E. 1979. "Transaction-Cost Economics: The Governance of Contractual Relations," *Journal of Law and Economics,* Vol. 22, October, 3-61.

Wilson, D. and Moller, K. 1988. "Buyer-Seller Relationships: Alternative Conceptions," *IBM Report,* 10-1988, Pennsylvania State University, University Park.

Wilson, D.T. and Mummalaneni, V. 1986. "Bonding and Measuring Buyer-Seller Relationships: A Preliminary Conceptualization." *Industrial Marketing and Purchasing,* Vol. 1, No. 3, 44-58.

Wilson, R.W. 1970. *Learning to be Chinese.* Cambridge, MA: MIT Press.

Winter, R. 1987. *Action-Research and the Nature of Social Inquiry: Professional Innovation and Educational Work,* Hants, England: Avebury Gower Publishing Co. Ltd.

Wong, Y.H. 1997. "A Buyer and Seller Relationship Model for Chinese Enterprises," Unpublished PhD thesis, Queensland: James Cook University of Northern Queensland.

Wong, Y.H. 1998. "Relationship Marketing in China: The Magic and Myth of Guanxi?" *Journal of International Marketing and Marketing Research,* Vol. 23, No. 1, 3-13.

Wong, Y.H. 1999. "Can Relationships Be Segmented? The Chinese Guanxi Approach," *Journal of Segmentation in Marketing,* Vol. 3, No. 2, 23-41.

Wood, A. 1995. "Hercules: Gradually Building Strength in China," *Chemical Week,* August 30-September 6, 15.

World Economic Forum. 1995. *South China Morning Post,* Hong Kong, September 6.

Xin, K. and Pearce, J.L. 1996. "Guanxi: Connections As Substitutes for Formal Institutional Support," *Academy of Management Journal,* Vol. 39, No. 6, 1641-1658.

Yan, A. and Gary, B. 1994. "Bargaining Power, Management Control, and Performance in United States-China Joint Ventures: A Comparative Case Study," *Academy of Management Journal,* Vol. 37, No. 6, 1478-1517.

Yan, A. and Gary, B. 1995. "The Formation Dynamics of U.S.-China Manufacturing Joint Ventures," *China Business Review,* Vol. 22, December, 31-49.

Yang, C.K. 1959. "Some Characteristics of Chinese Bureaucratic Behaviour," in Nivison, D.S. and Wright, A.E. (eds.), *Confucianism in Action,* Stanford, CA: Stanford University Press, pp. 134-164.

Yang, K.S. 1979. "Research on Chinese National Character in Modern Psychology," in Chung I., Wen (ed.), *Modernization and Change of Value,* Taipei: Wen Shih Che Chu Pan She.

Yang, K.S. 1981. "Social Orientation and Individual Modernity Among Chinese Students in Taiwan," *Journal of Social Psychology,* Vol. 113, 159-70.

Yang, M.M. 1986. *The Art of Social Relationships and Exchange in China.* Berkeley, CA: University of California.

Yang, M. 1988. "The Modernity of Power in the Chinese Socialist Order," *Cultural Anthropology,* Vol. 3, 408-427.

Yau, O.H.M. 1988. "Chinese Cultural Values: Their Dimensions and Marketing Implications," *European Journal of Marketing,* Vol. 22, No. 5, 44-57.

Yau, O.H.M. 1994. *Consumer Behaviour in China.* London: Routledge.

Yin, R.K. 1981. "The Case Study Crisis: Some Answers," *Administrative Science Quarterly,* Vol. 26, March, 58-65.

Yin, R.K. 1982. "Studying Phenomenon and Context Across Sites," *American Behavioural Scientist,* Vol. 26, No.1, 84-100.

Yin, R.K. 1989. *Case Study Research: Design and Methods,* Newbury Park, CA: Sage.

Yin, R.K. 1993. *Applications of Case Study Research,* Newbury Park, CA: Sage.

Yin, R.K. 1994. *Case Study Research: Design and Methods* (Second Edition), London: Sage.

Young, I. 1995. "BOC Inflates Gases Position in China," *Chemical Week,* August 30- September 6, 12.

Zhou, C.X. 1997. "How Should the PRC Implement National Treatment for Foreign Invested Enterprises," *Hong Kong Manager,* Hong Kong Management Association, October 2, 19-22.

Zuber-Skerritt, O. and Knight, N.C. 1986. "Problem Definition and Thesis Writing," *Higher Education,* Vol. 15, No. 1-2, 89-103.

Index

Page numbers followed by the letter "f" indicate figures; those followed by the letter "t" indicate tables.

Order Your Own Copy of
This Important Book for Your Personal Library!

GUANXI
Relationship Marketing in a Chinese Context

_____ in hardbound at $79.95 (ISBN: 0-7890-1289-8)

_____ in softbound at $34.95 (ISBN: 0-7890-1290-1)

COST OF BOOKS_____

OUTSIDE USA/CANADA/
MEXICO: ADD 20%____

POSTAGE & HANDLING_____
(US: $4.00 for first book & $1.50
for each additional book)
Outside US: $5.00 for first book
& $2.00 for each additional book)

SUBTOTAL_____

in Canada: add 7% GST____

STATE TAX____
(NY, OH & MIN residents, please
add appropriate local sales tax)

FINAL TOTAL____
(If paying in Canadian funds,
convert using the current
exchange rate, UNESCO
coupons welcome.)

❏   **BILL ME LATER:** ($5 service charge will be added)
(Bill-me option is good on US/Canada/Mexico orders only;
not good to jobbers, wholesalers, or subscription agencies.)

❏ Check here if billing address is different from
shipping address and attach purchase order and
billing address information.

Signature_____

❏ **PAYMENT ENCLOSED: $**_____

❏ **PLEASE CHARGE TO MY CREDIT CARD.**

❏ Visa   ❏ MasterCard   ❏ AmEx   ❏ Discover
❏ Diner's Club   ❏ Eurocard   ❏ JCB

Account # _____

Exp. Date_____

Signature_____

Prices in US dollars and subject to change without notice.

NAME_____

INSTITUTION_____

ADDRESS_____

CITY_____

STATE/ZIP_____

COUNTRY_____ COUNTY (NY residents only)_____

TEL_____ FAX_____

E-MAIL_____

May we use your e-mail address for confirmations and other types of information? ❏ Yes ❏ No
We appreciate receiving your e-mail address and fax number. Haworth would like to e-mail or fax special
discount offers to you, as a preferred customer. **We will never share, rent, or exchange your e-mail address
or fax number.** We regard such actions as an invasion of your privacy.

Order From Your Local Bookstore or Directly From
The Haworth Press, Inc.
10 Alice Street, Binghamton, New York 13904-1580 • USA
TELEPHONE: 1-800-HAWORTH (1-800-429-6784) / Outside US/Canada: (607) 722-5857
FAX: 1-800-895-0582 / Outside US/Canada: (607) 722-6362
E-mail: getinfo@haworthpressinc.com
PLEASE PHOTOCOPY THIS FORM FOR YOUR PERSONAL USE.
www.HaworthPress.com

BOF00